8 to GREAT

How to Take Charge of Your Life and Make Positive Changes Using an 8-Step Breakthrough Process

MK MUELLER
Author of *Taking Care of Me: The Habits of Happiness*

wisdom tree

Cover and Layout Design: Elina Diaz

First published in India in 2020 by agreement with Mango Publishing Group

ISBN 978-81-8328-544-5

Published by
Wisdom Tree
4779/23, Ansari Road
Darya Ganj, New Delhi-110 002
Ph.: 011-23247966/67/68
wisdomtreebooks@gmail.com

Printed in India

“The *8 to Great* book changed how I lead. Now I hand it out to my team members like candy.”

— Dave Tracey, CEO Xpress Group, Ontario

“The *8 to Great* advantage is like the weight room in sports. It helps each individual go into the game of life that much stronger and internally prepared to do their best!”

— Jon Rowberry, CEO Nextstep

“I picked up *8 to Great* with some reluctance, in part because I am always weary of yet another so-called self-help book from some unknown guru from across the pond. But I picked it up upon recommendation, determined only to skim and bin. Well, you can only but guess my complete shock when my surface skimming became more like deep sea diving and my life is now transformed. Strong words, I know, in such a short time period (I picked up the book twelve days ago) but the insights and wisdom are mind-blowing. My energy levels are — like the good Lord — Most High, and each day I chase the dream. Thank you for this bloody brilliant book. You have given me, and all of us, a priceless gift: the permission to be great.”

— Ray Lewis, Mayor’s Council on Youth, London

“What really impressed me is the Three Promises that are made at the start of the book. MK has absolutely delivered on these three promises and I am seeing results every day since. I have started sharing some of these lessons with my two children and will be giving them each their own copy of the book. I am very grateful to the person who connected me to MK and her wonderful book *8 to Great.*

— Allan Dubyts, Canada

"MK Mueller offers people of all ages tools such as the world's simplest (and therefore, most powerful) positive attitude formula at a time when they are more needed than ever."

— John Lenhoff, Ph.D. Omaha, NE

"*8 to Great* offers a life-changing recipe for success that is full of easy-to-understand ingredients. With hundreds of "aha" insights, readers will be able to take MK Mueller's processes and put them to work immediately."

— Bill Byrne, author of *Habits of Wealth: 111 Proven Strategies that Will Change the Way You Do Business Forever*

"In my view, this book puts MK Mueller in the history books as one of the revolutionary thinkers of our time."

— Avery Rose, horse trainer, Ocala, FL

"...Over the years I've read and listened to many of the authors quoted in this book — Ziglar, Robbins, Dyer, Waitley, Hill, Canfield, and on and on. Finally, now, I have something that I can actually use... something that will let me practice these concepts daily to hone them into a newer ME. God bless MK!"

— William A. Brown, Nebraska

"Reading *8 to Great* helped me realize what I want out of life and that I'm in control of getting it! In the past year I've gone from blaming others to being grateful every single day. I am a better teacher, stronger basketball coach, and more caring parent thanks to the 8 High-Ways."

— Jeff Hofeldt, head basketball coach and math teacher, Grand Island, NE

"The world's most practical text on the seemingly impractical topic of joy."

— Barbara Shousha, M.Ed.

"I finished *8 to Great* this morning at 7:30, stood in front of my large bathroom mirror, and hummed a rock & roll song as I danced happily. Then I kissed the book — with a great big smackaroo."

— Bob Bosco, Ph.D., art professor, Creighton University

"I have been reading the chapters in *8 to Great* each night and finding such joy and excitement with each page. Thank you for the peace, serenity, and joy you bring through your words."

— Amy Kilgren, middle school teacher, Michigan

"As a Christian, this book has awakened God's spirit within me. I can't help but turn each page and find not only hope in life, but a place for my dreams to live."

— Deb Haget

"I was allowing things from my past to prevent me from being successful. Now that I've been listening to *8 to Great* while in my car, I've learned that when I take responsibility for myself and become honest with myself, I'm able to move past things which I allowed to hold me back. I begin every day with my gratitudes and it starts me 'off and running. "I am becoming the person I have dreamt of becoming."

— Brian Bethel

"*8 to Great* has really changed my life! I finished it in two days and then gave it to my parents to read. By going through the 8 High-Ways it has even brought our volleyball team together. We are playing much better together and are doing great!"

— Kari S., high school senior

"Thanks to *8 to Great* I'm having my fourth and fifth grade students write three gratitudes in their assignment books daily. It is only the third day and already they are reminding each other to do it rather than me having to say anything. I'm also playing gratitude games with my fifth graders, which they love and want to do again and again!!"

— Megan Abresch, elementary teacher

"Reading this book is one of the best things that I have ever done for myself. Everyone can become a better person from using its systematic strategies."

— Marcia Kay, Counselor

"MK Mueller is a genius, and I literally owe her my life."

— Michael Sterns, FL, Children's Author and Speaker

Table of Contents

Foreword

I met MK Mueller on a cruise I hosted in the Caribbean. It was an "adventure" sponsored by my website, where like-minded people could explore the philosophical "jungles of time and space" in between my every-other-day lectures. She was easy to recognize as somebody special. Kindness and enthusiasm shone from her eyes. Yet, admittedly, and I am not proud of this, I didn't grasp the depth of her understanding nor the passion of her conviction to change the world.

Reading ***8 to Great*** has changed everything. It's not just a powerful book from cover to cover, revealing the greatest secrets to thriving within time and space that have ever been shared, but its lessons are made easy. They're taught in plain English by the kind of teacher we need. Someone real. Someone who's learned by trial and error. Someone skilled at telling stories with a message and humor. She has turned ancient wisdom into modern day tools, and above all, she's remained authentic, conceiving of and framing each of the 8 High-Ways in one of the most original presentations I have ever read.

I'm often asked what's going to rock the world, psychologically, next. What, after ***The Secret***, that is. And the answer is that people are going to be discovering the truth about their absolute power and their absolute responsibility for living their lives consciously and deliberately. People will be learning that ***The Secret*** was about far more than positive thinking or a way of looking at life; it's literally how reality unfolds. The concepts of victimhood, failure, luck, and blame are about to be swept into extinction like the philosophical dinosaurs they are.

We're now at the dawn of a new era: spiritual giants waking from a deep slumber, during which we reacted to the world around us instead of molding it. People will soon be realizing for the first time in recorded history that we are all capable of living as richly and happily as we can imagine, and that nothing can rob us of our power to conceive of, believe in, and achieve whatever our heart desires (using MK's C-B-A Formula). Whether this next wave of enlightenment will be sparked by a single book or a collection, I'm not sure, but I do know that ***8 to Great*** will be part of it.

Mike Dooley

As featured in ***The Secret***, and author of ***Infinite Possibilities: The Art of Living Your Dreams,*** www.TUT.com

Acknowledgments

Words are incredibly inadequate for the gratitude I feel to all who loved and supported me through this work, but until I write the song that's in my heart, they will have to do.

First, my forever thanks to The Source. I feel like I downloaded the 8 High-Ways because they came to me so powerfully. Being an envoy for a process this powerful has reminded me that the branch with the most fruit bows the lowest.

Then, for my beloved children. Zach, your daily "How was your day, Mom?" and caring about my answers were sunshine on the cloudiest days. The song I sang to you when you were little still shines true. Jo Bear, your sweet smile and gentle spirit meant more than you will ever know. I was the teacher then. Now you are the teacher I look up to with incredible pride and gratitude.

Tessa, when I count my blessings, you're on the page twenty times. Thank you for the miracle that you are.

Jules, green truly is the new color of unconditional love. Thank you for the beautiful "shutter release" that you have been for my soul.

To Anya, the Supersis who never let me question myself while writing this book, thank you. You are the "gifted gifter" who has been my teacher in so many ways. Love you muchly!

Coco, from our morning intendings to your healthy dose of hilarity, you are a friend for the ages. Thank you, Soul Sister, for your love and laughter and offering me a Home Sweet Holmes.

Abby, your friendship and disciplined dedication to this material have brought life to both ***8 to Great*** and to its author. Love you Dear Friend!

Tammy, I am overcome with gratitude about your gifts of words. Thank you for taking this book home.

Dana, every soul needs to be seen. There are no words for my gratitude for your seeing mine. I cannot imagine this journey without the depth of our connection. Love you!

John Joseph, your generous gifts to the kids freed me to find my inner CEO. Namaste.

Paul, your unwavering support of my work and my worth has been the anchor that steadied me amid the storms. Thank you for believing Dear Bro!

Teresa, your generosity and faithful friendship humble me. You have held the vision and held our village in your magnificent heart, and we all share in the deepest gratitude to both you and Dana!

Momma Ruth, thank you for your unconditional love and for the freedom to blossom and be!

To my editors Cia, Becky, Colleen, Angela and Michelle, thank you for taking this to the next level of light and love!

To Mango Publishing: Chris, Hugo, Brenda, and Michelle, thank you for your vision and for putting your hearts and talents into taking this message to the world. I am forever grateful!

Finally, to the man who left his wings behind so that I could fly: Dad, I never learned how to play your beloved bridge, but have dedicated my life to becoming one. Thank you for the love I feel from you every day and for following your dream so that I could do the same.

Gratefully,
MK

I cannot tell you any truth

that deep within you don't know already.

All I can do is remind you of what you have forgotten.

Eckhart Tolle

The Foundation

If you can't describe what you're doing as a process,
you don't know what you're doing.
W. Edwards Deming

I didn't know that I didn't know.

I had no idea that happiness, health, and success were the results of following a simple but powerful process. I thought it was all about hard work, being nice, and trying to fix everything that was broken in the world. Boy, was I wrong.

So wrong that I ended up in a shelter for domestic violence at the age of thirty-four.

Despite having won numerous teaching, music, and acting awards, my personal life was a mess. I didn't realize I was in an abusive marriage until I was knocked to the ground. The first time he hit me I threatened to leave if he ever did it again.

The next day I followed through on my promise and left.

Over that month in the shelter, I discovered there were extraordinary life lessons waiting to be learned and lived. One was that there are steps to forgiveness.

I recall my counselor asking me the second day I was there, "Why are you smiling? You're describing awful things, yet you're sitting here smiling."

"Am I?" I asked, my naïveté wide and deep. "It must be because I've forgiven him."

"Hardly!" she replied. "You haven't even faced what's happened to you. You certainly aren't ready to forgive it. I want you to go to your room, write down every abusive incident over the past six years, and show me the list tomorrow."

Eleven and a half single-spaced pages later, I was no longer smiling. I realized the three steps to forgiveness: I began to face my feelings, experience them fully, and eventually *was* able to forgive.

The Pupil Becomes the Teacher

Like the steps of forgiveness, my life lessons kept showing up, and I kept writing them down, because I never wanted to forget them.

The day I left, I asked that same counselor why we weren't teaching these life principles in schools and businesses. "Maybe you will be the teacher," was her reply.

I knew that the best way to learn something was to teach it, so I started sharing the lessons in a support group in my home I called, "Taking Care of Me." It quickly grew from five neighbors to twenty-five, moving into church basements and corporate training rooms, eventually resulting in national and international conference keynotes.

The week after 9/11 I was scheduled to speak in Hawaii. When it was canceled, along with all my other global engagements, I decided to take on a challenge I had received a few months earlier from one of my audience members.

A gentleman had come up to me after a talk and said, "I need the process. Don't just give me the ingredients. I need a recipe for getting my life back on track." Now I had the time to explore what that process might look like.

The Recipe for Results

Slowly the step-by-step process became clear. As I lived the steps and taught them, they began to change everything, first in my life, then in the lives of my audience members and clients. In the decades that followed, tens of thousands of individuals on four continents have come to acknowledge the power of these 8 steps. No matter their age or economic status, for those willing to be coached, its results have never wavered. Their success stories have confirmed that this is not a set of ingredients, as most self-help manuals offer, but a tried and true *recipe* for joy and peace beyond measure.

Over the years I've discovered that every proven process has similar characteristics: a few clear and practical steps that are simple to understand, deeply rooted in timeless truths, challenging to live, and rewarding beyond belief. This is true for processes such as Dave Ramsey's baby steps for getting rid of credit card debt, the 12 steps of AA and Al-Anon, and the SAAB program I created for getting off sugar addiction in my book, ***8 to Your IdealWeight.***

Today the global world is not perfect any more than my personal world is perfect, and yet, thanks to this process I am living my dream.

And I am not alone. At this time, over 2,500 others have been certified to train these eight life lessons. It has been taught in thousands of businesses, colleges, high schools and middle schools, places of worship, and juvenile detention centers, as well as to CEO's on cruise ships. All the while, the magnitude of its truth has never been questioned. No one has ever suggested to me that one of the eight steps is unnecessary or that the process is "missing something."

This *is* the process to get you moving toward greater *health, wealth, and happiness*. Some of us want to get to Hollywood; others just want to get out of hell. Whether you're longing for deeper, more loving relationships, to build a better business, or to recover your health and well-being, I am thrilled to share this 8-step process that is all-inclusive.

The success stories from those who have benefited from the 8 steps could fill another book — including how it helped one individual lose 140 pounds, how a fifty-year-old man found his first true love, how a CEO turned around his struggling business and won Small Business of the Year, how a forty-year-old woman finally forgave her father, how a teenager who had never been out of her home town got a scholarship to MIT, how a competitive golfer took eight strokes off her game in twenty-four hours, and how an entire small town healed a decade of hostility.

I have seen the benefits of this so dramatically, that I can make the following three promises:

Promise #1:

It will take you no more than three hours to learn this process.

Promise #2:

It will take you no more than three minutes each day to apply this process.

Promise #3:

This process will help everyone who embraces it.

Successful people know that success is a science more than an art. It's the result of practices and habits of thought and action that have been taught for thousands of years by the greatest among us. How else could every bookstore be filled with "How-To" guides that top the best-seller charts?

Despite this book buffet, people often fail to make lasting changes because they don't commit to one path long enough to see results. When we jump from process to process, it's similar to someone wanting to lose weight alternating days between a low carb program and one that is low fat. In doing so, they would not only ***not*** lose weight, they would gain it!

Then once we decide on a process, we need to be coachable.

This book will challenge you to change how you see yourself and the world. Here is your first coachable moment: write the following on a sheet of paper and put it where you'll see it every day for a year: *"Today is the first day of the best of my life."* Sign it and date it.

Now congratulate yourself and buckle your seatbelt, because you're in for the High-Ways ride of your life!

Defining Attitude

> *Go confidently in the direction of your dreams. Live the life you've imagined. — Henry David Thoreau*

Right now you *are* living the life you've imagined. You always have been. Your imagination is where your future comes to life, so you're living the result of what you've expected to happen so far. Are you ready to imagine better? As soon as you make that simple shift, imagining a life you love, your life will change dramatically.

And there's more good news. While your imagination determines your future, your attitude shapes your present. Everyone talks about "the importance of attitude," but no one has ever offered a definition simple and powerful enough to be universally accepted. Look at how various texts have defined the concept. The only thing that's clear is how *unclear* we are:

Attitudes have to do with your orientation towards something...

(*Boundaries*, Dr. Henry Cloud and Dr. John Townsend)

My definition for attitude is simple: Life!

(*Attitude Is Everything*, Keith Harrell)

Attitude: a manner of showing one's feelings or thoughts; a state of mind; one's disposition, opinion, etc.; a manner of acting...

(Webster's Dictionary)

It's time for a definition of attitude we can all agree on. If you could choose between the following three answers, which one would you say attitude is: a set of feelings and emotions, thoughts and beliefs, or behaviors and actions?

When I ask executives, sales teams, entrepreneurs, parents, nurses, educators, and counselors this question, their answers are equally divided between each option. If a fourth option is offered — "all of the above" — 90 percent will choose that answer, even though *it's wrong*.

There's only one correct response. Your attitude is based on your thoughts and beliefs. Attitude is mental, not emotional or behavioral. Emotions and behaviors are the results of our thoughts and beliefs. Once we get this, we can better understand how *we* are in charge of our attitudes.

Years ago, I created a diagram to demonstrate how attitude works. Since positive attitude is the key to personal power, ***8 to Great*** refers to this graphic as...

The Power Pyramid

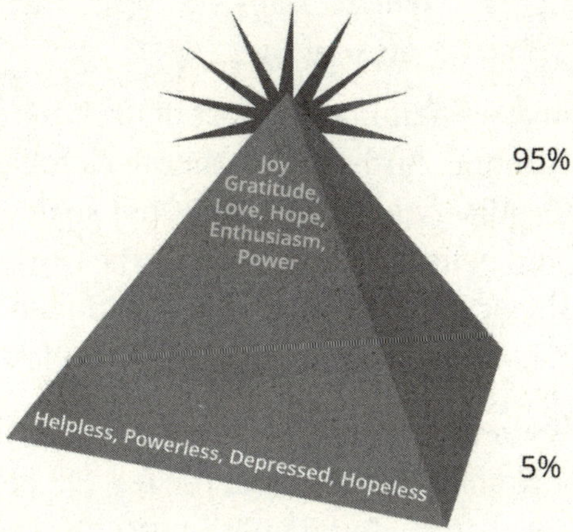

We are at "95" on the Power Pyramid when 95 percent of our thoughts feel good. Another way of saying that is when 95 percent of our thoughts feel good, we're using 95 percent of our power.

We are at "5" on the Power Pyramid when only 5 percent of our thoughts feel good. That's because when only 5 percent of our thoughts feel good, we're only using 5 percent of our power.

Most of our lives we are hovering somewhere between "5" and "95." As you become more aware of how your thoughts feel with the 8 High-Ways, you'll not only be able to move up the Power Pyramid, you'll be able to do it quickly, by selecting the focus of your *next thought*.

Misery Loves Company, But...

Complete the following phrases:

What goes around...
Birds of a feather...
When it rains, it...
Misery loves...

The adages above are familiar to most of us. What goes around comes around. Birds of a feather flock together. When it rains, it pours. Misery loves company, but so does joy! The thoughts and beliefs you have about the world are like boomerangs: they come back to you, often immediately. This universal truth is often referred to as the Law of Attraction.

On the Power Pyramid, at any moment in your day, you're between the bottom (5 percent) and the top (95 percent). When you're down at a "5" and only 5 percent of your thoughts feel good, you feel like a victim — hopeless and powerless. As a result, you either attract others who feel the same or you bring out the worst in those around you.

Conversely, when you're at the top at "95," and 95 percent of your thoughts feel good, you attract others who feel powerful, grateful, joyful and hopeful, and bring out the best in those around you. At the top of the pyramid, you're full of energy, enthusiasm, and appreciation. You're confident about your destiny and understand that what you focus on determines how your life will play out.

Your Attitude Score

You can use the Power Pyramid at any time to gauge how positive your attitude is. Are you feeling powerful right now ("95-ing")? Or are you giving away your power by complaining, blaming, regretting, or worrying ("5-ing")?

We all have something we could be complaining about or worrying about right now. We also all have something we could be grateful for right now. The decision between those good feeling (powerful) thoughts and the not-good feeling (powerless) thoughts will determine which direction our life is going.

As you grasp the concept of the Power Pyramid, more and more aspects of your life will start to make sense. For example, you'll see that "5" and "95" personalities do not choose to be around each other. When we're "5-ing" and having a bad day, and come across a "95-er" who is having a great day, we tend to write them off, label them as fake, or assume they're just "lucky."

Not only that, but when we look at the "what goes around" principle, it's clear that because there is a smaller circumference at the top, what goes around (the good stuff) comes around faster up there. When we're choosing thoughts that feel good, what we desire shows up quickly. We often call those manifestations "luck," "coincidence", or "miracles." But this wonderful power we've been given by our Creator is not random. It's at work every moment of every day.

> *Success is not the way to happiness. Happiness is the way to success. — Albert Schweitzer*

Choosing Your Focus

How can you choose to focus your thoughts more deliberately? Right now, think back to your last great vacation. Remember how much fun you were having? There, you just changed your focus. It's that simple. The next time something goes "wrong," remind yourself that focusing on something that you're grateful for is a perfectly painless and side-effects free way to feel better immediately. That, in itself, will be your motivator.

Will it work? The truth that your thoughts create your reality has been written about in a myriad of ways by some of the greatest teachers of all time.

In ancient Scriptures:

Everything you ask for, believe you have it already, and it shall be yours.

Mark 11:24

In government:

The empires of the future are empires of the mind.

Winston Churchill

In philosophy:

Great men are those who see that thoughts rule the world.

Ralph Waldo Emerson

In motivational literature:

When you are grateful, fear disappears and abundance appears.

Tony Robbins

In sports:

They said I was too small, but I just knew that the Seahawks would pick me and I would make the other 31 teams regret it. I remember my Dad asking me something that's always stuck with me, "Why not you, Russ?" Why not me? So speaking to our football team earlier in the year I asked, "Why not us?" We believed that we could get here and now here we are.

Russell Wilson, MVP Super Bowl 2013

The message is consistent: your life is like it is because of what you choose to think about, focus on and believe in.

Thoughts That Feel Good

You're thinking about something right now. That thought either feels good (moving you higher on the Power Pyramid) or it doesn't (taking you lower on the Power Pyramid). Your homework is to travel the road of the thoughts that feel better. When you get detoured onto thoughts that don't feel good, catch yourself, make a legal "you-turn," and return to a better feeling place.

For example, imagine you've just finished a presentation at work and are feeling good about it as you drive home, but then realize you forgot a key point. There's nothing you can do about it now, but you can focus on gratitude for the car you're driving, or your great spouse, or your health.

Or perhaps you awaken feeling good but then hear your teens arguing about who's been in the bathroom too long. You could take a deep breath, accept that teenagers argue, and imagine what you would be missing if you had lived your life without them.

I'm often asked how long it takes to change your life using the 8 High-Ways. My reply is always, "As long as it takes you to think your next thought." Try it right now. In the next moment, choose a thought that feels good, such as...

- ✓ *admiring the beauty of a tree outside your window*
- ✓ *appreciating the love and support of a good friend*

- ✓ *delighting in your child, grandchild, or pet*
- ✓ *relishing a recent accomplishment*
- ✓ *dreaming of "Won't it be wonderful when..."*

When you can't seem to find a thought that really feels good, find a thought that at least feels *better,* such as...

- ✓ *accepting that it's okay to cry*
- ✓ *realizing you probably won't remember this pain five years from now*
- ✓ *you don't have to do anything right now...but just be*

Take a moment right now to be grateful for your ability to read the words on this page. At this writing, 775 million people on the planet cannot read a book. Then wiggle your toes. Realize that when you were born, someone was very grateful that you had ten of them! Notice how these thoughts are affecting how you feel? That's the work we'll be doing in this process, but it will often feel more like play.

The FGH Formula

So, what are the best ways to get to the top of the Power Pyramid and stay there? Simply choosing your mental focus and going to thoughts that feel better. Since every thought is about the past, present, or future, I define Positive Attitude in a simple three-letter formula, FGH:

F*orgiveness of the past,*

G*ratitude for the present,*

and **H***ope for the future.*

Once I discovered the power of FGH, I shared it with anyone who would listen. I began seeing its effects in my children as well as in the lives of thousands of my coaching clients and seminar participants. The results were never short of astounding.

Nearly every holy book, guru, saint, and mystic has spoken of these three virtues in some manner as the path to peace, freedom and enlightenment. This book will take you through the 8 High-Ways process to a positively powerful life. Before explaining how the 8 came to be, let me summarize them.

The 8 High-Ways in a Nutshell

High-Way 1: Get the Picture

Visualizing the outcome *until it feels real* is the first step to any dream or goal. Once you're clear on your destination, keep thinking about it until you can get excited by what it will be like. Then, from that good-feeling place, the next step will reveal itself as surely as the next yellow brick showed up on Dorothy's road to Oz. Visualize yourself getting the diploma, driving the new car, or laughing with loved ones. It'll take you straight to "95" on the Power Pyramid.

High-Way 2: Risk

Once your dream starts to take shape, your next step will be to take a risk to follow it. Those who we refer to as "cowardly" have the same amount of fear as heroes, but they use their fear as an excuse to stay stuck. Heroes feel the fear and do it anyway. Whether it's the risk of telling the truth or pursuing a dream, the bigger the risk, the bigger the reward. Risking is letting go of security as the world defines it for a larger safety net — being true to yourself. Risk is never running from (our fears) — it's always running to (our dreams). Imagine, if you had no fear, what would you do?

High-Way 3: Full Responsibility

As we travel down the Risk High-Way, obstacles and detours will inevitably appear. We can curse the inconveniences of life, and blame and complain, but not without being pulled down the Power Pyramid. Full Responsibility is the fundamental shift that moves us from B.C. (Blaming and Complaining) to A.D. (Acting and Dreaming). Until we realize that we're in charge of our thoughts, and therefore our lives, we will be trapped in a prison of resentment, bitterness, and confusion. When we acknowledge the power of our focus, we realize that we were never prisoners in the first place.

High-Way 4: Feel All Your Feelings

As challenges arise, allowing yourself to Feel All Your Feelings takes you to a childlike freedom, where emotions can come and go without guilt or denial. When we realize that there are no "bad" feelings, we stop getting stuck in one feeling to prevent feeling another. We realize that we can feel mad and sad and still have a positive attitude. Once we're freed up emotionally, we "feel" better physically as well. Finally, as we overcome the fear and judgment of our own emotions, we can more easily accept the feelings of others.

High-Way 5: Honest Communication

Once we get in touch with our emotions through High-Way 4, we're ready to practice communicating them honestly with others in a self-responsible way. The practice of non-defensive listening and assertively asking for what we want empowers us and deepens our connection to those around us. When we risk taking responsibility for our feelings rather than blaming others for them, we combine the first four High-Ways into an "inner-state" of loving joy.

High-Ways 6, 7, 8: The FGH Formula

Together, the sixth, seventh, and eighth High-Ways make up the world's most powerful positive attitude formula. Since attitude is mental, not emotional, and since all thoughts are either about the past, present, or future, we only need to practice three kinds of thoughts: FGH.

High-Way 6: Forgiveness of the Past

...is knowing we were all doing the best we could at the time with the information we had.

High-Way 7: Gratitude for the Present

...is focusing on appreciation and celebration of the good in every person and situation.

High-Way 8: Hope for the Future

...is the light within us, no matter how small, that helps us persevere through the darkness. It's knowing that our destiny awaits.

How 8 to Great Came to Be: The First Five High-Ways

As simple a concept as FGH has been for my clients and audiences to understand, when I first began to teach it, there were often people who seemed unable to change their negative thought patterns. Despite their longing for greater happiness, they acted almost hostile toward the concepts of forgiveness, gratitude, and hope. I was determined to find out why.

By talking with them week after week, I learned that some were stuck in rage and depression — angry about their anger and sad about their sadness. They didn't realize that it's possible to be mad and sad and still have a positive attitude because they'd been taught to label those feelings as "negative." I saw that their inability to accept and acknowledge their feelings was keeping them stuck. At that point, I added High-Way 4: *Feel All Your Feelings* to my process.

It became clear that once an individual got in touch with their feelings, good communication skills were necessary to give those emotions a voice. Because many had never learned those skills in childhood, I added High-Way 5: *Honest Communication.*

I noticed another pattern as I came across those who had lost touch with their dreams. They had no sense of their purpose and were simply going through the motions. *Get the Picture* became High-Way 1.

For those who could verbalize their dreams but were hiding in their comfort zones and afraid to follow them, I added High-Way 2: *Risk.*

Finally, for those who were stuck in Blaming and Complaining and who didn't understand that power only comes with *Full Responsibility*, I added that as High-Way 3.

In coaching clients to greater freedom and fulfillment, I now teach the first five High-Ways to clear the way for 6, 7, and 8 — F, G, and H. The exciting reality has been that the 8 High-Ways work every time for those willing to invest in the process.

I've found that luck is quite predictable. — Brian Tracy

The Science of Luck

Most of us claim we don't believe in luck, yet refer to it almost daily when discussing coincidental occurrences. When things go very well or terribly wrong for someone we know, we talk about that person being "fortunate" or "down on their luck." But good and bad fortune are neither random nor mysterious. On the contrary, the way your life plays out is the direct result of your thoughts and beliefs. When we get this, we get it all.

Luck or the Law?

I got to see The Science of Luck in action a few years back after speaking at the International Jaycees conference in Barcelona. I started to feel sad about leaving. As the airport shuttle pulled up, I decided to change my mood by imagining a truly interesting and fun ride to the airport.

Once I got on the shuttle, I was "fortunate" to enjoy a half-hour chat with the winner of that year's World's Top Young Person award. I knew as I listened that Tim Lawrence lived all eight of the High-Ways. He was upbeat, optimistic, and had a contagious "can-do" confidence that had helped him accomplish everything from running for office to swimming the English Channel. Today he is Lt. Col. Timothy J. Lawrence, and holds a Ph.D. in Electrical and Satellite Engineering.

Was this wonderful encounter a coincidence? Of course not. I could have stayed in self-pity and pouted all the way to the airport. Instead I invited joy and received it.

It All Adds Up

You've had a thousand little regrets — a thousand big and little disappointments. So, when you're ready to release those old patterns and begin living the life of your dreams, answer the following: What percentage of your life isn't working right now? Is it 10 percent, 50 percent, 90 percent? Take a moment now to come up with your number.

Even if it's 100 percent, just be honest with yourself. What percentage would you like to trade in for an upgrade? Okay, got the number? *That's the percentage of your thinking that has to be reprogrammed.* That percentage tells you how often you have forgotten your power to shift your focus. When you choose thoughts that feel good, your positive thoughts will all add *up*.

When You Feel Good

Before we move on, here's an activity you can use to feel better right now. Take a moment to complete this phrase five times: "When I feel good I..." (For example, "I have more energy.")

Answers like "I smile more," "I laugh more," or "I'm more patient" often show up on this list. You may have written: I feel better, am kinder, more creative, or more productive. Whatever your answers were, they can be summed up this way:

When you feel good, good things happen.

Ever noticed how often people say, "I'll be happy when..." but *when* never arrives? Happiness is your choice in this moment, and it's an inside job.

> *There is no way to happiness. Happiness is the way.*
> *— Dr. Wayne Dyer*

Your Gratitude Heartwork

You will never change your life until you change something that you do daily.

John Maxwell

Although Gratitude is its own High-Way (7), it's such a simple way to get to "95" quickly, I'm going to start you on that part of the process now. It will make all of the other High-Ways easier, I promise.

Each day, take a minute to think of three things you're grateful for from the past twenty-four hours, no repeats. Then, share them with someone in your life, either verbally or in writing. In order to see the best results, do this each morning or evening for the next thirty days.

The most important components of this heartwork are sharing it and remembering not to repeat. If you are grateful for "sunshine" tomorrow morning, for example, you're done with sunshine for life! Why? Because repeating the same phrases over and over (health, job, family, etc.) can get stale and lose their ability to evoke a positive result. Stay fresh by looking for new things every day to be grateful for. You'll be amazed at how easy this will become over time.

My Gratitudes on an average day might look like:

1. *the gurglings of my guinea pig*
2. *new blooms on my Peace Lily*
3. *the taste of bananas on my oatmeal*

Or:

1. *the beautiful full moon last night*
2. *my sweetheart's midday phone call*
3. *that someone figured out how to make the next Kleenex pop up!*

That's it! Whether it's your nice big deck, your iPod, your mail carrier, the change in your pocket, or your contact lenses, you'll start to see life through grateful eyes. There may be some days that are more challenging, but trust the process and share three Gratitudes a day, even if one of them is "I'm grateful I remembered to share my Gratitudes today!" If you ever forget for a few days, weeks, or months, just FGH yourself: Forgive yourself for forgetting, be Grateful that you remembered when you did, and have Hope that you'll remember better next time.

If you're feeling down, off balance or like your heart is broken,keeping a gratitude journal will change your life. I guarantee it!

Oprah Winfrey

1

High-Way 1: Get the Picture

Think It 'Til You Feel It

Defining Get the Picture

We're never given a dream without the power to make it come true.

Richard Bach

Emma's Dream Job

I met Emma at one of my workshops. She sought me out at lunchtime to talk about how unhappy she was at her accounting firm. She didn't feel as if she shared the values of her employers and longed for things to be different.

When I asked what her dream job looked like, she chuckled, as though the concept of finding it was ludicrous, but eventually she not only told me, but also started journaling about it. It was the first step on her road to success.

What would your life be like if you woke up tomorrow with a magic wand?

Imagine that all you had to do was wave your magic wand in a figure eight, say your wish aloud, and it would come true in the next day, week, or month. How would that power change your life? I hear some of you thinking, "I'd win the lottery." Great. Then what? Where would you go? What would you do? Who would you be?

High-Way 1 is a reminder that you do have the power to co-create wealth, health, romance, and the job of your dreams — powers you've forgotten and therefore haven't been using to their full capacity. Your power has nothing to do with your bank account, your job title, your waistline, or your age. Your power lies within.

Spend any time around toddlers and you'll recall that we were all born with the boldness to ask for what we want, but as we grow, the litanies of "life is hard" and "get your head out of the clouds" take their toll. As a result, too many of us abandon our dreams. We start to see ourselves as helpless prey to life's circumstances, unworthy of life's greatest gifts.

The exciting news is that we can release those self-imposed limits by using the first ***8 to Great*** High-Way: **Get the Picture**.

The Magic "Want"

Instead of a wand, you have a magic *want*. Every time you **Get the Picture** and think about something you desire, your thoughts send out energy — like a magnet to attract that very thing to you. The more you think about it, the more real it becomes, until the thought of it feels as real as the chair you're sitting on. The easiest way to move from conceiving (thinking a new thought) to believing (feeling excited) is by using your imagination.

The C-B-A Formula:
If you **C***onceive it and* **B***elieve it, you will* **A***chieve it.*

> *The biggest thing I've been thankful for is my imagination. When people said, "It's impossible; it can't be done," that's where my imagination came into play.*
> *— Michael Phelps*

As children, daydreaming and pretending came naturally and occupied much of our time. Then, as we grew, many of us started to forget the fun and magic of "acting as if." Yet the happiest, healthiest, and most successful adults never stop daydreaming. They understand that their thoughts become their beliefs which then become their future.

Goals vs. Dreams

Part of understanding the power of dreams is to see how they differ from goals. Most books on goal-setting remind us that a goal is a target achieved by following specific steps to a desired outcome. In the Gratitude heartwork at the end of the Foundation chapter, for example, I coached you on how many Gratitudes to do and when to do them. Your goal might be to do them five days this week. Goals are extremely beneficial to a healthy life.

Dreams — the ones you have when you're awake — are very different. Books on dreams are even in a separate section on the bookstore shelves. That's because a dream is bigger — so large in fact, that people are often reluctant to share theirs out loud. If they do, it's only to a select few, because tears can flow when we touch this sacred place within.

Meanwhile, when your big dreams become clear, the steps necessary to achieve them are often hidden from view, which can feel frightening or overwhelming. Following a dream is a leap of faith that can discourage weaker hearts from ever getting started.

Leap and the net will appear. —Julia Cameron

A simple way to distinguish between a goal and a dream is as follows:

A Goal is S.M.A.R.T. =

Specific, Measurable, Attainable, Realistic, and Time-Based

When we set a goal, we know Who, What, When, Where, Why, How, and How Long. For example: I will walk for thirty minutes, five days a week, in my neighborhood to get back in shape.

A Dream is B.I.G. =

Bold, Innovative, and Grand

When we allow ourselves to dream, we disregard Who, When, Where, How and How Long. Instead, we focus only on What (we want) and Why (we want it). The other W and H questions are *head* questions that can take us from fantasizing to fretting, while What and Why are *heart* questions. They're the "turn-ons" that we can feel in the depths of our being.

"Johnny, Stop Paying Attention and Start Daydreaming!"

Remember the well-meaning teachers in our past who would scold daydreamers during class, telling them to "pay attention" and to "snap out of it?" Some such "challenging" students known for "excessive daydreaming" were Albert Einstein, Thomas Edison, J.K. Rowling, Lewis Carroll, and Eleanor Roosevelt. Not a bad gang to be associated with!

So how do you start believing the impossible is possible? I once asked an airline pilot how much his plane weighed. He lit up as he told me, "That's my favorite question! About 266,000 pounds, fully loaded!" That day I realized that if I could believe that a one-hundred-ton metal machine could fly, I could believe anything. So can you. As the White Queen pointed out to ***Alice in Wonderland***, it just takes practice.

> *Alice laughed. "There's no use trying," she said. "One can't believe impossible things."*
> *"I daresay you haven't had much practice," said the Queen. "When I was your age, I always did it for half an hour a day. Why, sometimes I've believed as many as six impossible things before breakfast." — From Lewis Carroll's* ***Through the Looking Glass***

Why is this such good news? Because the imagining is almost as much fun as the experiencing, and studies have shown has virtually the same effect on the body. Since the mind can't tell the difference between a thought and a reality, you can feel better instantly by going to that place in your imagination and crafting your ideal scene. Think of it as a free Virtual Reality ride.

Often, we only dream dreams that are similar to our daily experience, but the more we read and listen to the stories of great dreamers, the more we realize that even the sky isn't the limit when our heart is in it.

What can you expect from expecting miracles? Recently, a high school student told me that using **Get the Picture** to imagine working with his dad to restore an old car helped him stop fighting at school, thereby allowing him to graduate. Imagine that!

Strong Desires and Big Dreams

As children, many of us were warned by well-meaning adults that strong desires were "bad." Yet the word for "de-sire" is French for "of the Father." (Even the desire for no desire is a desire.) Desires naturally burn within us from the moment of birth and are the fuel for our dreams.

Passionate desires and big dreams are the common thread linking the most successful and "luckiest" people in the world. This can be seen in the true stories that have become film classics such as ***Coach Carter, Music of the Heart, Rudy, Sea Biscuit, Invincible, Milk, Erin Brokovitch, Hidden Figures,*** and so many others. Each hero in these stories was branded as "out of their minds" by those around them. They were out of their minds and into their hearts. As with all dreamers, their dreams had moved from their heads to their hearts.

> *Desire is half of life; indifference is half of death.*
> *— Kahlil Gibran*

Mary Lou Retton

In 1984, the first perfect 10 score in the history of the United States Olympic team was achieved by a sixteen-year-old named Mary Lou Retton. When the reporters swarmed around her after her flawless performance on the vault, someone asked, "How does it feel to have received the first perfect 10 for the U.S. team?"

Her answer was, "Like it's always felt!"

"But no one has ever done it before!" the reporter challenged.

"I've done it thousands of times in my mind," was her reply.

A belief is a thought you keep thinking until you feel it.

Mary Lou understood that nothing is impossible once you believe it to be true. For years she thought about the excitement of achieving a perfect 10. The only impossibility was that she would *not* achieve it.

> *Your hopes, dreams, and aspirations are legitimate. They are trying to take you airborne, above the clouds, above the storms, if you only let them. — William James*

Barcelona Baby

Years ago, when speaking to a group in Minneapolis, I was "95-ing." Sharing the speaking docket with Patch Adams for a large healthcare organization, I was getting paid to do what I loved and I got to see some dear friends. One was Brian McDermott, my agent, who had come to hear me speak. Add to that the warm first-week-of-spring weather, and you can imagine how good I felt. When we're "buzzing" at this high level, we're like Jack and his Magic Beans. Anything we plant will grow more quickly.

After I finished my talk, Brian and I went for a walk. "So, what's new with you?" I asked.

"The wife and kids and I are leaving for Spain next week," Brian replied, glowing.

He then went into colorful detail of what markets, music, and museums they were looking forward to, as well as the bullfights they'd probably skip. It was a glorious day-dreamy discussion, during which we both got more and more excited about his trip to Barcelona. (Let me note that I had never had the tiniest desire to travel to Spain before that day when the seeds were planted.)

The following day, as I was unpacking my bags back at home, the phone rang. It was Brian.

"How would you like to go to Barcelona in November?"

"With you?" I asked, stunned.

"No, with the International Jaycees. They want you to be the keynote speaker. Pack your bags, baby. You're going to Barcelona!"

That was how my first international talk was translated into seven languages and I got to share the stage with one of my favorite authors, Edward de Bono. It is a memory that can still take me to "95."

> *Most people associate the word 'abracadabra' with magicians pulling rabbits out of hats. It's actually an Aramaic term that translates into English as, "I will create as I speak." — Pam Grout*

The Get the Picture Process: Believing Is Receiving

The ***8 to Great*** process defines success as "setting a goal or dreaming a dream and achieving it." What always amazes me is that the greatest stumbling block for most people is the first half – acknowledging our goals and dreams. The majority of us don't take the time to get clear about our desires because we've never learned how powerful this process can be. Yet it's as simple as listing what you want.

What You Want to Receive/Experience

To fully experience the power of this concept, create a list of things you'd like to receive or experience. We'll call them intentions. You may list anything, as long as you're willing to believe it's possible for you to receive them. For the fun of it, make your intentions different sizes — some smaller and some larger.

Smaller Intentions

Experiencing an exceptional sunrise or sunset
Surprise money
A delightful surprise
Receiving a compliment from a stranger
An "aha" insight
Hearing your favorite song
Eating your favorite food
An invitation to a celebration
Having a belly laugh
Hearing from an old friend/ distant relative
Finding something you've misplaced
Receiving flowers
Attracting a new client

Larger Intentions

Getting a big promotion or new job offer
Finding a solution to a long-standing problem
Meeting your true love/ a new lifelong friend
Finding out you're pregnant
A new car, boat, or RV
Winning a competition or getting a scholarship
Being asked on a national talk show as an expert
Having a health challenge disappear
Receiving a surprise gift of $10,000
Running/Winning a race/marathon
Making it to a Hall of Fame

Inventing something that saves lives/the planet

Donating enough for a building on your favorite campus

Being part of the team that finds a cure

Receiving an honorary Ph.D.

An invitation on a safari/cruise/adventure

I recall a beautiful young seventeen-year-old named Maddie who showed up in one of my classes with a big dream she had basically given up on. She dreamed of studying in Spain her senior year. Her biggest challenge was that none of her applications for scholarships had been accepted. It was now May of her junior year, and in her mind, she had "missed all her chances" by three or four months.

I was so grateful that she was extremely coachable and willing to give the process a chance. In getting clear on her dream, I invited her to let go of "when" her trip would happen. She relaxed. She released her internal struggle ("5ing"), and started to talk about the trip as though it had already taken place ("95ing").

Shortly thereafter, she met someone from a local Rotary Club. When she asked what Rotary did, he shared that one of things they did was to send students abroad on scholarships. He added that, to his knowledge, they still had one left for the upcoming year that had not been assigned.

She applied, and within a few weeks got confirmation that her senior year would be spent in Barcelona. In her words, "*I had given up on going to Spain until I learned this process. Writing down my dream list and talking about what I wanted got me believing again. You just feel it on a whole different level. Then my passion helped me visualize things — like what I was going to do when I heard the news that I got accepted to a program.*

Within three weeks I had won a scholarship to study in Spain for an entire year. All I can tell you is, this process works!"

> *Your dream must be bigger than what you think you can do. — Mary Manin Morrissey*

Why Writing Helps

Every thought is an intention, but the ones you write down and/or share aloud will manifest more quickly because thinking about them and then writing them down helps bring the picture of your dream into focus. It's important to keep that written record to encourage you. As you look back over your journaling and see the intentions you've written start to appear, "95-ing" automatically results.

When you're ready to allow miraculous manifestations into your life, pick one of your intentions and do the following visualization.

Get the Picture 3-Minute Visualization

Make yourself comfortable, take a nice deep breath and close your eyes.

In your mind, go to the day when your dream is coming true. See it in full color. Notice what you're wearing, who's there with you, what fragrance is in the air, what people are saying, and especially how you're feeling. Stay there for a minute.

Next, in your dream, notice someone walking excitedly toward you. Hear them say that they have a dream similar to yours and want to know how you did it. Take a minute to tell them that you released the "How," simply imagined the good feelings of the end result, and Got the Picture of it coming true. Enjoy that conversation for a minute.

Then, keeping your eyes closed, imagine yourself returning home after that dream-come-true day. In your mind's eye, walk in the door and see your mail lying on the counter. Notice that the top letter is addressed to you. Sit down and open it. As you read it, discover that it's full of even more good news. It may be a love letter, a check, an announcement that you've won an award, a scholarship, or a thank-you letter from someone whose life you've touched. Be there with your feelings for a minute. When you're finished, open your eyes.

How did that feel? Inspiring? Hopeful? Exciting? When we focus on our dreams it feels good and lifts us to "95!"

> *What we think determines what we feel, which determines what we do, which determines who we are.*
> *— Anonymous*

Flexing Your Imagination Muscle

People sometimes tell me that they've "forgotten how to dream," but that simply means they're out of practice using their imagination. Imagination is natural to us. It's what a child exercises while packing for summer camp, what an actor uses to create a role, what a new home owner uses to decorate, or what a chef draws on to create a new dish. It's a muscle we all have that can be flexed and strengthened whenever we're ready to spend time on it.

Get the Picture is learning to harness that wonderful power — to see the checks as though they're already coming in, feel your clothes fitting loosely, smell your new love's cologne, or hear the laughter as your co-workers interact with all your new customers. In that instant, you are powerfully drawing your dreams into physical reality.

Thinking a Thought Until You Feel It

As we think a new thought, we're transformed. I can start thinking of myself as having a great memory for names. You can practice thinking of yourself as healthier and more energetic than you've ever been. Who do you think you are? Whatever your answer, that's who you're becoming. On any given day, you can practice believing that:

- ✓ *money is hard to come by*
- ✓ *there's no time to do what you really want*
- ✓ *you have trouble making new friends*

OR you can practice believing that:

- ✓ *more than enough money flows to you effortlessly*
- ✓ *you get everything that needs to be done accomplished with time to spare*
- ✓ *you make and keep good friends easily*

How can you tell what you believe now? Look at your life. Are you getting what you desire? I have a dear friend named Phil who always gets the parking spot right in front of the restaurant we're meeting at, no matter how full the parking lot. He jokingly calls it "Phil's Space." He expects to get the perfect parking space, and life becomes a mirror of his thoughts.

> *You have within you a GPS system that never asks where you've been or why you've been there so long. It simply listens to the now, and is set up to take you where you want to go by following thoughts that feel good.*
> *— Abraham-Hicks*

Waiting vs. Expecting

Perhaps the most challenging piece of dreaming is releasing the How and When and allowing a dream to show up in its own time and in its own way. Expecting is an apt description of the "95" frame of mind. Like the mother anticipating the birth of her child, you take your focus off of "wondering if" and move it into "preparing for."

When we stay focused on What we want and Why we want it, it will come to us at just the right time. This understanding is crucial because when we can release our attachment to the When of our dreams, we'll have the freedom to enjoy each and every moment of the present.

> *Infinite patience produces immediate results.*
> *— Dr. Wayne Dyer*

Getting frustrated can actually delay your desire from reaching you. Whenever you're drumming your fingers and looking at your watch as you await a particular dream-come-true, get back to "95" by noticing three things you're grateful for. Then let your imagination paint a picture of how perfect your dream will be when it arrives!

Remember to be gentle with yourself. Intensity can be a good thing, but tension is counterproductive when you're doing your intentions. Bringing dreams to life requires focus, not force.

Why Pushing Against Doesn't Work

Our brains are like computers — they can't take a joke. When we keep pulling up a mental picture, even one we don't like, we are focusing on it, and then are more likely to call it into being. I recall speaking to a woman after one of my talks in North Dakota. Her two friends were a few feet away and loudly exclaiming how they did not want to slip on the ice on the way to the car because they were all dressed up.

"They're going down," I said softly to the woman next to me. She looked confused, so I continued. "Even though their focus is all about not slipping, the picture in their minds is of slipping."

"You should warn them!" she told me.

"I just spent two hours warning them. I don't think they'd believe me."

As we spoke, the two women headed out the door and fell down within seconds. Fortunately, we were able to help them up and walk them safely to their cars.

This concept - that pushing against something actually attracts it to us - can take a while to wrap our minds around. We start to realize that:

- ✓ *Every time we criticize someone for a mistake, we are encouraging them to make more mistakes.*
- ✓ *Every time we think about how fat we are, we are more likely to gain weight.*

✓ *Every time we complain about bills, we attract more bills.*

So how do you not fall into these thought patterns? Impossible. Trying *not* to do them will simply bring more of them. Instead of worrying about a problem, we can exchange it for imagining how it will feel once we have the solution. Fortunately, positive thoughts are a thousand times more powerful than negative thoughts, and so it only takes a few minutes of dreaming a day to see amazing results.

Plugging into Your Power

You can't access your power while you're focused on what you don't want. You'll be like a lamp whose plug can't find the outlet. But once you "plug in" by focusing on thoughts that feel good, there's no dream or goal you can't bring to light.

After hearing about these concepts in his ***8 to Great*** class, one high school junior took the message to heart. During class, he did the gratitude exercises, then spent three minutes visualizing winning first place in his swim meet against a tough team later that afternoon.

> *Stay away from people who belittle your aspirations. Small people do that. But the truly great people in the world will make you believe that you, too, can one day become great. — Mark Twain*

Five hours later, he not only won first place, but took two full seconds off his personal record. After seeing his time, he jumped out of the water and ran up to his coach yelling, "She was right! That lady was right! When I believe it, I can achieve it!"

He became the motivational coach for his team that season, and the last time I saw him, was enjoying his full scholarship to art school. When I offered him a small card with the High-Ways on it, he asked, "Isn't the old one good anymore?" He had held onto it all those years.

Why We Don't Ask and Believe

We handcuff the heavens when we don't ask.

Caroline Myss

Take a moment to answer the following:

When it comes to *asking for what you want*, which of the following is most true:

A. The most selfish people do it all the time.

B. We should only ask when people are in good moods.

C. It's a risk that often ends up badly.

D. The happiest and healthiest people do it all the time.

The amazing thing is that only 10 percent of people get the answer correct the first time. The answer is D. One morning I got a glimpse as to why...

Santa Claus or Fairy Godmother?

"Can I talk with you for a minute?" asked a handsome twenty-something man after my ***8 to Great*** class at a homeless shelter. (I later discovered that although he was homeless, he'd been a professional model.) He walked me to my car and along the way told me how much he'd appreciated my presentation. Then he shared what was on his mind.

"If I start asking for things every day like you suggest, isn't that like believing in Santa Claus? If it were that simple, why wouldn't we all have what we want?"

I thanked him for his powerful question, then asked him to sit with me for a few minutes to do a visualization. He agreed, sat down, and closed his eyes as I began:

"Imagine that your fairy godmother appears to you tonight while you're sleeping. She sprinkles magic fairy dust over you and says, 'As of tomorrow morning, you'll be blessed with more money than you could ever spend. Everywhere you go, you'll increase your wealth. But there's one spending rule: you may keep it or spend it on yourself, but you may only give it to others if they ask.'

"Now imagine it's a month later. You're grateful for having money and all the things money can bring, and excited about visiting family members in another state. As you drive up to their small home, you can't wait to begin sharing your wealth. They greet you with hugs and start asking questions about your amazing new car. You explain about your fairy godmother and that all they have to do is ask and you can give them as much abundance as they want.

"'No way,' says your brother. 'That money's not mine. I can't take any of it.'

"'We haven't done anything to deserve it. It wouldn't be right,' explains your sister-in-law.

"'I don't believe that crazy story,' challenges your nephew.

"'I'm happy the way I am, son, but thank you,' adds your mom.

"A few days later, you drive away, confused and sad that you couldn't give your nephew a scholarship, your brother a hunting trip up north, your mom a comfortable recliner, or your sister-in-law a new minivan. You understand now why most people don't get. Most people don't ask."

Tears were rolling down his cheeks by the time I finished. He hugged me, thanked me, and walked back to his living quarters. The next day, he started to dream of getting back into shape. That week, someone donated like-new tennis shoes in his (very large) size to the shelter. Six weeks later, he had a good job and had lost twenty-five pounds. Six months later, he called to thank me for helping him turn his life around.

> *"We do not need magic to change the world, we carry all the power we need inside ourselves already: we have the power to imagine better." — J.K. Rowling*

The Reasons We Don't Ask

Happiness is always knocking at the front door, yet many of us run out the back. As I discussed at length in my first book, ***Taking Care of Me: The Habits of Happiness***, here are the four main reasons why:

1. We're afraid of getting our dream.
2. We're afraid of being disappointed by losing our dream.
3. We believe we don't deserve our dream.
4. We'd feel guilty about enjoying happiness when others are still unhappy.

A phone call I received one day made me shake my head and smile. An intelligent, happy, and healthy friend who'd been listening to me talk and receiving my emails for years was helping me proofread an article. In the middle of reading about High-Way 1, he decided to give this stuff a try. He picked up the phone to tell me:

"I got it. Today I got it! I'd been trying to get through to this one business for an hour on the phone, so I finally got fed up and stopped trying. Then I read your **Get the Picture** article and decided to test it. I said to myself, 'Someone will pick up on the third ring and we'll have a wonderful and loving conversation.' I only half believed it, but that's exactly what happened - third ring and all! Today was the first day I really and truly understood this isn't just formula, it's the truth!"

Clearly, the reasons we don't ask and believe make no logical sense. They're simply thought patterns we learned from our parents, who learned them from their parents and passed them along. They were all doing the best they could at the time, but with new information, we can now do better.

> *Imagination is more important than knowledge.*
> *— Albert Einstein*

If He Would Have Asked...

How important is asking for what we want to our happiness and well-being?

The following is an excerpt from a letter I received from a fifteen-year-old boy who had been sentenced to twenty years in prison:

"I find it hard to ask for help from friends and family," he began. "I've always been this way - as far back as I can remember. When I ask for help, it feels like I make the person I ask a better person than me and I'm less of a person for having to ask. I feel like there's something wrong with me and that if I need help I'm not a whole person. I also feel that when someone is helping me I must be lazy. This is the way I've felt all my life, but now as a person aware of himself, it is something I wish to change. I know you're helping me do that."

When I asked him a few weeks later what one message he'd send to young adults if he could share his insights with them, he said, "Reach out for help. There's always someone there. People really do care. God cares. Just ask for help."

> *The reason some of your thoughts haven't yet become things is because other thoughts of yours have.*
> *— Mike Dooley*

Whether it's asking another person or the Source of all that is, many of us are out of practice. When I was growing up, I often heard adults say to the kids in the neighborhood, "You asked for it." We're always asking for it. Every thought is a request. Knowing this, we can become more focused and much better at hitting our mark.

Get the Picture Success Stories

Wealth consciousness comes before the physical manifestation of abundance, not after.

John Randolph Price

I was once asked by a young man if he should follow his dream or follow the dollars. I replied that as I've watched people succeed and fail and succeed again, it had taught me that when you follow your dream, eventually it will take you to the dollars. If you follow dollars, however, they can detour you from your dream.

Asking for Money

Over the years, one of my favorite intentions has been asking for surprise money. It's an easy way to "keep score" of how well you are believing and manifesting miracles. I quickly realized that I had nothing to lose in asking and that when I received it, it felt like winning the lottery without buying a ticket!

At first, I found dimes and quarters everywhere I went. Then one summer day, I asked for hundreds of surprise dollars for a project I was working on. When I came back from the mailbox, my son noticed that I was frowning.

"What's the matter, Mom?" he asked.

"Oh, nothing, honey. I just asked for some surprise money, but there weren't any checks in the mail. I expected it, so I'm a bit confused."

"Money can come in more ways than just the mail," my brilliant twelve-year-old pointed out.

"That's true," I said. "Thanks for the reminder. I'll just keep expecting it and let you know how it shows up."

I do voice work at four recording studios in my area, most often phone messages for Fortune 500 companies. It's fun work that pays well. Only one of the four studios pays me the same day I do the work. An hour after the conversation with my son, I got a phone call from that studio, asking if I could come in on short notice because they had a boatload of work they needed to get out right away. I was paid hundreds of surprise dollars that afternoon.

A few months later, I was explaining the concept to a friend, but she'd have none of it.

"That's so silly," she said. "That wasn't an answer to your request. It was a coincidence."

I asked her to pick an amount of money she wanted me to ask for to convince her.

"OK, $10,000," she said without hesitation.

I got excited and agreed that I'd receive at least that much in the next few weeks. Two days later, I got a surprise phone call from my printer.

"What do you want me to do with these boxes of books?" he asked.

"What boxes are you talking about?" I replied.

"Last year, when you moved into your new house, you asked us to hold half the shipment. They're all paid for, but we have forty boxes sitting here that we need to deliver somewhere."

The total value of that book "find" far exceeded the $10,000 amount I'd requested. My skeptical friend started asking for and receiving surprise money the following day.

One Harvard study showed that ten years after graduation, the MBA graduates who were writing down their dreams were making an average of ten times as much money as those who were not.

Helping Our Children Get the Picture

When he was twelve, my son's nationally renowned children's choir was invited to China to sing at the Great Wall. I immediately contacted the director.

"Don't tell me I can't go," I challenged him. (He sometimes was concerned that having parents along was too great a distraction.) Eventually he gave me permission to lead a parents' tour, with a warning that I'd have to find nineteen other parents to join me. Eight emails and one month later, thirty-nine of the singers' family members had signed on.

Throughout that time, my finances were tied up in a video series we were producing. I wasn't sure where the extra money for the trip would come from, but I wasn't worried. I continued to get our group ready for what promised to be a glorious time, never giving the money a second thought. Two months into the planning process, I received a call from the tour director's office that my trip would be paid for due to my efforts in coordinating the group.

A few days later, Zach asked me for $250 to spend while in China on gifts for family and friends. I knew I could have said yes, but I also knew it was a perfect opportunity for him to learn to manifest abundance for himself.

"Believe that you'll have that much spending money by June, honey," I told him.

"But how will I get it? Shoveling walks? Doing chores for you?" he asked.

"Maybe so. Lots of opportunities will present themselves," I said. "Intend and be grateful that it's already on its way!"

On a snowy day two weeks later, he was in a friend's car on the way to choir practice when they were in a fender bender. Neither of them were hurt, but a month later, we got a call from the other driver's insurance company.

"Ms. Mueller," a voice asked, "Who did you want this check made out to?" I assured him that Zachary had no injuries whatsoever, but the man was insistent. "You don't understand, ma'am. The money has already been issued. I have to write a check to someone. Who would you like it to go to, Zachary or yourself?"

The check addressed to Zach arrived two days later — for $250.00.

Intending a Delightful Surprise

My favorite type of intention is "a delightful surprise." I always ask for these to be "knock your socks off" surprises — and they always are!

> *The important thing is this: To be able at any moment to sacrifice what we are for what we could become.*
> *— Charles Dubois*

One day I hosted a Gratitude Group in my home and nine people showed up. We spent an hour sharing what we were grateful for and saying our intentions out loud. Then we practiced feeling the good feelings we would experience once our intentions showed up. At the end of the evening amid the hugs and goodbyes, one woman asked if she could stay after for some help.

"I'd love to get some CDs to listen to on the days I don't have this group," she began. "Can you recommend some?" We went to my computer and I pulled up a list.

"I have everything by this author except Volume Two," I said. "They're all good, and I'm going to order Volume Two soon because I hear it's great."

She thanked me, gave me a hug, and left. I walked across the room to where my son had left the mail and sat down to read through the pile. When I got to the last item, a small package, I didn't recognize the return address.

"Who do I know in Vermont?" I wondered. I opened the package to find a note from someone I hadn't seen in a year. The note read, "MK, I know you love this author and I've listened to this set many times, so I wanted to share it with you."

It was Volume Two.

The Oscar Dream

I love watching the Oscars — but not for the dresses. I watch the show to hear the inspiring acceptance speeches, like Hilary Swank's when she received her first Oscar for Best Actress.

> *"This is for those dreams that started all those years ago in a mobile home court..."*

I love nothing more than imagining little Hilary looking out the window and imagining winning an Oscar in a gorgeous dress, smiling in front of millions of viewers. If you don't know her story, Google it. It's a classic example of a mother and daughter Getting the Picture while everyone around them was saying, "Impossible!" It is the hallmark of all the greats.

> *I'd be lying if I said I hadn't made a version of this speech before. I was probably eight years old and staring into the bathroom mirror. And this (holding up her statuette) would've been a shampoo bottle. Well, it's not a shampoo bottle now! — Kate Winslet, 2009 Oscar winner of Best Actress*

Love Was Looking for Her

I have seen countless examples of how when we are looking for our dream to be realized, it is looking for us.

Kathleen attended one of my trainings six happy years into her marriage. Over dinner one evening she shared a wonderful story. A few months before her graduation from college, her boyfriend had broken up with her, leaving her devastated. Soon after receiving her diploma, she decided to take charge of her attitude and her love life. It started with a Gratitude list for all the good times they had shared with each other.

“There were so many things to be grateful for. I focused on those and then started dreaming about finding my True Love,” she told me.

She was amazed that just a few days after making her list, love songs were no longer painful to listen to. Instead, she heard the songs as though “he” (her imagined new love) had requested them for her. It wasn’t long before “he” had a name.

It happened when she went to the movie ***A Walk to Remember*** and was completely taken by the actor Shane West. She began to daydream and soon started talking about him to her friends as though they were a couple.

“I’d tell people that Shane was taking me out on Saturday” she told me, “but he wanted to surprise me and wouldn’t tell me where we were going. It was my silly game.”

A few weeks later, a classmate of hers called to say she was looking for someone to ride across the country with her as she moved to Arizona. Kathleen thought the adventure sounded like fun and agreed to go.

> *You've been telling the truth. You've just been telling it in advance. — Zig Ziglar*

"I'll never forget the day we drove through Iowa," Kathleen told me. "We were both in "95" moods. It was a picture-perfect summer day with blue skies, just the right amount of white fluffy clouds, and green rolling hills as far as the eye could see. Then I saw it: a lovely white church steeple peeking out from between the hills. I squealed, 'Look at that. It's perfect! I could live here. I could meet someone wonderful, fall in love, and be deliriously happy!'"

High on hills and hope, Kathleen and her friend stopped at the next town to find a motel for the night. As they were checking in, Kathleen caught the eye of the gentleman behind the counter. Once they started talking, he wouldn't let her out of his sight.

The gentleman's name behind the counter was...Shane. They fell in love over the next few months, and a year later, Kathleen married *Shane*, the man she had met while driving *west.*

Emma Gets Her Job

Remember Emma, the woman I asked to write down her dream job requirements? Before I tell you how things turned out, I need to note that Emma's son was such a phenomenal hockey player that his parents sent him to a year-round hockey instruction program at fifteen-years-old. He was traveling the continent playing his favorite sport. Now see if you can guess what happened. The list of specific intentions for her new job included:

- ✓ *A team-oriented environment*
- ✓ *A growing company that encourages me to venture into new arenas*
- ✓ *An environment that enables me to reach out and meet others*
- ✓ *A job where I don't just sit at a computer all day*
- ✓ *A job where I can mesh my accounting with my operational and management skills*

After not getting the third job she had interviewed for that month, Emma came home one evening to a circled paragraph in the local paper. "Look, honey," her husband began, "a professional hockey team is relocating here. They're going be hiring, why not check it out?"

She did and passed through one interview after another. At the end of her final interview for the highest-paying position for her skills, the team's manager leaned forward at his desk and got serious. "Emma, we're very impressed with you. I'd like to hire you, but I have to ask one more question. Do you know anything about hockey?"

Within weeks Emma was managing the budget for that multi-million-dollar professional hockey team, got to work in a "team-oriented" environment, and regularly ventured into "new arenas" as she lived the life she'd imagined!

> *All big dreamers see things in the soft haze of a spring day, or in the red fire of a long winter's evening. Some of us let these great dreams die, but others nourish and protect them, nurse them through bad days till they bring them to sunshine and light, which always come to those who sincerely believe. — President Woodrow Wilson*

Putting Get the Picture into Practice

When you're ready to follow the ***8 to Great*** process, it will start with your first thoughts each day.

Partnering for Your Daily Gratitude Richual

For this daily practice, you'll want to first ask for someone to be the receiver of your daily Gratitudes. You can share them in person, via text, in writing, or over the phone. You can share them with a child, spouse, sibling, friend, parent or co-worker. That individual does not need to reciprocate, only be willing to receive your Gratitudes. Then take a few minutes to share your three Gratitudes each morning or evening — three things you're grateful for from the past twenty-four hours with no repeats.

Note: Most partners share their Gratitudes by email or text. If you share your Gratitudes with your partner over the phone, do them on a separate Gratitude Call. Have the same person initiate the call each morning at the same time. If the recipient doesn't answer, the caller can leave a message. Stay focused on sharing Gratitudes, keeping the call to no more than two to three minutes. If you let the calls lapse into "What's new?" they will soon expand to five to ten minutes and you could eventually decide that you are "too busy" for them.

A Weekly Manifasting Game

In ***8 to Great,*** we use the word "mani*fast*ing" to refer to manifesting *faster* by getting to a feeling place and acting as though it's already occurred.

Once you've been doing your daily Gratitudes for awhile with your partner, you can add one more game. This is a weekly ten to fifteen-minute call. You can do it with the same partner or someone else. You'll be amazed at how playing it once a week will accelerate and expand your manifasting ability!

In ***8 to Great,*** we use a code phrase to let people know that a mani*fast*ion is still coming, and hasn't been experienced on a physical level yet. The phrase is, "I'm so grateful now that...." If someone familiar with ***8 to Great*** says, "I'm so grateful *that...*" we know that this is an intention/manifestation that has occurred. If they use the "*now that*" phrase, we get excited, but we don't book our plane tickets yet, because the manifestation they're intending is still on its way. They are both part of what we call **The Congratulations Game**.

The Congratulations Game

To begin, with your game partner, decide who will be Person 1. Then follow the **ABCD** process...

A. Person 1 **A**sks the other person, *"What is one of your dreams?"*

B. Person 2, the **B**uddy, responds by sharing one of their dreams.

C. Person 1 then says, *"**C**ongratulations!"* (If in the same room, high-five Person 2).

D. Then Person 1 asks Person 2 **D**ream Interview questions such as:

   How did it feel?

   What was one of your favorite parts?

   What did the reporter ask you in the interview?

   Who came up to thank you when it was all over?

You'll both be acting as though it's already happened. Once you learn a person's dream, you open a window to their soul.

> *The only limit to our realization of tomorrow will be our doubts of today. — Franklin D. Roosevelt*

Changed Fore-ever

One of my favorite stories about using **The Congratulations Game** happened with my brother Paul.

While visiting him and his family on lovely Whidbey Island in Washington, he gave me a tour of the country club where he was a member. We passed some very large, beautifully framed photographs and I asked, "Are these the former presidents of the club?"

"No," he shared. "Those are the winners of the annual Club Championship Golf Tournament. My photo will replace this guy's next year!"

I didn't realize my brother was just having fun with me... that at that time he'd *never* won a golf tournament, and that he wasn't sure he could. But during our round that day, I interviewed him. "What color sweater did you wear for the Champion's photo?" "Who was the most fun to beat?" "Who was the first person you called to say that you'd won?"

He answered each question with enthusiasm. His answer to the last question was, "Well, since my family was here watching me, the first person I called after I won was you."

Three weeks later my phone rang, and my brother, amid tears of gratitude and joy, shared that he had just won the tournament. He has since won that annual honor three more times along with a variety of other championships. We are all so proud of and excited for him!

If you can dream it, you can do it. — Walt Disney

On the days that you're not sharing dreamings with a partner, you can practice the same manifasting thoughts on your own. I remember a time years ago when I was feeling low on the Power Pyramid. I realized that I felt a bit unsupported as I flew across the country to speak at a national conference, so as I was getting into a car to take me to the hotel, I spent a few minutes getting back to a "95" by being grateful for how I *was* supported.

I'm grateful for the way the earth supports me every day. I'm grateful for the airline crew offering me drinks and a snack. I'm grateful for being able to pay a driver to take me to the hotel.

Then as we drove, I wrote some intentions in my journal as if they had already happened:

I'm grateful now that I have met so many wonderfully supportive people at the hotel. I'm actually feeling more supported than I've ever felt at a hotel. The people here are amazing. And they take care of their guests with smiles on their faces and delight in their eyes!

Just imagining and writing those intentions felt great. (And when we feel good, what happens?)

When we arrived at our destination I watched in amazement as my visualization unfolded. After we pulled up to the hotel, I never touched my bags, I got checked in within four minutes, and as the conference keynote, was given a key to a private floor. (A first!)

Once on that top floor, I had a glorious view of an exquisite snowfall on the river. Meanwhile, there were chocolates waiting on my pillow, a beautifully wrapped welcome gift next to fresh flowers on the dresser, a whirlpool tub, a crackling fireplace warming the room, and best of all, *my own personal valet* asking if I would like coffee or tea, could he prepare a fruit and cheese tray, and would I like my outfit pressed for the following day.

> *You must learn a new way to think before you can master a new way to be. — Marianne Williamson*

Super-Sizing Your Dreams

It doesn't matter what size your intentions are. Intending little things at first can build up your "believing muscle" and prepare you to realize you can manifest bigger things. Remember to focus on how you want to feel with phrases such as: "I'm so grateful ***now that*** I have such great close friends" or "I'm so grateful ***now that*** I'm hearing so many congratulations."

Note: Being disappointed means you're impatient. Remember to let go of the when's and who's and just have fun with the what's and why's. Know that today's intentions will turn into tomorrow's Gratitudes when we stay grateful and "95-ing." I've never known anyone to do this process and not have their intentions start showing up *within a week or two*. Soon your friends will be asking for your secret!

"Hogwash!" shout the skeptics. "Tom Foolery!" cry the critics. Maybe it's a truth only fools and children can see. Ever wonder why they call it "make-believe?" Because by *believing* it, we access our God-given power to *make* it so.

The Teacher's Story

As part of my high school curriculum of ***8 to Great***, I recommend a special ceremony, during which students who have completed the class can share their success stories and receive certificates of participation. I'll never forget one young English teacher in our first inner-city school.

On a May afternoon, I dropped by one of her classes the day of the ceremony. I heard one junior share that he had added thirty-four points to his competitive bowling score, while a classmate of his had contacted her father for the first time in years. Each student had an amazing story to share. When the students finished, I turned to their teacher and said, "You've been participating through all the sessions. Have you seen any changes in *your life* that you'd like to tell us about?"

She teared up as she began, "I wasn't planning on sharing today, but I guess this is as good a day as any. In college, I was in the pre-med program. My first science test my junior year was especially difficult and I flunked it. Panic-stricken, I went to the instructor to request special help, telling him I needed a good grade to get into medical school. He laughed at me and said, 'There's no way that someone who flunks my exams can make it in med school.' Heartbroken, I dropped his class and changed my major the following day."

She paused to compose herself before continuing.

"I love teaching, but after hearing this program, I realize that I need to follow my dream, so last week I turned in my resignation. I'll stay until the end of this year, but I've already applied to medical school." Her students applauded her.

That woman was — and still is — one of my heroes. She taught in the most powerful way, through her example, how to **Get the Picture** as well as how to practice High-Way 2: **Risk**. We're not only much stronger *than* we imagine, we're much stronger *when* we imagine.

Q & A on Get the Picture

Q: *I went to lunch with a friend last week and we had so much fun talking about our dreams and memories that I went home feeling great. When I got to the office the next day, I had a message about a huge contract. Is it true that people can be "good luck" charms?*

A: Anything that makes you feel good — a smell, a taste, a touch, a beautiful sight, or a fun lunch with a friend — instantly moves you up the Power Pyramid. If you and your friend spent almost an hour "95-ing," that positive vibration was building on itself, heightening the effect. Staying at a high vibration for an hour will have a greater impact than a minute a day for sixty days. It's like a laser beam. The longer you hold a laser in one place, the more intense the effect.

Q: *When I was in my mid-30s, I was the golden boy at a huge advertising firm, often handling million-dollar accounts. Before every major project started, I'd spend two days mentally "walking through" what I'd wear, what I'd say, every meeting, every shoot, and every editing session in my mind. Sometimes I'd replay a "scene" in my mind three or four times until it felt right. I thought I was doing it because I was afraid of making a mistake. Now you're telling me that all along I was Getting the Picture?*

A: Yes. Isn't it great you can return to those mental habits so easily?

Q: *When I discovered the* **Get the Picture** *concept years ago, it worked beautifully for me, but then I lost my "magic touch." How can I get back to manifesting what I desire with ease?*

A: You may be experiencing a very natural effect of taking the process for granted. What happens is that rather than imagining having what we want, we sometimes just *think about* thinking about it. We don't ever get to the feeling excited place.

"Yes," we think, "there's that yellow convertible. I could think about owning that." Then we stop there. **Get the Picture** doesn't work that way. You have to really put yourself in the picture and let it change how you feel. Don't just dip your toes in the water. Swim in the pictures of your imagination. Go test drive the car. Go visit the college. Take time each week to feed your imagination through listening to music, watching videos, journaling, or daydreaming until you feel grateful for already having it!

Q: What does being at "95" have to do with asking for what I want? Can't I ask for what I want when I'm in a really crummy mood, too?

A: You can ask from there; you just can't receive from there. Let's say you're in an unhealthy relationship and want a better one, so you break up with boyfriend X and imagine boyfriend W (for Wonderful). In the moment you're imagining Mr. W, you're at "95."

Now it's the next day. You don't do your Gratitudes. Instead, you look in the mirror and tell yourself you hate your puffy eyes. You almost trip over the dog, so you start yelling at him. You listen to the news on the radio on the way to work and decide the world's falling apart. Once you get to work, you mutter to yourself about all the impossible deadlines.

Look where you are. From your position at the bottom of the Power Pyramid, that new salesman who is your "95" prince charming is going to stop by your office today, but neither of you will notice the other. You're not a match. He's "95-ing" and you're "5-ing." Instead, your ex-boyfriend is going to call and ask you to forgive him, and you'll consider it because you have lost hope that anybody "really good" is out there.

Now, let's replay the day.

Take 2: Another possible scenario...

You wake up to a phone call from your Gratitude Partner. You both take a few minutes to share your three Gratitudes with each other. She shares that *you* are one of her Gratitudes for the day!

You look in the mirror and are grateful for the stylist who helps bring out the best in your hair. From this relaxed state, when you see your dog sitting in your path, you pet him up and know that he just wants a little extra attention today. After a few minutes of dog time, you make your favorite breakfast, grateful that the milk hasn't soured, even though it's past its due date.

On your drive to work you notice a flock of birds and marvel at the miracle of being surrounded by a creature so beautiful to see and to listen to.

You get to work, look at the number of emails you have to return, and are grateful that you have a job where you're busy, unlike the last one, where you were bored.

Now what happens when the new sales guy walks into your office? He only has eyes for "95's," and his eyes are on you!

Q: I had a question come up in my ninth-grade class today and I told them I'd email you. The student asked, "Will there ever come a time when I say, 'I can do it' but it just doesn't work out for me and ends up that I really couldn't do it?"

A: Your thoughts create your reality. The only thing that might stop your "success" is that you got attached to the "when" or the "how" and gave up one minute before the end of the game. You might consider having the students watch the movie ***Rudy***, about a college student who gave up very close to the finish line and had to be talked back into a "95" place by his custodian friend.

Q: How do you continue believing when you've been waiting for your dream for a long time?

A: I read success stories to remind me that everything is coming in its own perfect time. Find yourself a ***Chicken Soup for the Soul*** book full of hopeful stories and remember that its creator, Jack Canfield, was rejected by 123 publishers when he first proposed the idea for his book. At this book's printing, that series has sold over 80 million copies in over fifty languages. More on **Hope for the Future** in High-Way 8.

Q: What do I do with the naysayers in my life?

A: I suggest you only share your dreams with dreamers. The ancient Scriptures remind us not to cast our "pearls before swine." It's not that some people are swine. It's that they don't know the value of dreams and will treat them just like everything else in the trough. Arguing with naysayers is draining. Simply say something like, "Thanks for sharing," or "I'll take that under consideration," without malice or cynicism. Then...go prove them wrong.

Q: When are dreams just fantasy? I have a dream of driving a black Mercedes - it's something I've always wanted. I don't know that it would serve much of a bigger purpose. Isn't that selfish?

A: First, the "purpose" of getting your Mercedes is that you'll remember who you are and that you've been given the power to manifast anything in your life. You'll become so joy-filled with this understanding that you'll spread it to people, young and old, who are caught up in darkness and despair. Now that's a lot of "mileage" to get out of one Mercedes!

When you're ready, you'll upgrade your definition of dreams from "fantasy" to "fantastic." You'll see that your dreams are sacred and realize that being called a "dreamer" is a very high compliment.

Finally, remember that the Mercedes won't bring you genuine happiness. It's your genuine happiness that will bring your Mercedes. Remembering your power to **Get the Picture** and choose your focus is the key that unlocks it all.

*(For more on living this High-Way and honing the art of visualization, check out my ebook, **Becoming a Magnificent** at* www.8togreat.com.*)*

The only thing that's keeping you from getting what you want is the story you keep telling yourself.

Tony Robbins

2

High-Way 2: Risk

Run To, Not From

Defining Risk

Only those who dare to fail greatly can ever achieve greatly.

Robert F. Kennedy

Merriam-Webster's dictionary describes risk as: "possibility of loss or injury...peril...danger." Most parents would agree. Yet the skill of creative risk-taking and thinking out of the box is a prerequisite for happiness and success. Obviously, our culture sends us very mixed messages about risk, but the greats among us have always agreed — No Risks, No Rewards.

If you want to increase your success rate, double your failure rate.

Thomas Watson, Sr., founder of IBM

Stop being afraid of what could go wrong, and start being excited about what could go right.

Tony Robbins

Do one thing every day that scares you.

Eleanor Roosevelt, former first lady

Don't be that kid standing at the top of the waterslide, overthinking it.You have to go down the chute.

Tina Fey

Even those who acknowledge that moving out of our comfort zones is a good idea sometimes hesitate to take the chance. Why? Because risks are risky, and when they don't turn out, they can deal a seemingly crushing blow to our self-esteem.

Therein lies the catch: on our lowest days, when we least want to risk, risk is the only way back up the Power Pyramid.

When we take a risk and it doesn't turn out, we can use our supposed "failure" as an excuse for guilt, regret, or self-doubt. From this place on the Power Pyramid, the courage to risk can feel out of reach, but we can't let our fears stop us.

> *To be nobody but yourself, in a world which is doing its best to make you everybody else — means to fight the hardest battle which any human being can fight; and never stop fighting. — E. E. Cummings*

The Happiest People

As children, risking was as normal for us as breathing. We all start out as risk-takers, but over the years we slowly shut down to play it safe.

Research by Dr. Sidney Simon at the University of Massachusetts revealed that two psychotherapists went around the world to study thirty-three different cultures with one intent: to find out what the happiest people had in common. Their findings were surprising. The most common characteristic wasn't love, money, or fame. Neither was it good looks, lots of friends, perfect health or perfect grades. It was Risk.

When she heard these results for the first time, one GED student moved right to the heart of it by asking: "What kind of risks am I supposed to take?"

I looked into her wise young eyes and asked, "What's the greatest risk you could take from now 'til the day you die?"

"To be myself," she replied.

"And that, young woman, will remain your greatest risk for as long as you live."

A Different Drummer

One sure sign of maturity is when we begin to follow our inner voice more than the outer voices around us. The challenge is that internal wisdom will often lead in the opposite direction of external wisdom. "Follow your heart" may directly contradict your co-worker warning you not to "rock the boat." Your family of origin may want you to take a job close to home while your intuition is telling you to do what you love and follow your dreams.

> *The reward for conforming is that everyone likes you except yourself. — Rita Mae Brown*

Whether you refer to this inner counselor as your gut, your instinct or your sacred knowing, you've undoubtedly heard it tell you to do something that would result in disapproval from those around you. The journey of the risk-taker inevitably includes times of trial, pain, and solitude. Yet risk we must.

Risk vs. Escape

In ***8 to Great,*** we define risk as facing our fears, as opposed to trying to escape from them.

Risk is running to, not from.

Notice in the following list that some risks are running to and others are running from:

- ✓ *sharing your improvement idea with your boss*
- ✓ *asking for a raise*
- ✓ *lying to a friend*
- ✓ *not applying for a job out of fear*
- ✓ *getting drunk*
- ✓ *parasailing*

Sharing your improvement idea, asking for a raise, and parasailing are risks because they are running *to* a goal or dream. On the other hand, we would all agree that that lying, not applying for a job out of fear, and getting drunk are escapes — examples of running from our fears. The "Run To" always takes courage.

Fear Has No Favorites

Who do you think has the most fear, cowards or heroes? Most people assume it's one or the other, but the surprising fact is that we all have the same amount. The high dive at the swimming pool is scary to every ten-year-old. Heroes feel the fear and do it anyway.

On any given day we can use fear as an excuse to stay stuck or we can tap into our innate courage and dive into our next risk. If you haven't been taking risks, your resistance to what's new and different has probably grown strong. As one CEO told me after my seminar, "I've created a security blanket that's suffocating me." He was ready to throw off his fear of change and start living again.

> *A ship in the harbor is safe, but that's not what ships are built for. — Rear Admiral Grace Hopper*

Fear has no favorites. It plagues us all from time to time. I'll always remember the evening a good friend of mine called to ask if he could come over to talk. The next morning he planned to ask his bank for a ten million dollar loan, even though he already owed them double that amount. I listened as he talked and held him as he shook with fear.

There are some who could not imagine being in such a situation. Those who are the most miserable and stuck often criticize risk-takers and are quick to point out when we fall and skin our knees. The fact is that to find happiness and success, instead of being scared to death we must risk being "scared to life."

Who Makes More Mistakes?

There are certain questions about risk that, when asked, almost everyone in my audience will get wrong. Here is one:

Successful people make how many mistakes as compared to unsuccessful people?

a) half as many

b) the same number

c) twice as many

d) five times as many

e) twenty times as many

Very few guess the correct answer: e) twenty times as many.

The good news is that risks don't have to be huge to be beneficial. Everyone has the potential to take small risks every day. Maybe Broadway auditions aren't for you, but there's always the risk of singing a solo at church. Maybe you won't be called on to donate a kidney, but there's always an opportunity to donate blood, join a dance class, run for the school board, learn to play pickle ball, or strike up a conversation with your new neighbor.

The Risk of Risking

As I've shared earlier, I love the Academy Awards. It never fails to amaze me how top entertainers continue to grow and risk. I recall one year learning that Clint Eastwood was not only a magnificent actor and director, but also a producer, a former mayor of Carmel, California, and *an Academy Award nominated composer of film scores.*

I hear you thinking, "It's easy for him to risk, he's Clint Eastwood."

I would rephrase that as: "It's easy for him to be Clint Eastwood because he takes risks."

What Have You Got to Lose?

We often don't risk because we feel we'll "run out." What do you fear running out of? Time? Take the risk of slowing down. Money? Take the risk of donating to your favorite charity. Youth? Take the risk of telling someone your age and feeling grateful for it.

> *It is not because things are difficult that we do not dare.*
> *It is because we do not dare that things are difficult.*
> *— Seneca*

In the past, perhaps we tried something new, hit a snag, and jumped to the conclusion that we weren't "supposed to" be on that path. We mistakenly interpreted a detour as a cosmic STOP sign.

Perhaps you wanted to go back to school but didn't get a loan. Perhaps you called to ask someone out but they turned you down. Perhaps your first month of sales yielded no results. None of those are out of the ordinary or a sign of defeat. Rather than failures, they were feedback. Those who want success on a silver platter have forgotten what the road to success looks like.

> *The jump is so frightening between where I am and where I want to be...but because of all I may become, I will close my eyes and leap!*
> *— Maryanne Radmacher-Hershey*

The Road to Success

On a sheet of paper or in the air in front of you, draw what you think the road to success looks like. Start at A on your left-hand side (signifying where you are now) and end at Z on your right-hand side (signifying where you want to arrive). About half the people in my seminars draw a zigzag line from point to point, while the other half draw a straight line. The confusion reminds me of a student who once asked, "Do you want me to draw what I believe or what's true?" ***8 to Great*** teaches that:

The road to success is *never* a straight line.

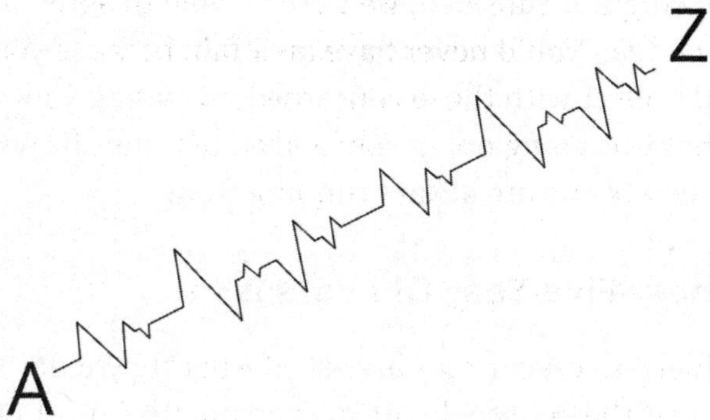

The Risk Process:

Run to, Not from

Life is an ongoing process of choosing between safety (out of fear) and risk (for growth). Make the growth choice a dozen times a day.

Abraham Maslow

Once you're ready to face your fears and move through them, you can begin using the following formula for making the best, most loving decisions every time. The next time you have a decision to make, just ask yourself:

"If I had no fear, what would I do?"

Affair Question?

The first time I asked a large corporate audience the decision-making question, "If you had no fear, what would you do?" I received a surprising response. A gentleman sitting in the back of the room yelled out, "Did you say if I had an affair, what would I do?"

After the laughter subsided, we were all able to agree that if you had no fear, you'd never have an affair, because you'd be open and honest with those concerned, including yourself, about what was going on. Affairs and addictions always involve secrets and are always running from.

The Ninety-Five-Year-Old Vote Is In

When ninety-five-year-olds are asked what they'd do differently if they got to do life over again, they most often reply they'd have taken more risks. It isn't the risks they *took* that they regretted, but the risks they *didn't* take. That would mean that asking the "dumb question" in your meeting at work might be the smartest thing you can do.

> *Some people live for ninety years. Others just live one year ninety times. — Dr. Wayne Dyer*

The Risk of Believing in Our Dreams

The word "courage" comes from the French word "coeur," meaning heart. The most courageous people are those who follow their hearts to places their minds would never approve of. Believing in our dreams takes great courage because our dreams often don't make logical or financial sense.

I once knew a man who was rising to great heights as a corporate dealmaker. One day at lunch I asked him the "if fear wasn't a factor" question.

He challenged me, saying, "You don't understand. I just closed a five-million-dollar deal. I don't have any fears."

I continued, "Then tell me, if you had no fear, who would you *be*?"

He paused for a moment before he shared something he'd never told anyone. "I'd be a math teacher to fifth graders at an inner-city school." Then he added, "But if you ever tell anyone it was me who said that, you're dead."

> *Life is either a daring adventure or nothing.*
> *— Helen Keller*

No Risk, No Reward

When an employee can't risk saying "No," they're headed for burnout, for no one can do it all. The ability to say "No" is the only way our "Yes" means anything. When we agree to something, we are agreeing not to do other things. The glory of the human experience is that we can have it all — but not all at once.

Setting boundaries is honoring that we want to protect something important. Whether we're in a recovery program, on a weight loss program or making sales calls, there are always distractions attempting to lure us away from our path. Assertiveness is needed to stand our ground and stay the course. At a time in my life when I was new at saying "No," I found the following tenets from S. R. Lloyd extremely helpful:

Tenets of Assertiveness

1. By trying to govern our lives so we never hurt anyone, we end up hurting ourselves and others.
2. Not letting others know how we feel and what we think is a form of selfishness.
3. Sacrificing our rights usually results in training other people to mistreat us.
4. If we don't tell others how their behavior

negatively affects us, we are denying them an opportunity to change their behavior.

5. We have the right to refuse requests, to feel and express anger, fear, and hurt, to make mistakes in order to learn, to have opinions that are different from those of our family and friends, to be treated as capable adults, and to have our needs be as important as anyone else's.

Rewarding Your Risks

I'm a firm believer in recognizing and rewarding risks, whether or not they are successful. **Rewarding others for risks can in itself be rewarding.** I often challenge corporate leaders to embolden their teams to think and act out of the box with "Risk Rivalries" or "Risk Rewards." It can be anything from giving a bonus to the team member who takes the biggest risk each month (whether or not it succeeds), all the way to a get-away trip for the team that comes up with the most unusual marketing ideas during a week of brainstorming.

If you're a team leader or project manager, do most of your team members speak up at meetings or is it the same few every time? If it's the latter, consider starting with handing out cards for everyone to write ideas or questions on each month. Then move to a team bonus if everyone speaks up at a given meeting, or taking them all on a ropes course adventure to get the risk-taking rolling.

> *To believe yourself brave is to be brave; it is the only essential thing. — Mark Twain*

The same is true for young children. When my son turned six, I was concerned because he wasn't going underwater at the pool. To try and "fix" that problem, I signed him up for swim lessons, certain that the lifeguard would help remedy the situation. Unfortunately (for my agenda), Zach was smart enough to simply move to the back of the line when the instructor wasn't looking every time there was an underwater activity.

One day as I watched this fascinating foil take place, the teacher announced that as a special treat at the end of class, anyone who wished to could jump off the diving board. Knowing that such a thing was out of the realm of possibility for my son, I started to walk toward the locker rooms, but my thirteen-year-old daughter stayed put at the fence.

"Psst! Zach! Come here!" she whispered.

Her younger brother obeyed and walked over. I was curious, too.

"If you jump off the low diving board, Mom'll take you to get an ice cream cone!"

"Will you, Mom?" Zach asked.

"Um...of course I will, sweetheart," I hesitantly replied.

To my amazement, after many small swimmers backed down from the diving board, Zach walked out to the edge, looked at the instructor holding out her arms to catch him, jumped into the water in the opposite direction, and swam over to the ladder unaided.

Zach got his ice cream cone that day — and I got an amazing life lesson. My daughter knew that rather than waiting for life to reward us for risks, we can reward ourselves.

Getting a Return on Your Risk

When it's just you, here are some examples of how you can reward yourself for risks. Note that it isn't the outcome that earns the rewards, it's the risk-taking.

Risk Reward

1. *Doing a Facebook Live or YouTube video about your product = dinner at your favorite restaurant*
2. *Joining a dating site = a professional massage*
3. *Showing up for your first racquetball or pickleball lesson = getting a pedicure*
4. *Asking for a raise = taking a whole Saturday off without doing anything*
5. *Trying out for a play = going to dinner with a friend before the cast is announced*

Build in your favorite little pats on the back for immediate rewards. Start referring to yourself as a risk-taker. You've read this far in this book. What does that tell you?

Courage is the price that life exacts for granting peace.

Amelia Earhart

Why We Don't Risk

There came a time when the risk to remain tight in the bud was more painful than the risk it took to blossom.

Anais Nin

If so many self-help gurus agree that risk is the key to happiness, health, and wealth, why don't more of us turn off Reality TV and embrace our own adventures? Perhaps the answer is nestled somewhere between stock market and insurance industry jargon, which teach that "low-risk" is the way to go.

> *People can do extraordinary things if they have the confidence and take the risks. Yet most people don't. They sit in front of the TV and treat life as if it goes on forever. — Philip Adams*

I recall a high school junior who barely blinked during the first hour of my program because he was so engrossed. He shared with me after class that he had never considered the possibility that risk could be a good thing.

When he left for school the following morning, his mother sent him off with her usual, "Okay honey, be safe!"

"No, Mom!" he countered. "I'm learning from this lady at school that successful people take risks, so from now on, tell me to take some risks."

"Okay, honey," she replied hesitantly, taking her own gamble. "Go take some risks!"

Over the next six weeks, that young man went from all Cs and Ds to As and Bs, excelled as a football player, improved his relationship with his girlfriend, and according to his mother, "was barely recognizable as the same person because he was so helpful."

A Question of Who and When

One day after realizing a certain book agent wasn't going to work out, I was feeling disappointed and discouraged. The next day as my sixteen-year-old son and I were talking, he asked me a powerful question: “Mom, why don’t you use the stuff you know to stop having ups and downs?”

I thanked him for his question, and then asked him to show with his fingers how big a risk most people take. He showed me an inch. Then I asked how big the risks were that I usually took. He showed me about twelve inches. I agreed with his guestimate.

“They’re called risks because they’re risky,” I reminded him. “There’s no way to protect yourself from big losses or big disappointments when you’re going for the gold.”

Somehow, he had heard what I’d been saying all those years as something like “once you do these steps, your road to success will be a straight line,” so I had to set the record “straight.”

“Honey, what I teach is to believe that good stuff is coming and to let go of the how and the when. You and I thought this agent was going to be the how and we got all excited. Now we just have to step back, take a deep breath, and watch for when the real ‘who’ shows up.”

> *We learn more from our messes than we do our successes. — John J. Smith*

Making Friends with Change

Want to make friends with Change? Rather than dreading its knock at the door, try inviting it over for dinner. I once spoke to a group of railroad employees who averaged twenty-seven years with their organization. The topic for my talk was: “Shift Happens: Tools for Transition.”

To begin, I asked them to write down what changes they would incorporate into their workplace if they were in charge. Out of seventy-nine men, seventy-eight wrote: "profit-sharing." We then spent thirty minutes brainstorming risks they could take to unite as one voice on that issue to get the attention of those in charge, amid mutterings such as, "She just doesn't understand how this place works."

My talk was evidently well received, and I was invited back the following year. Again I asked everyone to list the changes they'd like to see at work. Not one of them listed profit-sharing. When I asked why, they told me, "Oh, we have that now!"

Their willingness to dream the solution and take a risk led to their desires being fulfilled.

> *Those who say it cannot be done should not interrupt the person doing it. — Chinese Proverb*

The Money Excuse

It's common to hear people say that they can't take risks because they don't have the money. Here are some famous businesses whose founders refused to buy into the money excuse:

- ✓ *Domino's Pizza was started with a $900 loan.*
- ✓ *Pink's Hot Dogs in Hollywood was started with a hot dog cart in 1939 and in 2007 made 2.5 million in revenue.*
- ✓ *Calvin Klein was started when a friend loaned him $10,000.*
- ✓ *Ben and Jerry's began when they took a $5*

correspondence course on making ice cream and got a $4,000 loan.

- ✓ *When Fred DeLuca was 17, he received a $1,000 loan to open a sandwich store. He put ads in the paper for used appliances. Deluca Pete's Super Submarines was almost sunk when the city required a $550 sink to be installed, prompting a second $1,000 loan. DeLuca held on, opening three more stores in rapid succession. Today his chain is known as Subway.*
- ✓ *Anita Roddick started a skincare specialty shop in 1977 with a $6,800 bank loan. Mixing ingredients at home, Roddick created unique skincare products and created a story for each one. After switching to a franchise model, Roddick's store spread all over the world and was purchased by L'Oreal for over $1 billion.*
- ✓ *Apple got its start when Jobs and Wozniak sold their van and two calculators. That $1,300 provided their initial funding. Its worth at this writing is 800 billion dollars.*

None of the above businesses had an easy road to success. All had to face huge disappointments and adversity. In life as well as in business, great risks don't always require great amounts of money, but they do require great courage, great belief, and great perseverance.

Jim Carrey's Early Risks

Some of us run from risk because we don't want to "hit the rocks." The great news is that there are no rocks. From all my experiences and hearing the stories of others, I've discovered Rock Bottom is more like a trampoline. The harder you hit it, the higher you can spring back if you'll only release your self-judgment. The same "rocky" experience that deters one person from risking will be the catalyst for another to take a chance.

When Jim Carrey was ten and his family needed money to pay the bills, he sent his resume to the star of the top comedy show on TV - Carol Burnett. Although he never heard from her, it did not deter him from dreaming big dreams and taking bigger risks later in life.

> *Avoiding danger is no safer in the long run than outright exposure. — Helen Keller*

Nineteen years later, when he had only a few dollars to his name, he drove to the most beautiful area of Beverly Hills in the middle of the night and got out of his car. He sat on the curb and stared at his dream home. He refused to get up until he could believe that he lived there. Five years later, he was living in his own mansion and commanding $10 million per film.

"What have I got to lose?" is embedded in our universal unconscious for just that purpose — so that when all else fails, we'll take our boldest risks and end up with our best results.

There was a very cautious man
Who never laughed or played.
He never risked, he never tried,
He never sang or prayed.
And when he passed away one day
His insurance was denied,
For since he never really lived,
They claimed he never died.

Anonymous

Risk Success Stories

I've been absolutely terrified every moment of my life, and I've never let it keep me from doing a single thing I wanted to do.

Georgia O'Keeffe

No guts, no glory. No risk, no story. If fear wasn't a factor, our question moves from "What do I have to lose?" to "What do I have to gain?" Every adversity can make us bitter or better. We are the ones who get to decide.

The Three Greatest Risks

When I pass from this earthly life, my eulogy will likely be filled with stories of the risks I took that worked out, but there have been many more that did not. Throughout all my risking, I've found three kinds of risks that are the riskiest of all: believing, trusting, and setting boundaries.

1. Believing in our Dreams

Renna had been unhappy for years because her job had become more paperwork than people work. After eighteen years with a solid company, she told me she was leaving. Without another job lined up, she had decided to take some time off to figure out what she really wanted to do. Renna was a risk-taker!

It was a thrill to watch her adventure unfold. She'd always wanted to work in a bookstore, so for five months she worked part-time for $7.00 an hour and broke every sales record they had. But after a while, she longed to return to a "career" and began applying for full-time jobs. Two months into that process, her self-confidence and faith in her ability to find that great job had begun to wane.

"I have a job interview tomorrow, but..." her voice trailed off during our phone conversation.

"But what?" I asked.

"It's my dream job, but I'm probably not going to get it. There are so many people out there more qualified."

"Just curious," I said. "What have you got to lose by believing you'll get it?"

"I might be disappointed," she replied, but then realized that she'd been disappointed before and had survived. With that insight, Renna took the risk of believing, and the following week she was offered the position.

2. Trusting

"I like you and I like most of what you're saying, but I can't work your program," said the young man sitting before me. "See, I don't have any dreams or goals, but I think that's okay. And there's no risk I can think of that I'd be afraid to take, so I can't do the homework." I thanked him for his input and we chatted awhile. He told me he'd recently quit a job because of an unethical employer.

As he was explaining his decision he added, "One of my favorite phrases is to keep your enemies close but your friends at a distance."

I asked him to explain.

"Well, you know what your enemies are capable of, but you don't know what your friends are capable of."

"So why not expect them to be capable of wonderful things?"

I asked. "I live a very different philosophy. Trust, trust, and when in doubt, trust. If you're betrayed, that's their issue, not yours."

His eyes lit up as he said, "That's it! That's what I've been looking for!"

"What is?" I asked.

"That's the one risk I have never taken. I don't trust anybody right now. I want to learn how to trust."

He looks back on that day as a turning point in his life.

> *Cautious, careful people, always casting about to preserve their reputations can never effect a reform.*
> *— Susan B. Anthony*

3. Setting Boundaries

"I feel like I bite my tongue all day long. I just don't know what to do," shared a seventy-year-old woman who was in a fairly new relationship.

I asked her to explain.

"He's so good to me. When I'm not feeling well, he goes and gets my prescriptions and all sorts of things like that, so when he wants me to do something I don't want to do, I feel guilty if I say no. Yesterday he pointed out to me, 'I never say no to the things *you* ask *me* to do.' I can't tell what's healthy or loving at this point."

I reminded her of the formula for making every decision and knowing it's the right one for you: "If you had no fear..."

"If I had no fear, I'd tell him what I feel and let him sort out his feelings from there," she stated clearly. "That's it, isn't it. I need to be real with him. He deserves that." Thanks to the formula, her confusion and doubt disappeared. She acted with greater self-confidence. The relationship flourished and at this writing they have been together for fifteen years.

Boundaries are the key to self-love. — Brene Brown

Idling to Idoling

When I met him that July, Michael was eighteen and floundering. He'd just started singing in my choir on Sundays, but not much else was going on in his life. He'd considered going to the local community college, yet was anything but excited about it. Then in August, he lost his job because his car broke down. That week, he called to say he couldn't make it to choir practice. I let him know that my car would work all the way to his house, and he accepted my offer.

On the way to rehearsal, I asked him what I ask everyone when I get the chance: "Tell me about one of your dreams, Michael." Without hesitation, he told me he wanted to be a performer and singer. "Then you're auditioning for **American Idol** in Minneapolis in a couple of weeks?"

He corrected me with a simple "No," explaining that he'd "been there and done that" the year before and it hadn't worked out. "There were incredibly long lines, and I didn't even make it past the first audition."

"Well, 18 is a good age to give up on your dreams," I replied, trying to egg him on.

He sat up straight and countered, “Did you forget why you’re driving me to church today? How am I supposed to get there without a car or money?”

I challenged him. “You’re going to let a $120.00 round-trip bus fare stop you from reaching for your dream? Surely there’s someone you could ask for help.”

“Nope, my family is all asked out.”

“Well, I could pull over while you think of someone to ask.” He finally got my hint.

“Well, I could ask you, but I’ve only known you a few months.”

“True, and if you did ask, the worst thing that could happen is that I’d say no and you’d be a little disappointed. The best thing that could happen is you’d get the money to go and win a ticket to Hollywood.”

Finally, Michael got up his nerve and asked me. I wanted to see how serious he was, so I told him no, but that I had some ideas for how he could raise the money. That weekend he stood in front of a restaurant in 95-degree heat and handed out fliers offering to sing if someone would help him get to Minneapolis. He made a little money doing that, proving his willingness to take risks, so my choir, pastor, and I pitched in to give him more than enough funding the following Sunday.

> *Great people do things before they’re ready. They do things before they know they can do it. If you’re not good at it, who cares? You tried something. Now you know something about yourself. — Amy Poehler*

That first big audition day in Minneapolis, as Michael entered a stadium with more than 17,000 other hopefuls, he took another risk and called me at 5:30 in the morning.

"I know even God isn't up yet, and I'm sorry to bother you so early, but can you tell me that stuff you tell people? I could use a boost."

"I'm glad you called. Thanks for taking that risk. My question is, why are you there, Michael?"

He paused, and then said, "To claim what's mine."

"Then go do it."

And he did. He made it through the first few rounds. Once in front of Randy, Paula, and Simon, Michael took his next big risk. When asked what song he was going to sing, he replied, "Can you keep a secret?"

The judges looked at each other and then told Michael they could.

"Meeeee and Mrs. Jones..." he began to croon. "We got a thing goin' on..."

They laughed. They also fell in love with his voice and decided that Michael would be one of only sixteen people from Minneapolis that year who got a gold certificate and a week in Hollywood.

> *I want to stay as close to the edge as I can without going over. Out on the edge you see all kinds of things you can't see from the center. — Kurt Vonnegut, Jr.*

The first four days of that exciting week, I got calls from California to tell me he'd made it through the next round of auditions, but on Friday, the last day before the top twenty-four, he was sent home. Even that didn't keep Michael from taking risks.

On the flight home, his conversation with a woman sitting next to him in first-class began with, "If you can smell rejection, that would be me."

"I beg your pardon?" she asked.

"If I start weeping, it's because I just got cut from **American Idol**," he said, tongue-in-cheek.

"Oh, my," she replied. "If you made it that far in Hollywood, you must be exceptional! My name is Nancy, and I run a talent agency. This is how I met Ashton Kutcher."

Before the plane landed, Michael was offered a $10,000 scholarship to study acting, modeling, and performance at Nancy's agency in Minneapolis. Six months later, the agency flew him to New York for a competition that included actors, singers, and performers from around the world.

When all the votes were tallied, Michael had won seven awards, including Male Vocalist of the Year 2007, Best Duo Vocals of the Year 2007, and Entertainer of the Year 2007. He has since been featured on a music CD and has acted in six films, including ***April Showers,*** the story of the Columbine shootings. As Michael will tell you, he now takes risks every day.

Putting Risk into Practice

When you asked me what I would do if I had no fear,

I immediately thought, that's easy, I'd change the world.

Jaimee, a junior at an inner-city high school

Take a moment to write down your answers to the following question: **What are three risks you've taken that you're glad you did?**

One woman's answers to this question were:

- ✓ *I'm glad I risked having my baby even though I wasn't married.*
- ✓ *I'm glad I risked not marrying the baby's father.*
- ✓ *I'm glad I risked coming to this class today.*

One man's answers were:

- ✓ *I'm glad I risked walking up and talking to the woman who became my wife.*
- ✓ *I'm glad I risked following my weight loss program and losing the weight.*
- ✓ *I'm glad I risked getting another dog after ours died.*

Next. write down three risks you'd like to take, but haven't yet.

Many people consider themselves poor risk-takers until they start to take their own Risk Inventory. We all take risks from time to time, and honoring that can help us expand our risk range and build our courage.

When you're finished, write down your answers to this question: **What are three risks you'd *like to take*, but haven't yet?**

The answers to the second question will be riskier to admit. Congratulate yourself on acknowledging them. Then, looking over the three risks you'd like to take, decide on the one you're going to take a step toward this week. Ask yourself how you could prepare yourself mentally and/or physically. Then take that step.

> *Courage is the first of human qualities because it is the quality which guarantees the others. — Aristotle*

The Decision-Making Formula

We must all start where we are. By risking small things (like talking to a stranger on an elevator, singing karaoke, or learning yoga) we become better at risking big things (like starting a not-for-profit, moving to a new city, or running a half marathon).

Whatever size decision you're facing now, remember that ***8 to Great*** offers a formula that will help you know your best-answer-for-you every time. For each decision during your day, ask yourself the question:

"If I had no fear, what would I do?"

Another way of phrasing it is, "If I had all the courage in the world, what would I do?"

One option in each moment will require the most courage. That is the option that will take you to greater happiness, health and success. What you risk isn't important, only *that* you risk. Whether you're Bill Gates or Billie Smith, finding the edge of your comfort zone and crossing it will make you feel more alive, giving you the boost of confidence needed to follow your dreams.

Friendly Feedback

Finally, as you learn to take bigger and bigger risks, whether in business, the arts, politics, or your personal life, remember there's no such thing as failure. It's only Friendly Feedback, reminding you, "Don't stop here; keep looking."

Can you recount the ups and downs in the lives of the people who inspire you? If not, read the biographies of your heroes. Make it a regular ritual to watch true-story movies like ***McFarland USA*** with Kevin Costner, ***Freedom Writers*** with Hilary Swank, ***Pursuit of Happyness*** with Will Smith, ***Blind Side*** with Sandra Bullock, ***We Bought a Zoo*** with Matt Damon, ***Moneyball*** with Brad Pitt, and one of my all-time favorites, ***Hidden Figures*** with Taraji P. Henson and Octavia Spencer to see risk in action. You'll find yourself in their stories.

Twenty years from now, you will be more disappointed by the things that you didn't do than by the ones you did do. Dare. Dream. Discover.

Mark Twain

Q & A on Risk

The greatest risk is the risk of riskless living.

Stephen R. Covey

Q: Why does it always seem to be darkest before the dawn?

A: What a great question. I've also heard this question asked as, "Why does every great achievement seem fraught with frustrations?"

My belief is that there is a Divine Order to The Universe, not some "whimsical" or "moody" deity who withholds good in order to teach us patience. My desires, prayers, and dreams sometimes put *each other* on hold while another is being answered, but they're answered in perfect time. Along that line, I don't believe we're being "tested" by setbacks. When we ask, "Why do I have to face trials before triumph?" We're asking the wrong question. Instead, we can ask, "Why is there so often great triumph after trials?"

When adversity hits hard, we long for its opposite. If you forget something important, you immediately dream of your life as being more organized. If you overdraw at the bank, you instantly issue a silent cry for financial abundance. Ask, believe and receive are the core of High-Way 1. You'll discover that it's in response to your greatest challenges that you'll ask for and attract your greatest miracles.

The Constitution only guarantees the American people the right to pursue happiness. You have to catch it yourself. — Benjamin Franklin

Q: Can you expand on the "if I had no fear" concept?

A: I recall being invited to speak to a group of high school juniors. Because I was feeling especially courageous, I sang them a song I'd written that morning entitled, "If I Had No Fear."

"I may never sing that song again," I told them, "but that's not important. My goal is to live a no-regrets life. Would anyone here like to fill in the phrase: If I had no fear...?"

Two students raised their hands. I called on a young woman first.

"I'd sing again," she began. "I used to sing in church, but my legs shook so badly that I could hardly stand up, so I quit. I want to start singing again." I thanked her for sharing.

Then a young man said, "I'd find a job outdoors this summer, but I'm not sure what I'd do."

I thanked him as well, then added, "My brother once dreamt of having an outdoors summer job. He started asking around and applying for lots of positions. Within a month he was offered a job living on the side of a mountain shooing bears away from a fish pond for pay. If you'd like his number, I can give it to you."

"As for you, dear singer, I direct a choir and I'd like it very much if you'd join us this Sunday."

She took my cell number and promised she'd call me...and she did.

Later that day I got a call from their teacher. More than half of the students wanted to buy my book. She'd never seen anything like it.

Taking risks raises us from "surviving" to "thriving." Now I'm asking you: If you had no fear, what would *you* do?

Q: *Do we tend to take more risks if our parents did?*

A: Not necessarily. I'm an avid risk-taker, yet both of my children went through periods where they weren't. I think at times they felt as if the sky was falling and that someone had to hold it up because Mom was so "out there." I believe it helps that I have supported them when they have taken risks, both those that worked out and those that didn't.

On that note, let me thank the two amazing risk-takers that raised me. When I was twelve, I asked if could attend a "parents only" meeting at school concerning new school uniforms. As the only student in the hall that night, I remember waving my hand for some time before receiving permission to speak. I argued for the uniform I thought was the most comfortable and easiest to play in. Although the one I suggested wasn't voted in, I'll always be grateful for my parents' love and support that evening. I can't help but believe experiences like that one helped mold the risk-taker I am today.

Faith is taking the first step, even when you can't see the whole staircase. — Dr. Martin Luther King

Q: *Why do so many people tell us to play it safe?*

A: I remember watching a scene in the true-story movie ***Rudy*** where the young man's dad meets him at the bus station to try and talk him out of his dream of playing for Notre Dame. For many like his father, the memory of having one dream take a wrong turn can feel excruciating, almost life-threatening. Those well-intentioned people in our lives truly believe they're saving us from pain, suffering and even death if we take a risk. Little do they know that we can die inside if we don't.

Q: *I feel like I'm in a rut these days. Help!*

A: It's time for you to return to Nike's motto,"Just Do It." Whatever you've been doing, do something else! Here are some possible risks to get you started:

Adopt a pet

Answer an ad and apply for a job...any job

Ask someone out

Become a Big Brother/ Big Sister

Call the family member you haven't spoken to in some time

Climb a tree

Dye your hair

Eat sushi

Get a massage

Go back to school

Go on a cruise, on a Ferris wheel, to a nude beach, to a sweat lodge

Hire a Life Coach

Join a meetup group or singles group

Learn to play bridge or chess, use sign language, repair your own car

*Read **The 4-Hour Workweek** by Timothy Ferris*

Rent a convertible

Ride a train, in a hot air balloon, on a rollercoaster

Run in a race

Say "No"

Sign up for a computer class, dance lessons, a Martial Arts class, swim lessons

Sleep under the stars

Teeter totter

Travel abroad

Try out for a play

Visit a synagogue/Buddhist temple/Baptist church

Volunteer at a homeless shelter

Walk in the rain without your umbrella

Write a tweet thanking someone

> *In a world that's changing really quickly, the only strategy that is guaranteed to fail is not taking risks.*
> *— Mark Zuckerberg*

After evacuating for a Florida hurricane in 2017, I had gotten out of the habit of exercising for three weeks. When it was time to go back to yoga class, I found myself hesitating because I felt I had fallen behind on my skills. I helped myself take the risk again by calling a friend and saying I would meet her there. I knew I wouldn't let her down and I didn't.

You know what you need to do next. Stop listening to what everyone else thinks you should do and do the thing that you know is right for you, even if it means you *stop* "doing" for a while. Your stillness may birth your greatest miracle ever!

If there is one thing I would banish from earth, it is fear.

And the only way to do that is to see that there is nothing to fear, nothing in all of life to be afraid of.

Henry Ford

3

High-Way 3: Full Responsibility

Life Is Your Mirror

Defining Full Responsibility

One thing to be grateful for each day is that you are only responsible for you and no other person, and only responsible for now and no other time.

Abraham-Hicks

Responsibility is defined in various dictionaries as "a duty; an obligation; a binding," which makes it sound somewhere between a burden and a prison. On the contrary, taking Full Responsibility for your life is one of the most freeing experiences you can have - but that freedom comes with a price. You must be able to accept the hard news in order to hear the good news.

First the Hard News

Once while speaking to a group of ninth-grade girls in a small Midwestern community, I asked, "Why, out of all the men I was dating in my twenties, did I decide to marry a man who would become physically abusive?"

One young woman in the front row quickly answered, "Because he treated you like you believed you deserved to be treated." I told her she could go to lunch because she obviously didn't need my presentation.

As the student pointed out, the hard news is that the greatest problem in our lives is, and always will be, ourselves. Until I become 100 percent Fully Responsible for my life, the world can feel unsafe.

We've all met people who believe they are victims. "Why even try?" they ask. They are hovering at "5" on the Power Pyramid.

Now the Good News

The world is as we are. — Ayurvedic saying

Once we're ready to embrace the concepts of **Get the Picture** and "what we think about, we bring about," everything starts to change. When we understand that our thoughts attract our experience, and we're therefore co-creating our lives, we awaken our unlimited potential. The resulting sense of freedom is exhilarating. I remember my own wake-up call.

No Victims

At thirty-four, when I walked into the domestic violence shelter believing I was a victim, the first thing the counselor told me was that I couldn't talk about "him" or even mention his name during the weeks ahead, because *I* was the only problem I needed to solve. It was the best and the worst news I could have heard.

It was the *worst news* because I'd given up my job, my friends, and most of my self-esteem in an attempt to save my marriage. As a result, I was sick all the time and had become increasingly lonely and sad. In short, my life had fallen apart.

It was the *best news* because if I was the problem, I was also the solution. I began to take **Full Responsibility** for my life. To this day, working High-Way 3 continues to be one of my greatest challenges, but it is the foundation of my happiness and hope. When I stopped looking to others to "make" me happy, my life improved dramatically. I was no longer imprisoned by despair. Now I see this High-Way's transformative power almost every day.

Let's start with a simple definition:

Full Responsibility is acknowledging that life is my mirror, every thought is a request, and the only thing I need to change right now in order to be happier is *me*.

When we aren't willing to take responsibility for ourselves, we give our power away by waiting for someone or something else to change so that we can be happy. This takes us down to a "5" on the Power Pyramid. While we're in a hopeless and helpless mindset, we can't possibly attract the life of our dreams. Fortunately, we can return to "95" by moving from B.C. to A.D.

From B.C. to A.D.

B.C. generally denotes "Before Christ," but in ***8 to Great*** it stands for Blaming and Complaining. Many of us get caught in the trap of B.C.ing about the aspects of our lives we don't like, but as we learned in High-Way 1, our lives are like they are because of what we choose to think about and focus on. When we move into **Full Responsibility**, we stop Blaming and Complaining, and realize we are the architects of our lives.

An incident occurred in the late '90s in a Kohl's parking lot. The painful scene involved a young mother who was caught on camera beating her four-year-old in the backseat of her car. After she was arrested for doing so, she was questioned on TV as to her motivation. She said that she was enraged and lost control because Kohl's hadn't given her a cash refund for a return item. Are we to believe that if Kohl's had given her cash, the scene wouldn't have taken place? Kohl's was just the anger trigger (more about emotional triggers in High-Way 4), but she was responsible.

Once we're ready to get out of B.C., we can move into A.D. Rather than Anno Domini, in ***8 to Great*** the letter A stands for Action and/or Acceptance and the letter D stands for Dreaming.

Sometimes there's an Action that I can take. Other times, there is nothing to be done, but Accept the person or situation as they are. Either way, the next step then, is to Dream — to visualize being in a new place with the situation or person, whether that means releasing it/them or becoming closer to it/them.

We B.C. - Blame and Complain - when we feel like a victim.

We A.D. - Act/Accept and Dream - when we understand our power.

Unsuccessful people B.C. and stay stuck around "5." Successful people A.D. and float up around "95." We get to choose which category we fall into.

The Hurting Husband

I recall a coaching client who had challenges in two areas. He'd been out of a job for six months and his wife was threatening to divorce him. By helping him start daily Gratitudes and turn his focus to what he wanted rather than what he didn't want, within a few weeks he was offered his dream job, for more pay than ever. He was ecstatic, but his wife didn't respond as he'd hoped.

He expected her to immediately forgive all the money problems and the less-than-desirable behaviors he'd used to cope during their hard times. When that wasn't happening, he plunged into B.C. Even his daily Gratitudes became tainted with Blaming and Complaining:

- ✓ *I'd be grateful once she has seen that I'm not a bad person and that we should work through our problems. (He'd feel better when she changed.)*
- ✓ *I'd be grateful once she spends more time with me. (He'd feel better when she changed.)*
- ✓ *I'd be grateful for a long happy life together. (He'd feel better when she changed.)*

Full Responsibility is based on the premise that we get back what we send out...period. I coached him that his helpless and blaming mentality was not only self-destructive, but potentially pushing his wife away. It's hard to be attracted to someone who needs you in order to be happy. The missing component for his happiness was to take **Full Responsibility** for feeling good by focusing on all the gifts in his life, such as his new job, his health, and his ability to manifest his thoughts.

> *Owning our story can be hard, but not nearly as difficult as spending our lives running from it. — Brene Brown*

The Job Reprimand

A friend called me one evening very agitated.

"I've never received a verbal warning from my boss before. I can't believe it. Everyone else does what I did and they don't get warnings. It's so unfair."

After a while, she asked, "What should I do?"

I replied, "Do you see yourself as responsible in any way?"

"How am I responsible?" she replied.

"You started mentally leaving this company three months ago. You've said nothing good about them during that time, and that was when you started actively looking for another job. Not only do you *not* look like a victim, but in my eyes you look incredibly powerful. You're about to get the very thing you set into motion."

> *The truth that you are in charge of your life will set you free only after it really irritates you. — Sky St. John*

Over time she'd fallen into a pattern of B.C.ing and focusing on what she didn't like rather than what she did. Once she saw the situation from the perspective of **Full Responsibility**, she acknowledged the part she had played and shifted to a mindset of gratitude. Due to that small shift, a year later, she was still working at the same job and loving it.

We often underestimate the power of our thoughts, thinking we can "get away" with Blaming and Complaining as long as it's just in our minds. Not true. As powerful as **Get the Picture** is for getting what we want, Blaming and Complaining are equally powerful in keeping it from us.

Who We're Not Responsible For

A key distinction of **Full Responsibility** is realizing who and what we're not responsible for. Byron Katie, my favorite author on this topic, defines this concept well:

> *There are only three kinds of business in the universe: mine, yours, and God's. Suffering only occurs when we are in business other than our own.*

"Mind your own business" is a common reprimand today. We go "out of business" when we find ourselves:

- ✓ *Complaining about the weather. Instead we could think, "It's cold. Nothing I can do about that. Glad I have an indoor job."*
- ✓ *Complaining about the way our spouse talks. Instead we could think, "She talks so loud. She's been doing it all her life, so there's not much I can do about that. Boy, am I grateful how many great friends she has and how she helps all of us laugh."*
- ✓ *Complaining that your teenager isn't getting good grades. Instead we could think, "I've reminded him about the effect his grades will have on scholarships so many times. Now I get to sit back and watch how he handles the events that will come his way. I'm grateful for the knowledge that like cats, we'll all (eventually) land on our feet!"*

One way to stay in your own business is to ask yourself, "If it's not within my ability to change it, how can it be my responsibility?" The only life we can live peacefully is our own.

People are just as happy as they make up their minds to be.

Abraham Lincoln

The Full Responsibility Process:
B.C. to A.D.

My drug use was my fault. My time in prison was my fault. But my successful business, my healthy relationships, my four years of sobriety, and the fact that I love my life today are also my fault.

Ryan S. (at twenty-four years old)

I recall talking to an old friend who'd just been reprimanded by his supervisor for something he didn't do.

"If they wouldn't have found that the error was made by somebody else, I could have been fired," he shared with me.

"And you would have been fine with that on many levels," I replied.

"What do you mean?"

We then talked about the fact that nothing ever happens "to" us without happening "with" us, "by" us, and "for" us. Life is our mirror. He admitted that he hated his job and was starting to think about leaving.

> *Freedom means responsibility. That's why most men dread it. — George Bernard Shaw*

Until we take **Full Responsibility**, we can't enjoy freedom, and without feeling free, we'll never find happiness. When we understand that our happiness is ours to hold on to or throw away, we stop feeling like victims rafting on ocean waves that can capsize us at any moment.

Working with coaching clients, I have found that the first step toward accepting **Full Responsibility** is to notice when we don't.

How We Avoid Responsibility

The primary ways we avoid responsibility are:

1. Believing we're helpless and not accepting our power.
2. Trying to control other people's business.

The first is a cycle that starts in our head with helpless or Blaming/Complaining thoughts.

Helpless Thoughts:

"I could never do that."

"No one will give me a chance."

"It's not my fault."

"I can't stop worrying."

"It's because of my childhood."

"Must be nice."

"My husband/wife won't let me."

"I'm too shy."

"If only I felt better."

"It's not that simple."

Helpless thoughts center on "I'm wrong" or "I can't." We convince ourselves that we're defective and don't have what it takes to get the job done or to be happy. It blinds us to the multitude of opportunities before us. When we don't acknowledge the power we have over our lives, we distract ourselves by trying to change someone else. Soon after helpless thoughts arise, we find ourselves in B.C., thinking or speaking phrases such as:

> *"How come you never..."*
> *"You're always so..."*
> *"You make me so angry."*
> *"I can't stand it when they..."*
> *"You should..."*
> *"People can't be trusted."*

I'm reminded of a story from my first book. For years my mom and dad were unhappy. Mom always seemed to be worried about something - my traveling for my job, her middle son climbing mountains, her youngest son being hurt in a game, and dozens of other possible calamities. She had lots of "shoulds" and shared them with us often.

After forty-five years of marriage, she and Dad separated (and months later reconciled in a very loving manner). During that time her "shoulds" for other people ceased. We were still traveling, climbing mountains, and playing sports, but because she was taking care of her business, she had no need to take care of ours.

As we say in *8 to Great*:

Don't "should" on yourself and don't "should" on other people.

Dealing with "Shoulds"

When we tell people what they should do, we're trying to control them, and eventually they'll rebel. Throughout my life I've dealt with control issues, often trying to convince other that I knew better. I recall a time when I was replaced in a Christmas musical revue one week before the performance for making "too many suggestions." I thought I was just being helpful. Talk about the Queen of Denial!

Giving advice that isn't solicited is codependent, unhealthy, and unpopular — even when it comes to our children. Giving instructions to small children is one thing, but giving advice to our young adults is something else. Sometimes we think that as parents and grandparents we're given a special pass that allows us to share endless opinions, but that's just an excuse for yielding to our addiction to control.

When we own **Full Responsibility** for our lives and release responsibility for the other adults in our lives, we acknowledge that we don't know how someone else should live their life better than they do. Releasing the need to change them frees us to come back into our own bodies and restores our sanity, well-being, and quality of life.

The best alternative to telling someone to change is to change yourself. Perhaps a job isn't a good fit for you. Rather than harping on someone about the behavior that's uncomfortable to you, let them know what upsets you, and if it doesn't change, you can either Accept (let it go) or as I did in my violent marriage, Act (go).

The next time you're upset or uncomfortable, ask yourself the following questions.

The Three Questions of Full Responsibility

1. Is there an action I can take?
2. Is there an action I can stop taking?
3. Is there a thought I can change?

1. Take an Action

The first option is to be proactive rather than reactive. Have you ever tried to tell a teenager what they can't do? They will often do more of it. What we fear most, we attract to ourselves. Whatever we push against, we get more of.

That's why nagging and begging don't work, because *what we resist persists*.

When you decide to take an action, look for one that empowers you rather than one you think will change someone else. Here are some examples of actions taken that brought greater peace and harmony to the individuals involved.

The Rebellious Son

JM: I don't know what to do. I'm a single mom and my 6'3" son has gotten out of control. Things are going from bad to worse.

MK: Give me an example.

JM: I tried to ground him last week and said he couldn't use my car, but he took the keys out of my purse, got copies made, and waved them in my face.

MK: What action would a really powerful parent take in this situation?

JM: Stop him.

MK: How?

JM: Take the tires off the car!

MK: Do you know how to take the tires off a car?

JM: Yes! And I have friends to help me do it. Thank you!

The Broken Bones

By the time this female physician and I spoke, she'd had three employees go to the hospital with broken bones, all from falls in her icy parking lot within a thirty-day period.

MK: Talk to me about how you're feeling.

Dr. T: I'm furious and frustrated by all this chaos! How am I going to run my business with three people in the hospital? They should be here to help me!

MK: You're feeling out of control?

Dr. T: That's right. One person fell, then the other two thought about it, got afraid of it, and then it became a self-fulfilling prophecy.

MK: What was your fear?

Dr. T: Well, after the first one fell, I was afraid that someone else would, especially after one of them said, "What would happen if I fell at 7:00 in the morning and no one was around?" That's exactly when she fell the next morning!

MK: **Get the Picture** really works. So, if you're saying, "They should have known better," that's about them and gives them all the power. Try on **Full Responsibility** and move from "they should" to "I could." Change "they should have known better" to "I could have."

Dr. T: I could have known better. Yes, I can see that I helped attract this. I could have redirected their conversations and shifted my focus.

MK: Action-wise, I would close the office for a day, and treat the entire staff to the Disney movie ***Enchanted***. Then have fun talking about it for the rest of the week. If any patients bring up broken bones, just listen, nod, and change the subject.

Dr. T: That will be a relief!

There were no more accidents of any kind that year at her office.

The Mother's Advice

> *Blaming mother is just a negative way of clinging to her still. — Nancy Friday*

CR: I feel like I'm suffocating. I've moved out but my mom is still giving me advice on my job, where I should go to church, and where my boyfriend and I should spend the holidays. It's driving me nuts!

MK: Are you fully responsible for yourself financially or is she still paying for some things? For example, who's paying for this coaching appointment?

CR: She is, and she's still paying my car payment and insurance.

MK: Full freedom requires **Full Responsibility**. Is there an action you can take?

CR: Yes. Even though it's going to be hard, I'm going to ask her to give me the car as a present for my birthday next month and I'll start paying my own car insurance.

At her next appointment, which she paid for, this young woman had nothing but great reports about her life and her relationships.

2. Stopping an Action

The second option after taking an action is stopping one. When we overdo in a relationship, it almost always results in the other person underdoing. Here are some examples of how stopping an action was the fully responsible thing to do.

L.O.V.E. = Letting Others Voluntarily Evolve

The Abusive Boyfriend

This woman had left her abusive boyfriend five times before she came to me.

RG: I miss him. Why do I love and hate him at the same time?

MK: You may never know why. You just do. What actions have you taken in the past?

RG: I leave after he has a fit, but then I always miss him and go back, and the whole cycle repeats.

MK: Is there something you can do or stop doing to find greater happiness?

RG: I could stop calling him.

MK: Yes you could. I recommend that you make one promise you feel capable of keeping. Only one. It has to become your number one priority. Everything else will take second place.

RG: I want to promise myself that I won't call him, no matter what.

MK: How can you support yourself in that resolution?

RG: It'll be hard, especially when other people tell me how he's doing.

MK: You can be clear with them that you no longer need or want that information.

RG: Yes I can. I think they'll actually be relieved.

This woman, true to her promise, moved out of town two months later and was happily married to a new love two years later.

The Doughnuts and the Diet

> *Have you ever noticed that when there is a problem you are always there? — Ho'oponopono teaching*

PJ: I can't seem to lose weight because of all the doughnuts people bring to work. The snacks are right next to the restroom and I can walk past them once or twice, but the third time, I eat two or three doughnuts. What's wrong with me?

MK: Nothing. You like doughnuts. Sugar is addicting. Is there more than one bathroom at your workplace?

PJ: Yes, but it's on a different floor.

MK: Is there an action you can take or stop taking?

PJ: I could stop using that bathroom and use the third floor restroom instead.

MK: A little extra exercise and you'll only have to use it until you're confident that you're strong enough to be around little, round, sugared circles without eating them.

He lost thirty pounds over the next four months.

There's always something you can do.

When we release the helpless thoughts of "there's nothing I can do" and the blaming thoughts of "it's all their fault," we can more clearly see the next action to take. For those times when there is no action to take, it's time for a thought-based remedy — Acceptance.

3. Change a Thought

When there's no action to be taken, it's time to release our "should" thoughts and exchange them for thoughts that feel better. We can go to a "higher" consciousness by confronting our problems, "getting over them," or "rising above them." As we heighten our awareness of the power of our minds, we move beyond our painful thoughts, and discard or replace them as we see fit.

> *If even one person has to change so that you can feel better, you have no power. — Abraham-Hicks*

I invite you to "rethink" your most recent challenges using the definition of **Full Responsibility**: **"Life is my mirror, every thought is a request, and the only thing I need to change in order to be happier is me."**

Life Is My Mirror

When I encounter a person or situation I can't change, I remember the power of acceptance. Acceptance of another person's "flaws" is easier when I remember that I couldn't be irritated by this quality in others if it wasn't in me. In **8 to Great**, we phrase this as "You spot it, you got it."

When we aren't willing to acknowledge our own shortcomings, we invariably find someone with the same core issue to criticize. When we don't honor our own gifts, we tend to find someone with those same gifts to idolize.

The Sorority Sister

HL: I've thought of quitting school three different times this week because I'm so tired of a couple of people I live with.

MK: Tell me about one of them.

HL: Where do I begin? Tori's always sticking her nose in other people's business. I've told her I don't need her advice, but she continues to do it. It's driving me nuts.

MK: And the other person?

HL: Katie's completely critical. I don't remember the last time I heard something positive come out of her mouth. All she can do is find fault with people. It's awful!

MK: Okay, thanks. Are you ready to feel better?

HL: Yes!

MK: You've found your judgment statements, so take a deep breath and remember that if these two traits weren't in you, you couldn't see them in anyone else. Can you accept that you sometimes stick your nose in other people's business? Tori's, for example?

HL: Oh, my gosh. I do!

MK: And are you sometimes critical of others?

HL: Yes, but not as often as —

MK: One of my favorite teachers, Byron Katie, reminds me to let go of the "but" when I want to feel better.

HL: Yes, I'm sometimes critical of others.

MK: Of course. We all are. So instead of catching *her* doing it, you can focus on catching when you do it and change the thought from "Katie should be more positive" to ...

HL: I could be more positive.

MK: How does that feel?

HL [giggling]: Painful and lots better!

First take the plank out of your own eye and then you will see clearly to take the speck out of your brother's eye.
— Luke 6:42

My Experiences with Full Responsibility

I had been practicing **Full Responsibility** in my own life for years when I came across Byron Katie's **The Work**. She has broken the process of taking personal responsibility into four steps, and offers us easy-to-use phrases, such as "release the 'but'" and "Is that true?" I strongly recommend her books for those ready to live in the freedom of this High-Way.

I want to end this section with some examples of my own journey as I moved from B.C. to A.D. The thoughts below are written as a dialogue because that's what they sounded like in my head. It was as if my calmer, wiser Higher Self (HS) was speaking to the Me that wanted to stay stuck in my anger or misery.

The Van Driver

I was dropping off my son at school on a beautiful spring day when a van ahead of me stopped right in front of the school door instead of moving to the designated area. When I tapped my horn, not only did the driver not move, but a student got out and gave me a "look," which irritated me greatly.

HS: Okay, you just fell from "95" to "5." Action (your honking) didn't work. Time to change your thoughts! What are you upset about?

Me: She was inconsiderate and irresponsible!

HS: That might be true or it might not be. Let's see, are *you* ever inconsiderate? For example, have you been inconsiderate to her? She might have other things on her mind. Maybe she just put her mother into a care center or just got a diagnosis and was distracted.

Me: That's true.

HS: Can you take **Full Responsibility** here and do Byron Katie's turnaround, changing "she should" to "I could"?

Me: I was inconsiderate of her. I get that, but how was I irresponsible? I wasn't parking in the...oh, I wasn't taking responsibility for my attitude. OK, now I feel relieved. I almost gave that incident permission to ruin my day, but I caught myself. It was really about me. That feels great!

By the time I drove out of the parking lot I was back to feeling free and peaceful.

The Litterer

On a fall afternoon, I was stopped at a stoplight when I saw the driver in front of me flick his cigarette butt out the window.

Me: Who does he think he is? We don't need his garbage. I just saw somebody do that last week. Why are people always littering public streets with their cigarette butts? Who's supposed to clean up their mess? How irresponsible! The Billboard signs need to read, "Keep America Beautiful, No Ifs, Ands or Butts!"

HS: They're irresponsible. Could that be true about you?

Me: I don't litter, that's for sure. At least I don't think I do. Let me think about it. [Two hours go by.]

Me: I figured it out. I have a whole lot of garbage I throw at people — mostly my judgments and unwanted advice. I sometimes make a mess and don't always clean it up.

As soon as I got that connection, I felt a shift. I didn't see anyone throwing a cigarette butt out their window for an entire year.

A Final Thought on Trust

One of the complaints I hear most often is that "people (lovers, neighbors, car salesmen etc.) can't be trusted." I've grappled with my own versions of that belief and offer this possibility:

Trust has degrees. Being attracted to someone is one thing. Trusting them with all your bank account information is another. When we take the job without checking on the company, hire the employee without a background check, or move in with a roommate who we didn't realize was dealing drugs, it's time to ask ourselves if we are being fully responsible. When you don't take the time to find out who someone is (and it always takes time), you assume that others are a carbon copy of you. Later, when you find out differently, you often feel stunned, disappointed and angry.

The real question is, did they "let you down" or did you let yourself down not following a responsible process? Trusting people is healthy, but it needs to be tempered with trusting them to be *uniquely themselves*. If we stay aware, they will show us clearly who they are.

The day we wake up to **Full Responsibility** is the day we step back into our power. The more I work with pregnant teens, the more I see a version of the following journal entry from an eighteen-year-old: "I thought he'd be my knight in shining armor. Now I can see that *I need to be that knight for myself.* I'm ready to take **Full Responsibility** for me. I know I can do it."

Be the heroine of your life, not the victim.

Nora Ephron

Why We Don't Accept Full Responsibility

We have not passed that subtle line between childhood and adulthood until we move from the passive voice to the active voice — that is, until we stop saying "It got lost," and say "I lost it."

Sydney Harris

The Choice to Grow Up

The aging process doesn't guarantee that we'll grow up. We grow up the day we take **Full Responsibility** for our lives. Many of us didn't have good modeling in this High-Way, but we can unlearn and relearn. Business leaders, sports figures, and literary greats agree:

Ninety-nine percent of all failures come from people who have a habit of making excuses.

George Washington Carver

The man who complains about the way the ball bounces is likely to be the one who dropped it.

Lou Holtz

If you don't like something, change it.
If you can't change it, change your attitude.

Maya Angelou

I am in charge of my life. I am not in charge of yours. How simple, yet how challenging those concepts can be.

The Exceptional Excuse

One of the biggest culprits when individuals struggle with High-Way 3 is the belief that their situation is the lone exception to the rules. Excuses for getting involved in other people's business, such as "My daughter will be kicked out of school if I don't..." or "My boyfriend will lose his job if I don't..." start to sound unexceptional in the coaching business. Our love of the "just this once" clause makes **Full Responsibility** much easier to embrace in theory than in practice.

The Disease of Codependency

Teaching my classes at recovery shelters for thirteen years taught me that the biggest difference between that population and my other adult audiences was that early in their recovery, addicts tend to be in everyone's business but their own. I found myself regularly reminding them of the second half of the **Full Responsibility** equation — that they were not responsible for others and that pretending to be so endangered their sobriety.

Again and again I see parents in crisis because of the rescuing they've attempted with their adult children. At a time when the young adult needs to be learning from life, we too often coddle them by softening the blows of natural consequences. Little do these adult children know that there will be a price for their rescue — their freedom. If the rescue is successfully completed, the parents often shove "shoulds" down their throats for decades, believing they have proven their child "incapable" of handling their own affairs.

"Shoulding" on those close to us takes place when we're lacking either clear expectations or clear consequences. I've seen healthy parents establish the same clear boundaries found in successful businesses.

> *When we are no longer able to change a situation, we are challenged to change ourselves. — Victor Frankl, psychiatrist and Holocaust Survivor*

Clear Consequences

If an effective employer wanted her employees to be on time, she wouldn't respond to a second tardy with, "You really should be on time, you know!" Instead, she would set clear boundaries and consequences with a statement such as, "If this behavior continues, there will be a written warning, which could lead to your dismissal. I don't want to have to do that, so I look forward to your coming to work on time from now on." Clear consequences free up both parties to speak/demonstrate their truth (which for the employee could be "I hate this job," and then moving on.)

Likewise, my best discipline experiences with my children involved being clear *before* their choices were made. The arguments that occur from our lack of clarity are much harsher than the pain of being grounded for a week as a result of coming home late.

The B.C. Fix

There are now theories that there's a chemical "fix" we can get from B.C.ing. That may explain the person who each morning stops at every workstation to tell the latest horror story before their first cup of coffee. For those of us ready to feel good and manifest our dreams, the time for excuses has run out. No matter what our reasons have been for staying in a less than fully responsible mindset, there will come a day when even *we* get tired of our woeful tales and yearn for our own Independence Day.

Once we really "get" **Full Responsibility**, everything changes. We no longer bring up stories of what "they" did to us yesterday or ten years ago. We no longer rail against "unfairness" or "mean people," realizing that they're only reflections of the same qualities within us.

The Good News

The good news is that once we hit rock bottom and realize that happiness will elude us until we stop B.C.ing, our turnaround is usually swift and strong. It often takes a spouse leaving, a job ending, or an illness taking hold of our body to wake us up to the fact that life is as it is because of what we have chosen to think about and focus upon. I celebrate those of you who are making that shift today. May yours be the next success story.

> *Tell everyone you know: "My happiness depends on me, so you're off the hook." And then demonstrate it. Be happy, no matter what. — Abraham-Hicks*

Full Responsibility Success Stories

Our deepest fear is not that we are powerless.
Our deepest fear is that we are powerful beyond measure.

Marianne Williamson

Peace Unearthed

One of my all-time favorite emails from an educator was this one:

MK, I did as you suggested. The **Full Responsibility** *work of "You spot it, you got it" wasn't a lot of fun. First, I looked at four things that I don't like about one of the teachers at my school:*

1. *He blames others when things go badly, but when things go well he takes the credit.*
2. *He's always trying to "one up" somebody else for the kids' attention.*
3. *It's all about him.*
4. *He talks about people behind their backs, even though he's friendly to their faces.*

OK, I admitted, I have those qualities too. Not all the time, but I do have them when I get honest with myself. (This was really hard to admit.)

Examples of how I also do each of the above:

1. *My wife and I both do this sometimes, not very often, but when the kids are fighting and we are tired, we want the other one to handle it and if it doesn't go well, we get upset with each other.*
2. *Life isn't a competition, but sometimes I make it out to be. For example, I always want to be "the person" my nephews want to play with when we all get together.*
3. *It's true. At times, I just focus on me and what I want. I'm a pretty caring person, but when I look at some things I do, I can also be selfish.*
4. *I'm embarrassed to admit this, but I used to talk about co-workers sometimes with my wife at home.*

I feel more liberated now because I am starting to be conscious of what I do. The lesson, I guess, is that people are what they are. They're not the problem, we are. It's great to know that you, by yourself, can make yourself feel better. Thanks so much for this amazing **8 to Great** *program.*

Things do not change, we change. — Henry David Thoreau

The College Student

I recall the day I looked up to see a red-headed college student enter my classroom. As I got to know him, I appreciated his openness and willingness to risk. As we worked our way through High-Ways 1 and 2, he shared that his best friend had committed suicide eight months earlier. When we got to the ***Full Responsibility*** *exercises, he bravely offered to talk about his deepest challenge.*

MK: Who in this class has a "should" about someone they're willing to share?

RM: My best friend should have been more open about his feelings.

MK: Thank you. When you take **Full Responsibility**, what does that sound like?

RM [beginning to cry]: I could be more open about my feelings... about his death. I've been holding a lot of my pain in. I get that now.

He finished the course with a new sense of energy and purpose.

All blame is a waste of time. No matter how much fault you find with another, and regardless of how much you blame him, it will not change you. — Dr. Wayne Dyer

The VP Who Was Very Perturbed

A female VP walked into our coaching session looking beaten down and tired.

VP: I have to get a different job. I'm working too hard and no one appreciates me. I feel stuck. The other day my boss asked if I minded if he missed a meeting. I told him I didn't, but the client really didn't get a great impression of our company when I was the only one who showed up. This happens over and over and I'm tired of it.

MK: Are you willing to try some new ways of being and thinking?

VP: Yes. Anything.

MK: Great. First, you're not ready for a new job yet because you're at "5" on the Power Pyramid where only 5 percent of your thoughts feel good. From there you can only attract another "5" employment situation. I suggest you move up to a better place before you make any changes or you'll take your "5-ness" with you. Let's start by describing your perfect job.

VP: I don't want a boss who —

MK: Can you tell me what you want, rather than what you don't want?

VP: I want respect, appreciation, honesty, clarity, not to have to take work home at night, and my evenings and weekends free for personal and family time.

MK: Wonderful! I wrote those down as you were talking. Now let's move to Risk. Real risk is when we run to, not from. Right now, quitting your job right now would be...

VP: Running from. I can see that.

MK: We call that an Escape, and it's a "5" behavior that can only attract more "5" jobs. Now let's move to **Full Responsibility**. Give me three "shoulds" that your boss should do or be.

VP: My boss should be more honest, affirm me more, and be more responsible.

MK: Great. So "he should be more honest." Did *you* tell the truth when your boss asked your opinion about not coming to the meeting?

VP: I could be more honest with my boss. That's true. And yes, I could affirm me more and I could affirm my boss more. I could be more responsible - Oh Wow!

MK: You could choose **Full Responsibility**, instead of B.C.ing about your boss. Remember, we can only see traits in others that are in ourselves. That truth works both ways. Your boss can only criticize you for making a stupid mistake if he's been beating himself up about the same thing.

VP: So I've been taking his criticisms personally when they were how he feels about himself?

MK: Yes. Until you forgive and get grateful for your boss, you can't feel good or attract what you really want. Once you've done your **Forgiveness of the Past** (High-Way 6) and **Gratitude for the Present** (High-Way 7) work, you'll be soaring at "95." Then you can stay at the job or go. Either way, you will feel better.

VP: I feel like you've lifted 1,000 pounds off my shoulders. I've never thought of it like this before. Thank you!

At whatever point you judge another, it is you who do the very same thing. — Romans 2:1

My Parents Should Forgive Me

When I met James he was at an interim juvenile detention facility on his way to court and a more permanent placement. He signed up to work with me and asked for help to turn his life around.

MK: Thanks for taking the risk of working with me. Let's start with High-Way 3 today. James, who are some people you think *should* change?

JA: That's easy. My parents. They should forgive me. They should believe in me and give me another chance.

MK: How have you been feeling lately?

JA: Angry. Frustrated. Hopeless.

MK: Are you ready to feel better?

JA: Yes, ma'am.

MK: Then take a deep breath and start to take **Full Responsibility**. Keeping the same phrasing you used to say what your parents *should* do, move from "they should" to "I could" statements and see if they're true.

JA [after a few moments of silence]: I could forgive me. I could believe in me and give me another chance. [As he began to cry.] I deserve it. I do.

The Neglected Wife

This woman in her early forties was extremely depressed when she came to my seminar.

FL: My husband doesn't treat me well. I'm considering divorce. He should take better care of me and do nice things for me.

MK: Thank you. Now see if you are willing to take **Full**

Responsibility. You couldn't recognize these things in him if they weren't in you. Change "He should" to "I could."

FL: I could take better care of me and do nice things for me. (She began to cry.)

MK: Why haven't you taken care of yourself, Dear One? Is it about money?

FL: No, there's plenty of that. I have a two-year-old son. I raised my first two children by myself. I thought I should be able to raise this one by myself, too, but I get so tired. I can see now that I can ask for help from my teenagers and pamper myself once in a while. I will.

My Son Should Get Help

God, grant me the serenity to accept the things I cannot change, the courage to change the things I can, and the wisdom to know the difference.
— The Serenity Prayer by Reinhold Niebuhr

This next father's challenge is a common one.

TW: My nineteen-year-old son has been a drug addict for three years. We've done everything we can and nothing seems to help.

MK: Are there things you could stop doing?

TW: Well, I don't use drugs. I guess I could stop drinking beer. I have a couple on bowling nights. Never more than that.

MK: Okay, that would help you understand how hard it is for people to change. That compassion might be good, yes?

TW: Yes, I suppose so.

MK: What about changing your thought from "he should" to the **Full Responsibility** of "I could." What are your shoulds about your son right now?

TW: He should get over his addiction. He should get help.

MK: Okay, and we can only see in other people what's in us, so where does addiction reside in you?

TW: Maybe I'm addicted to trying to get him to change? Maybe I could get help for that.

MK: Sounds like a fully responsible plan to me. Joining an Al-Anon 12-step group may be a good place to start for the family and friends of addicts.

Today there are dozens of different 12-step groups based on Alcoholics Anonymous, or AA. They offer free and open meetings in almost every community around the world.

The Son Who Lost His Scholarship

Mother: My son flunked a class and now he's losing his college scholarship. I'm furious.

MK: What are your most judgmental thoughts?

Mother: He shouldn't have flunked. He's irresponsible! He said, "It just doesn't count if I'm not paying for it myself." Where did he come up with that?

MK: If that's what he believes, then he was responsible for bringing it about.

Mother: But now what will happen?

MK: Whose business is what happens in his life next?

Mother: His, but he's always been so cooperative and easy to raise.

MK: He's still cooperating with his own plan and now he's raising himself. Isn't that what you always wanted, that he be happy and on track with his own agenda?

Mother: Yes. Yes, it is.

MK: Move from "he should" to "I could" and see how it feels.

Mother: I could be more responsible for my own happiness and stop worrying about his.

MK: How does that feel?

Mother: Great!

The Story of the Two Snakes

Two snakes were having lunch one day, when one said to the other, "I sure hope I'm not poisonous."

"Why?" asked his friend.

"Because I just bit my tongue."

Whatever we send out to others will always come back to us. You can tell by how you feel if your own thoughts are loving or poisonous.

How Will We Know?

"I am in charge of my life." Say it over until you believe it. It will change everything. One evening while on a cruise with a group of friends, I listened to the cruise director share stories of the most ridiculous questions he'd ever been asked. My favorite was:

"When I go to the photo gallery, how do I know which pictures are mine?"

Many of us seem to ask the same question about our lives. How do you know which life you're responsible for? The one you are in.

I am in charge of my life.

Putting Full Responsibility into Practice

No one can make you feel inferior without your consent.

Eleanor Roosevelt

I recall a beautiful young coaching client who tried to convince me that the problem in her life was her father not accepting her career choice. "This is really hard," she began. As we looked at the situation through the lens of **Full Responsibility**, her resistance softened.

I shared with her that the best person to take advice from about a job, a relationship, or a new car is one who *isn't* personally attached to whether or not you pursue it. Secondly, I reminded her that we attract people who mirror our own insecurities. As soon as we're completely comfortable with our choice, their comments won't bother us and will often cease.

Finally, we used Byron Katie's wonderful turnaround and changed "He should accept my choice" to "I could accept my choice" or "I could accept his choice not to accept mine." She wrote me a thank-you note the following week saying that she felt like a "95" on the Power Pyramid.

We are free to enjoy happiness the day we stop needing from others what we can only give ourselves.

The Hero's Wish

I have spent much of my life helping people pull themselves out of pain. Sometimes I have crossed the line and found myself working harder than they did. Lately I've become more comfortable with pain — in my life or the lives of my loved ones — and have seen how challenge and adversity can actually be a response to our intentions.

Ever think about what heroes have in common? "Courage!" is likely our first thought, but an equally true response would be "challenge and adversity." For most of us, there is nothing heroic about getting out of bed in the morning, but if you've been told you'll never walk again, as Olympic gold medalist Wilma Rudolph was, then your effort in the face of pain makes you a hero.

I saw this play out at a football game in November 2008. Nebraska (NU) was my team and this was going to be our comeback year. There was 1:43 left in the final game of the regular season and a decision had to be made. Down by a point, looking at 4th and 25, the head coach asked his two punters who thought they could make the long field goal. The younger player raised his hand and the coach sent in sophomore Alex Henery to try for a 57-yard field goal, even though Henery had never kicked one longer than 52 yards.

> *If I have lost confidence in myself, I have the universe against me. — Ralph Waldo Emerson*

While watching the young man run onto the field, I felt panic. I wanted to protect Alex from the "pressure" and said so to the football fans watching the TV screen with me. "That's asking too much!" I remember yelling.

But it wasn't too much for the young kicker. He booted the ball through the goal posts with room to spare and sent the crowd into a frenzy.

After the game a very different picture became clear to me. It was of a young man growing up wanting to play football for the Nebraska Cornhuskers. He dreamed of being a difference maker, so as he practiced endless field goal kicks over the years, he had visualized that scene a hundred times. It was always with a similar storyline: a big game is on the line and he is called in to save the day.

I wanted to "protect" Alex from being a hero and having a glorious moment of fame for his record-breaking kick. I now know that sometimes we need adversity to become better, and have become much better at sidelining my overprotective instincts.

Games for High-Way 3

Some simple games for this High-Way include:

The "Don't B-Lame" Game: Keep a note card in your pocket for one day. Every time you B.C. — Blame or Complain (even silently) — about someone or something, put a check mark on the card. At the end of the day, add up your marks. That's how many points down the Power Pyramid you moved, because it's how many times you gave away your power to something outside you.

> *Criticisms are like homing pigeons; they always return to their source. — Dale Carnegie*

"Whose Business?" Cards: How much we enjoy the holidays is all...well, relatives. I had a friend who made up "Whose

Business" (as in "Whose Business am I in?") business cards for herself and her husband before a family reunion. You can make your own. Then if you ever think your relatives need to talk softer, drink less alcohol, mind their own business, or buy a more fuel-efficient car, instead of "shoulding" on them with advice, pull out a card and read it silently, asking yourself, "Whose business am I in?"

When we remember to take our "Whose Business?" cards with us, it can be "relatively" simple to deal with the challenges of in-laws. The other fun part of this game is that if you find yourself wanting to give a "Whose Business?" card to someone so they'll stop shoulding, that means you are shoulding on them *not to should*. Simply pull one out and read it yourself.

Letting Go

From infancy on, we're all quite good at finding what makes us happy. I recall when my son was a senior in high school, and it felt like I needed to cut my "advice-giving" umbilical cords daily. I constantly reminded myself that in a few months he would be listening only to the voice in his head and that my silence gave that voice a chance to grow stronger. An anonymous poem that helped me through that time reads as follows:

Letting Go

To let go does not mean to stop caring, it means
I can't do it for someone else.
To let go is not to cut myself off,
it's the realization I can't control another.
To let go is not to enable,
but to allow learning from natural consequences.
To let go is to admit powerlessness,
which means the outcome is not in my hands, only my attitude is.
To let go is not to try to change or blame another,
it's to make the most of myself.
To let go is not to care for, but to care about.
To let go is not to fix, but to be supportive.
To let go is not to judge,
but to allow another to be a human being.
To let go is not to deny, but to accept.
To let go is not to nag, scold or argue,
but instead to search out my own shortcomings
and correct them.
To let go is not to criticize and regulate anybody, but to try to
become what I dream I can be.
To let go is not to regret the past,
but to be grateful for the present and have hope for the future.
To let go is to fear less, and to love more.

Q & A on Full Responsibility

Whatever you think is holding you back is not what is truly holding you back. What's holding you back is your thought that something is holding you back.

Ralph Marston

Q: I want to create a culture of **Full Responsibility** *at my office. Where do I start?*

A: A manager I admire greatly shared with me something he learned while in the military. On an employee's first day, he hands them three envelopes with the instructions to **only open them when problems occur and they need someone to blame**. The trick is, they may only open the first envelope the first month, the second envelope the second month, and the third envelope their third month. The only other alternative is to rip them all up and hand them back to the manager.

Many curious employees open them all the first day, of course. In the first envelope, they find their predecessor's name, inferring that the first month they can blame their predecessor for their problems. In the second they find their supervisor's name. In the third, their own name. He shared that 95 percent of his employees receive his message loud and clear and rip them up and hand them back immediately. If this manager's success is any indication, setting the tone of **Full Responsibility** builds an extremely dedicated and empowered team!

Q: In High-Way 1, you say to have high expectations, but my counselor says my expectations are too high because I expect to be treated with respect. I expect people to be responsible and do what they promise me they'll do.

A: Those are wonderful visions for the environment you want to live in. Now you just have to let go of the Who, What, When, Where, and How. If you continue to work this process, you'll have the life you describe, in which you and those around you act responsibly the majority of the time, but right now, life is your mirror. You're getting back what you put out because you're acting irresponsibly. How? You aren't taking responsibility for your own attitude.

Just as others are using their car breaking down or a poor memory as an excuse for *not* acting as they said they would, you're using their actions or attitudes as excuses for not feeling good. What if you *respected yourself* and took **Full Responsibility** for feeling good, no matter what happened or who was late or who forgot to call you back?

I am so grateful that when people show me "who they are" with their behaviors, I can choose to adjust how and when I interact with them. I don't have to judge them or be upset by them. I can just acknowledge where they are and respond accordingly.

Q: I'm trying to teach responsibility to the teenagers who work at my shop, but haven't had any luck yet. Do I need to buy them your book?

A: That might help. But let me ask if you expect them to succeed. Pull them aside, one by one, ask what their dreams are, and then refer to them as if they've already achieved them such as, "Professor Bryce, how's it going?" Let them know you believe in them. Listen to their input and give them special responsibilities. At the same time, be clear about your expectations and consequences.

Teens respond amazingly well to clear expectations. One of my favorite restaurant owners recently revealed his secret weapon for hiring and keeping good high school help. When they apply, he warns them, "If your mother calls me, you're fired!"

Q: I'm afraid that if I start believing I'm fully responsible, I'll feel so ashamed that I won't get out of bed.

A: You're playing the "I should have known better" tape in your head, which is keeping you in the past. The past is ancient history. The fact is that you *didn't* know better. Shame can only exist when we hang onto inaccurate assessments about our past. In this moment, your "now" is completely new, completely innocent and full of light. Keep an open heart and mind. You're on the right track.

The most powerful moment of my life was in MK's ***8 to Great*** *class years ago. She helped me move from being a thermometer that takes the temperature of the room to a thermostat that sets the temperature for the room. I realized from that day forward that I was the one who could cause amazing things to happen.*

Teresa R. Getman, *8 to Great* Master Trainer

4

High-Way 4: Feel All Your Feelings

Allow Emotional Freedom

Defining Feel All Your Feelings

The fastest way to freedom is to feel your feelings.

Gita Bellin

In the world I grew up in, talking about feelings and allowing yourself to feel them was either forbidden, or only for "sissies." In the world I live now, the healers I respect most teach that the primary cure for addiction, illness, rage, depression, and a long list of self-destructive behaviors can be summed up in one word: *feel.*

Feelings wield amazing power. They can motivate us to greatness or plunge us into despair. They're catalysts for everything from weddings to wars. We do what we do with one primary intention — to feel good. But in order to feel good, we must feel.

The alternative to feeling is to run from. Some of us avoid feelings through addiction to food, others through perfectionism, drinking, drugs, computer solitaire, or gambling. Even a seemingly virtuous act like volunteering for *every* church function can be an attempt to escape from dealing with feelings. But "running from" is always running in circles. Eventually, our feelings find us.

Pain is required, suffering is optional.

The Problem

For many of us, growing up meant shutting down. "Children should be seen and not heard" thinking has long labeled the quiet child as "good" or "easy." We've forgotten to give ourselves permission to feel the "noisy" and "messy" feelings. Politeness and peace-at-any-price have often replaced happiness and joy as our ultimate goals. Do any of these sound familiar?

> *"Please don't cry. I hate it when you cry."*
>
> *"You shouldn't be angry about that."*
>
> *"Stop crying or I'll give you something to cry about."*
>
> *"Don't raise your voice to me, young lady."*
>
> *"Don't cry. You'll upset the little ones."*
>
> *"You can't be mad at them, they're family."*
>
> *"You're just too sensitive for your own good."*

Once children start school they often receive more of these unhealthy messages. "I don't like your attitude, young man" is often thinly disguised disapproval of a student's anger. One large Midwest school system recently published their definition of positive attitude as "staying pleasant in times of adversity," an alarming implication that anger and grief aren't healthy and must be suppressed. My objective in this chapter is to invite you to consider that **there is no such thing as a negative feeling. Feelings just are**.

The Day Feelings Died

I recall a teacher telling me the story of the day she shut down her feelings. The year was 1998. In her rural school system, most of the eighth graders rode the same bus to school. One fall morning, they drove by the scene of an accident and saw a classmate receiving CPR from his mother.

When they reached the classroom, a distraught young girl voiced the fears of the class when she choked through her tears, "Is he dead?"

The teacher, grieving deeply herself, had been given a directive by the principal to keep everything as normal as possible "for the children's own good."

"We don't have word yet," the teacher said softly. "Please sit down and open your books so we can get started with class."

Word came later that morning that the young man had died in the accident and counselors quickly flooded the classroom. The following day classes were held as usual. Life simply "went on."

The teacher wept as she shared the rest of the story with me.

"We didn't know how to deal with the students' feelings — or our own, for that matter — so we didn't even try. The following evening, during parent-teacher conferences, the best friend of the student who'd been killed took his own life."

Give sorrow words. — William Shakespeare

Workplace Woes

Meanwhile, in many of today's workplaces, there is a continued assault on the natural flow of emotions. The person in the office or cubicle next to yours could be dealing with challenges ranging from divorce to a devastating diagnosis, credit card debt to defiant teens, heart palpitations to ailing parents, yet sharing feelings at work is often discouraged.

I recall a time I was speaking to an IT firm. During a break after teaching this **Feel All Your Feelings** High-Way, I was confronted by a supervisor.

"I don't want you talking about emotions anymore. Someone could have a...breakdown!" he said quite loudly.

I realized that he meant someone could have cried. Tears are common among my audiences and I am grateful for this healthy release. In fact, rather than a breakdown, I call tears a breakthrough. I listened to the manager and asked him to trust me to continue teaching the process. He later told me the seminar's evaluations were their "best ever."

The Price We Pay

The suppression of emotions exacts a high price. Addictions, illness, accidents, and destructive behaviors against ourselves and others are just some of the symptoms that surface.

1. Addictions

The "Just Say No" anti-drug campaign of the '90s fascinated me with its lack of understanding about why people use drugs. Drug addiction is never the result of peer pressure alone. Whether in a child or an adult, substance abuse is a desperate attempt to run from our feelings.

I recall a conversation with a thirty-something recovering alcoholic who was new to the homeless shelter where I was teaching. When I asked how she was doing, she quietly replied, "I've been shot three times, but the pain of having to face my feelings this past week has been worse than all of them put together."

She'd been using alcohol to avoid her emotional pain, but now she was processing a lifetime of stored up anger and sadness. No wonder it was hard.

2. Illness

Another price we pay for stuffing our feelings is illness. Years ago, I realized that I'd stopped getting colds. Back in my high school teaching days, I used to get three or four a year. When I saw that it had been ten years since I'd had more than a scratchy throat, someone gave me a book entitled ***You Can Heal Your Life***. Author Louise Hay studied indigenous cultures and found that lifetimes of wellness were as common for them as doctors appointments are in the Western culture. Hay's book helped me make the connection that colds and crying have the same physical symptoms.

"If you do not allow yourself to release toxins in the natural way, through crying, you'll have to release them in a more painful way, through a cold," she writes. Now when I get a scratchy throat, I journal, take a hot bath, and/or rent a three-Kleenex movie to help me cry.

> *It's what they've been asking us all our lives. "How are you feeling today?" You're either feeling all your feelings or not 'feeling well' and stuffing them. — Dr. John Meister*

3. Accidents

I remember the night my babysitter walked in the door crying. When I asked what was wrong, she told me she'd been in another car accident — her fourth that year — and she was afraid she was going to lose her license.

After she finished, I asked, "What are you so angry about that it makes you keep running into people? What is it you want that you're not getting?"

It turned out this Midwestern girl wanted to move to California but was afraid her mother would disapprove. As she admitted that she wanted to make the change, she calmed down and got very clear. She confronted her mom the next day and California has been her home for more than a decade now. Last I heard, she was still accident-free!

> *If you bring forth what is within you, what you bring forth will save you. If you do not bring forth what is within you, what you do not bring forth will destroy you.*
> *— Gospel of Thomas*

4. Destructive behavior against ourselves and others

When young Reggie's parents divorced, he was an award-winning athlete. Reggie assumed that it was their having to drive him to so many sports practices and games that had been the cause of their break-up. As a result, he quit the sports that he loved so much. With nowhere to release his pent-up anger and sadness, he turned them back on himself. The result was severe depression and suicidal thoughts.

Once out of high school, the pain continued and drugs became his best friend. When he was kicked out of college for selling narcotics he moved back home. When I met him at the request of his mom, he wasn't sleeping and was shut down emotionally, but he was coachable and open to whatever I could offer. I helped him get in touch with his strong emotions, and today this talented young athlete is following his dream to be a professional basketball coach.

The Energy of E-Motion

What are emotions, where do they come from, and why do they often overwhelm us? The word emotion stands for "energy in motion." Emotions are the energy that "moves" us, so the worst thing we can do is try and stop them.

Getting stuck in a feeling is a sign of resistance and always brings suffering. The two emotions that we refer to as "negative" are the ones we most often get stuck in: mad and sad. Once we realize that *there's no such thing as a negative emotion*, we can accept mad and sad as natural and healthy versions of "energy in motion."

The Mad/Sad Balance

It is evident to those who study our emotional makeup that we always feel mad and sad *at the same time and in the same amount* because these two emotions balance each other. These normal and natural feelings only become a problem when one is suppressed and the balance is disrupted.

When teaching this concept, I use the images of fire and water. Mad (fire) is a good thing, but too much of it is not. When there is too much fire, we need water to keep it in balance. Similarly, sad (water) is a good thing, but when there is too much of it, we need fire and heat to dry it up.

Where does the suppression begin? As small children, many of us heard phrases like "Dad's in a bad mood." We knew Dad was angry, so at a young age we made the inference that anger was "bad." In our efforts to be "good," we tried to stifle our normal frustrations, but it never worked and we ended up even angrier as a result.

Similarly, hearing "Leave Mom alone because she's feeling bad right now" was interpreted as "sadness is bad," so we went off by ourselves and either cried quietly in our pillows or just stuffed our tears completely.

In my first book, I shared a story about the time in my childhood when I saw my kitten get run over by a car. I was rushed into the house and told not to cry so I wouldn't upset my younger brothers and sister. I can see now that my loving and well-meaning parents were part of a culture that wasn't taught about the cleansing release of tears. They were parenting me the way they had been parented. It's time for a new model of emotional acceptance.

No Such Thing as a Negative Feeling

It amazes me that many popular self-help books today still refer to mad and sad as "negative feelings." Some feelings are more pleasant to experience, but as you'll see, they all have potential benefits. The healthiest and most positive people on the planet regularly feel both their sads and mads because they understand the power of feeling *all* their feelings.

Dr. Martin Luther King, Jr. felt all his feelings and even credited his angriest moment as a youth for inspiring his civil rights work. Regarding that first racially-charged incident as a boy, King wrote: "Riding the bus that day was the angriest I have ever been in my life."

Author Miriam Greenspan offers a possible replacement for the word "negative." She refers to these as our "dark" emotions and teaches that just as a seed must go into the rich darkness of the earth to germinate, we can learn to embrace our dark emotions and know that from them, something unexpected and beautiful can bloom.

> *The truth is that our finest moments are most likely to occur when we are feeling deeply uncomfortable, unhappy, or unfulfilled, for it is only in such moments, propelled by our discomfort, that we are likely to step out of our ruts and start searching for truer answers.*
> *— M. Scott Peck*

Mother Teresa was also known for her anger, which she used to fuel her passion to work with the poor. Many of our greatest leaders remind us that feelings of anger are not synonymous with acts of violence. Anger is merely energy for change.

Defining Anger as "Angergy"

When we talk about anger, we're referring to the energy/adrenaline rush we experience when we encounter a real or supposed injury or insult. From a lioness protecting her cubs to an employee upset at unethical behavior in a workplace, anger pulses through us to give us the energy to take action.

As we start to see anger in a more positive light, we can more easily give ourselves permission to feel it. To remind us of how anger energizes us into action, I blended the words anger and energy and refer to it now as "angergy." Angergy is a byproduct of passion — that wonderful life juice that tells us what we want to co-create next, whether it's an art piece, a winning team, a loving relationship, or a cultural reformation.

> *I never work better than when I am inspired by anger; for when I am angry, my whole temperament is quickened, my understanding sharpened, and all temptations depart. — Martin Luther*

Defining Sadness as "Release"

The other emotion we often get stuck in is sadness, which shows up with anger because it's the perfect release valve for our excess angergy. Just as the heart brings blood in through the veins and takes it out through the arteries (or as I call them, the outeries), angergy builds up energy for change and sadness releases the extra we don't use. A blockage of anger/angergy or sadness/release will cause physical or emotional problems, just as a blockage in the veins or the arteries will cause physical problems.

The Mad/Sad Diagram

When we're experiencing an upsetting incident, we always feel anger and sadness at the same time. Watch the natural emotion outburst from a small child. It always involves both emotions, anger and sadness. Mad and sad are like two sides of the same coin. In ***8 to Great*** we use the following diagram to demonstrate their relationship:

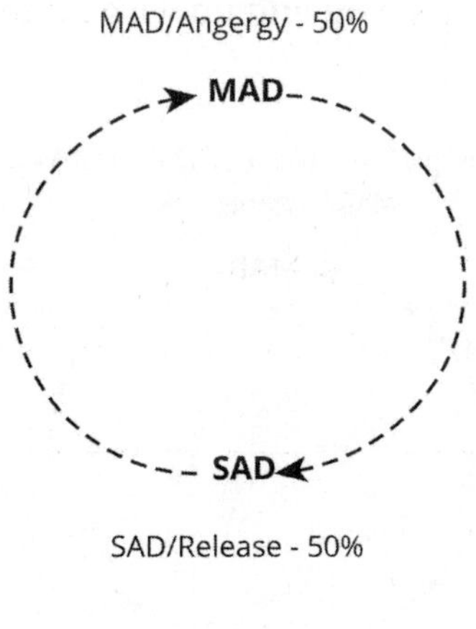

When there is deep grief, such as at the death of a loved one, there is often strong anger — anger that they "left" us, anger at the disease, or anger at ourselves for not having done more for them or appreciated them more while they were alive.

The Benefits of Sad and Mad

Many of us grew up in homes where there was a lot of shaming anger. As a result, we may have come to the conclusion that all angry people were "mean," therefore **cutting ourselves off** from feeling and expressing our own angergy/fire. What we didn't realize was that when we cut ourselves off from our fire energy — mad, we will eventually experience an overflow of water energy — sad. The most common name for being stuck in sadness is depression.

> *Only through emotions can you encounter the force field of your own soul. — Gary Zukav*

How much energy do you have when you're depressed? None. Why? Because you've cut yourself off from your angergy. By telling yourself that anger isn't appropriate and that only mean people get angry, you end up with all release/water and no angergy/fire.

No Angergy/Fire = Too much Release/Water

MAD/Angergy - 0%

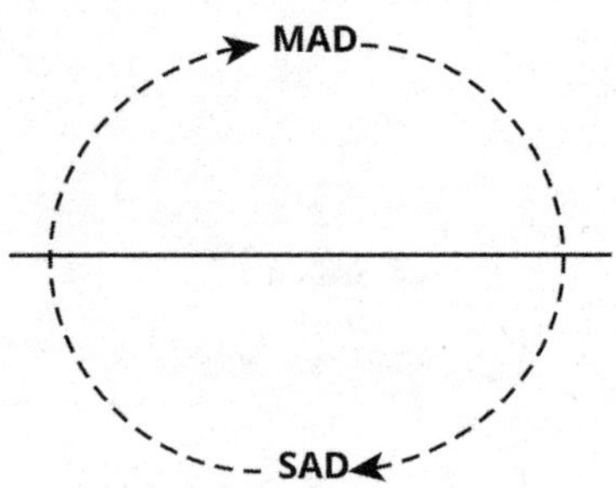

SAD/Release - 100%

Too much Release/Water = Depression

Others of us may have grown up in homes where a parent was sad a lot and didn't stand up for themselves or ask for what they needed. They looked "weak," so we decided that no one would ever see us as weak! The result was that we judged our sadness and would not allow ourselves to feel it. However, without our sadness/water, we got stuck in our anger/fire, which then ignited into rage. Rage is the problem maker, not anger. When you cut yourself off from your sadness, telling yourself that only weak people cry, you end up with all angergy (fire) and no release (water).

No Release/Water = Too much Angergy/Fire

Too much Angergy/Fire = Rage

MAD/Angergy - 100%

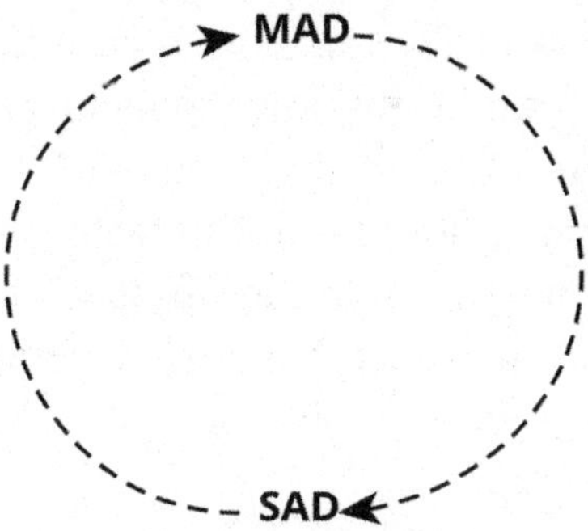

SAD/Release - 0%

We need both the Angergy of our anger and the Release of our sadness to stay in a healthy balance. When we don't feel our sadness, that emotion will "go to the dark side" and turn into its opposite: rage. When we don't allow our anger, we only get more and more water energy and get stuck in depression. Therefore, the way to diminish our rage and depression isn't to *stop* feeling so much, but to fully experience *both* our mads and our sads.

> *What we resist persists. What we embrace we can erase.*
> *— Anonymous*

"I'm Angry" Is Not True

We are not our feelings. To say "I am angry" is not only inaccurate, but the way the mind hears it, we have taken on our anger on as our identity. The reality is much less dramatic. Anger is something we feel, like the drops of a spring rain on our face or the heat of a winter's fireplace on our hands. We would never say that we *are* the rain or we *are* the heat. Similarly, we are not our emotions.

Instead, we can start to reframe our relationship to emotions with phrases such as, "Right now I'm feeling a little/really (angry, scared, sad, excited) about what just happened." It's similar to saying, "Right now I'm feeling a little warm from the sun shining through the window." See yourself as separate from the emotions that move through you. *You are not your feelings.*

The Mad/Sad Bowl Theory

What happens when we don't allow or express our emotions and bottle them up instead?

"Honey," I said to my unusually quiet seven-year-old son in the back seat. "You're usually singing on the way to school, but it's pretty quiet back there. Is anything wrong?"

"No, Mom," he said mournfully.

"Are you sure? Remember, we don't keep secrets about feelings in our family."

"I don't want to tell you 'cuz I don't want to make you feel bad." His statement startled me. I'd never realized my kids were suppressing their feelings because they wanted to "protect" me from feeling them. I pulled over and stopped the car so we could get out and talk a bit.

"The great news, sweetheart, is that you can't *make me* feel anything. Not sad or mad or glad. You can't make me feel, but you might be able to *help me* feel sad," I told him.

"What does that mean, Mom?"

"Well, honey, it's as if everyone has two bowls inside of them, a sad bowl and a mad bowl. If we let ourselves cry when we want to cry about something, our sadness bowl is empty. But if we don't let ourselves release our tears, like when Grandpa died or when our neighbors moved away, they get stored in our sadness bowl. Then, when someone we care about cries, it can help us pour out our tears by crying, too. That's how you'd help me cry by allowing yourself to cry."

"So what about the mad bowl?"

"Well, it works the same way. When something upsets me, I can talk it out, walk it out, or write it out, or I can store it inside. If I keep it inside, it will start to fill my mad bowl, not with tears like the sad bowl, but with kerosene! If I keep putting kerosene in my mad bowl, someday, someone with a match is gonna walk by..."

"And there'll be a big explosion!" Zach spouted.

"That's right, sweetheart, but an explosion is never about the match."

Little did I realize that this story I made up for my son would bring me such insight. The more I reflected on it, the more clearly I saw that when we explode in rage at someone, it is never about them, but about the kerosene we've been carrying. It is an insight that's changed my life.

We can learn to befriend all our feelings. There's no need to get depressed about our depression or angry about our anger. I've come to a place in my emotional life where depression is a rare visitor, but when it comes, I now "watch it," knowing it will only be with me for a while. When I observe it without judgment, it goes on its way more quickly. The last thing depression wants is acceptance.

> *Emotions are the next frontier to be understood and conquered. To manage our emotions is not to drug them or suppress them, but to understand them so that we can direct our emotional energies and intentions...*
> *— Doc Childre*

The Feel All Your Feelings Process:

In the last decade, researchers have found that even more than IQ, your emotional awareness and abilities to handle feelings will determine your success and happiness...

John Gottman

The process for feeling our feelings is as natural as breathing. We've been doing it all our lives. The key is to do it with every feeling, not just the ones that feel good. The benefits of becoming aware and accepting of all our emotional states are as numerous as the emotions themselves. We will have:

- ✓ *more energy*
- ✓ *more clarity and focus*

✓ *clearer boundaries*

✓ *more insight and access to our intuition*

✓ *more assertiveness*

✓ *more compassion for others*

To put it in the simplest terms, when we feel more, we feel better!

Awareness vs. Denial

"I'm not angry!" a young mother yelled at her children, unaware of how ridiculous her denial sounded to everyone in the store.

It reminded me of this acronym for DENIAL:

D*on't*
E*ven*
*k***N***ow*
I
A*m*
L*ying*

Acceptance means you allow yourself to feel whatever you are feeling at the moment. — Eckhart Tolle

Denial is a tool we use to cover up something we've been trained to believe is "bad." That's why we try to cover them up. The truth, however, is that suppression of anger causes much more harm than expressing it.

The Highly Sensitive Person

In her book, **The Highly Sensitive Person**, Elaine Aron writes, "I was convinced that I had a fatal flaw that I had to hide and that doomed me to a second-rate life. I thought there was something wrong with me." In fact, she was a Highly Sensitive Person, or HSP, along with 15% of the population. HSP's feel their feelings — both joy and pain — stronger than the rest of the population. HSP's other characteristics include that they:

1. Are often visionaries, artists, writers or inventors
2. Are highly conscientious and often work too much
3. Are often nervous about being observed or evaluated (could show up as test anxiety)
4. Are more sensitive to pain, light, loud noises and strong smells
5. Are more intuitive, have clear "gut" feelings, and are more aware of subtleties
6. Are easily moved by music, a film, or an encounter with a stranger
7. Are more easily overwhelmed when asked to multi-task
8. Ask deep questions, often reflecting on the meaning of life, or thinking about their own thinking process
9. May have trouble sleeping because of overstimulation
10. Often feel the need to shut down after highly stimulating experiences

If you are an HSP, your best gift to yourself is awareness and acceptance. Create a lifestyle that supports who you are, while watching for tendencies to "overthink" or overreact when in emotional pain. As an HSP, you are an incredible blessing to your friends, family and workplace.

Finding ways to decompress that honor your unique needs is a gift to you and to all those around you.

> *No, I'm not insulted at all when people call me sensitive. Feeling things deeply is my super power. I'm an empathetic badass.*
> *— Jess Colpean www.empatheticbadass.com*

Honoring the Balance

I recall a day many years ago when a co-worker was mocking me because he thought a question I had asked was naïve and stupid. I felt a gut punch, reminded myself that *only those who've been wounded can wound*, and then found a quiet place to get in touch with my anger. I didn't have to look very hard into my past before remembering being mocked by my teachers when I asked questions they thought trivial.

Once I acknowledged feeling sad and disrespected, I was also able to get in touch with the anger I had suppressed years ago over those incidents. I did my anger work (see the options below) and eventually my Forgiveness work, which we'll cover in High-Way 6.

We sometimes need to take an action to regain our emotional freedom. If you're feeling stuck emotionally, my favorite ways to get in touch with feelings are:

1. Walk 'em out
2. Talk 'em out
3. Write 'em out
4. Movie night 'em out
5. Art and music 'em out

1. **Walk 'em out could include:**

- ✓ *a workout at the gym*
- ✓ *hitting a pillow (perhaps yelling, "It's not okay!")*
- ✓ *throwing ice cubes at sidewalks*
- ✓ *dancing*
- ✓ *digging a garden*
- ✓ *going to the batting cage*

The above options could include anything that gets you breathing deeply.

2. **Talk 'em out could include talking with:**

- ✓ *your spouse*
- ✓ *a friend on the phone or in person*
- ✓ *a counselor or pastor*
- ✓ *a teacher or coach*
- ✓ *a hotline or support group*
- ✓ *your higher power*

3. **Write 'em out could include writing your feelings:**

- ✓ *in a journal (online or on paper)*
- ✓ *on a napkin*
- ✓ *as a short story or a poem*
- ✓ *in a letter that you burn*
- ✓ *as one phrase over and over*

If privacy is an issue, throwing the pages away or burning them can bring great relief.

4. Movie night ‘em out could include:

- ✓ *watching a movie at home*
- ✓ *going to a movie with a friend or by yourself*
- ✓ *attending a play or musical*

5. Art and music ‘em out could include:

- ✓ *going to a concert*
- ✓ *playing/singing a song*
- ✓ *listening to music*
- ✓ *creating a sculpture, a painting or piece of jewelry*
- ✓ *attending a drumming or crystal bowls ceremony*
- ✓ *visiting an art gallery*

> *Even if you're not at ease right now, being aware that you're not at ease embraces that unease and dissipates it. Learn to be with and accept what is. — Eckhart Tolle*

Author Matt Kahn encourages one more option in the honoring of feelings - meditation. He defines it as, “becoming comfortable with the seemingly uncomfortable.” He lists the three steps as 1) recognizing the distractions 2) acknowledging your feelings and 3) allowing yourself to find comfort within that feeling experience. No matter what you're going through, you're not alone in how you feel. Emotions are a universal language we all share. Whether by talking with someone or watching a movie, it's comforting to relate to another human being or character on the screen who's experiencing similar challenges.

Why We Don't Feel All Our Feelings

One of the deepest truths about the cry of the human heart is that it is so often muted. It is strange that members of a species renowned for communicative gifts should leave unexpressed some of their smoldering resentments, their secret hopes, their longings to serve a higher purpose.

John W. Gardner

Ultimately, there's only one reason that we, who began life kicking and screaming through all of our feelings, shut down emotionally. Fear is the culprit, but F.E.A.R. is nothing more than False Evidence Appearing Real. What makes fear even more interesting is that some of us are so frozen emotionally that we fear even admitting that we're afraid.

The alternative is awareness and acceptance of our emotions. Then, with our new perspective, we can decide to start feeling better from here on out.

Scrooging

One reason we don't **Feel All Our Feelings** is because we've been hurt in the past. In Charles Dickens' ***A Christmas Carol***, Scrooge wasn't born bitter. He became that way when he shut down emotionally. He was enjoying life and connecting with those around him until his fiancé left him. In order to protect himself from ever feeling that intense pain again, he decided to shut down his heart.

We have all "scrooged" to some extent, closing off our hearts after a painful incident. But when we shut down our hearts from feeling our sads and mads, we cannot feel our compassion or glads. Thank heavens there are alternatives other than being visited by ghosts in order to learn how to feel joy, hope, and love again!

Myths Around Emotions

Many of us don't feel our feelings because we carry so many misconceptions about emotions. Some believe that expressing anger isn't feminine, others that crying isn't masculine. While some have been told that getting emotional is a sign of losing control, others believe that people who display emotions are only doing so to manipulate others. Meanwhile, others believe that emotions are optional, and therefore taking time to feel or express them is a waste of time.

If we do not transform our pain, we will most assuredly transmit it. — Richard Rohr, OFM

I have heard each of the above sentiments from my coaching clients. Recognizing them as false is necessary to the "unlearning" process for **Feeling All Our Feelings**.

One morning I had the following conversation with a friend who had just dropped her daughter off at college.

"I'll bet you had a good cry over that experience," I shared.

"No, not really. On the way to the campus, my nine-year-old son said, 'You're not gonna cry are you, Mom?' and I promised I wouldn't."

I asked her if she would like permission to break that promise. In response, she began to weep.

> *When you suppress emotions, you numb your ability to feel your true desires. —John Gray*

"Real Men" *Do* Cry

When asked by a fellow actor how she cried so easily on set, Meryl Streep answered, "How can you not?" Unfortunately, tears from men in films have been longer in coming. One reason we don't **Feel All Our Feelings** is that we've bought into cultural stereotypes from our cinematic heroes. On a Hollywood set in 1995, while Clint Eastwood and Meryl were filming ***The Bridges of Madison County***, the actress noticed during one particularly moving take that there were tears in Clint's eyes.

According to sources on the scene, Meryl begged him to use that take, but he wouldn't do it.

"I don't cry," he said.

A decade later, things had changed. Anyone who has seen the Academy Award-winning film ***Million Dollar Baby*** knows Eastwood's character was required to get in touch with deep levels of grief. Al Rudd, the film's producer, recalled the day they shot the film's climactic sequence:

"Everyone was standing around the set crying. The makeup girl was crying. Hilary Swank was crying. Clint was crying. It was amazing."

The Royal Recovery

The British have been famous for centuries for keeping "a stiff upper lip." Since the lips tremble when one weeps, this refers to their determination not to cry when facing loss. But in 2017, emotions had an unlikely hero in Prince Harry, sixth in the line of succession to the British throne. He shared with **The Daily Telegraph** newspaper in the UK that he had "shut down all his emotions" for almost two decades after losing his mother, Diana, Princess of Wales, despite his brother, Prince William, trying to persuade him to seek help.

He shared that he was now seeking counseling after enduring years of "total chaos" while struggling to come to terms with the death of his mother. He shared how he only began to address his grief when he was twenty-eight after feeling "on the verge of punching someone."

"I can safely say that losing my mum at the age of twelve, and therefore shutting down all of my emotions for the last twenty years, has had a quite serious effect on not only my personal life but my work as well...My way of dealing with it was sticking my head in the sand, and refusing to ever think about my mum, because I thought, 'Why would that help? It's only going to make you sad. It's not going to bring her back.'

"So from an emotional side, I was like 'Don't ever let your emotions be part of anything.' I was a typical twenty-eight -year-old running around going 'life is great.' And then [I] started to have a few conversations and all of a sudden, all of this grief that I've never processed started to come to the forefront, and I was like, there is a lot of stuff here that I need to deal with."

Since learning to talk honestly about his feelings, he said he now feels able to put "blood, sweat and tears" into making a difference for others. Who know how many lives will be touched, or even saved, by Prince Harry's courage to share his emotional journey with the world.

Medicating Our Pain

Brits aren't alone. People around the world shut down from their emotions because the cultural message is that feelings aren't "cool." Rather than carry the stigma of being "emotional," we often turn to prescription drugs to medicate our pain away. In the U.S. the use of antidepressants increased nearly *400 percent* between 1995 and 2015, mostly among women between the ages of 40 and 60. As of this writing, over 10 percent of Americans take antidepressants.

Certainly, using an antidepressant to deal with a loss is nothing to be ashamed of, but the number of people taking antidepressants long-term — more than 24 months — has doubled in the past two decades, to 6 percent. Why has this become our go-to answer for dealing with pain?

When my seventy two-year-old mother was grieving the loss of my father, a psychiatrist put her on a strong antidepressant because she was "crying too much." Two weeks later, when she complained over the phone that she didn't feel any better, he simply doubled the dose — without even scheduling an appointment.

When we hear a fire alarm, our first impulse isn't to turn off the annoying noise, but to get to safety and call someone to deal with the fire, yet our medicine cabinets are full of substances that only "turn off the alarm." Numbing ourselves with medication is the equivalent of ignoring a warning signal that says we're out of balance physically, mentally, or emotionally. Taking a pill without allowing yourself to first **Feel All Your Feelings** is a sure prescription for more visits to the doctor and pharmacist.

> *All addictive behaviors are attempts to suppress and avoid feeling what we feel. —John Gray*

I was delighted when my Mom found a new doctor, a new support group, and a new acceptance of her strongest emotions. Eventually, she also found a wonderful new gentleman to share her life with!

Feelings at Work

A woman came up to me after a seminar a few years ago crying uncontrollably. Between sobs, I discovered that her job had transferred her *four times in three years*. Recently, she had been held back from a promotion because she was overheard crying in her cubicle after she arrived late, having driven to the wrong job site. The supervisor's report read: "has trouble handling stress."

As I honored her tears and urged her to take deep breaths, I reminded her that the person who had trouble dealing with stress and feelings was the person who wrote that report. We try to suppress only those emotions in others that we have practiced suppressing in ourselves.

Feel All Your Feelings Success Stories

To feel is to heal.

Eddie Buchanan

Recently, a gentleman came up after a seminar and told me, "Last time I heard you speak, I made a shift in my life. I had just lost my pet of twelve years. I was totally incapacitated and overwhelmed by grief, and your stories enabled me to get closure on an old wound. Years ago, my father accidentally shot one of my dogs in a hunting accident. In order to protect him from feeling any worse than he already did, I didn't grieve my first beloved pet. I realized that my intense pain was due to the fact that I was grieving both dogs at once."

The Secret Vows

Bill and Paulette were in their sixties when I met them. When Bill wandered into my seminar, they were separated. We talked afterwards and I heard a familiar story. He'd been raised by a German farmer who had no time for feelings. Bill's mom passed away when he was young and in his words, "the family went silent." He hadn't allowed himself to cry for years.

"So you raged at Paulette and she did all the crying for you?" I asked.

"Exactly."

I've seen it many times. It's as though some couples add to their wedding vows: "I'll do all the anger if you'll do all the sadness." When you are ready to feel better, you can change your relationship dynamics by **Feeling All Your Feelings**. Over the next few months Bill and I worked through the High-Ways together and the couple reunited. He wrote to me that on his sixty-fifth birthday he felt such immense gratitude that his tears saturated his piece of cake.

> *Feelings only come to pass, never to stay.*
> *— Kaylene Smith*

Seven Freshmen

I got a call a few years back from a private school saying they had a dilemma and didn't know who else to call. Seven of their freshmen were flunking every course and the school didn't know how to get through to them. They requested that I come and present my material.

No surprise to me, all seven were boys, full of more angergy and dreams than they knew what to do with. At our first meeting, I asked them to **Get the Picture** of what they wanted for themselves and their futures. Unfortunately, I asked them to do it aloud. (I've since learned to do this in journaling.) All their anger would let them admit was that they wanted fast cars and "hot chicks." The angriest young man said he just wanted out of the school so he could become a professional dirt bike racer.

As the bell rang at the end of that first session, they all ran out of class. I wasn't sure how I was going to help them because they all had so much fear of feeling that their dreams were being kept at a safe distance. After class, Charlie, the dirt biker, walked back into the room and asked if I had a minute to talk.

"Of course," I said.

"I lied, Ms. Mueller, and you don't deserve to have people lie to you when you came here just for us. I want something else. I want it bad, but I didn't have the guts to say it in front of the guys."

"What is it?" I asked.

"I want to make honor roll," he said, his eyes brimming with tears, "but I was afraid I'd start crying if I said it out loud. Thanks for listening."

The following semester, Charlie made the honor roll.

Physician Prescriptions for Health

Studies show that an inordinate number of heart attacks occur between 7:00 and 9:00 a.m. Monday mornings, when many people are heading to jobs they hate but have stuffed their feelings about. The medical community is becoming aware that having emotional outlets and allowing yourself to **Feel All Your Feelings** is a vital part of the healing process.

Once we regain our emotional freedom, we start to "feel" better physically! After feeling both their mads and sads at our ***8 to Great*** Institute weekends, people's migraines have stopped, their blood pressure has dropped, and they report sleeping better.

A few years back, as I addressed a group of physicians, I asked them to list "the real cause of their patients' problems." After that, I asked them to write a corresponding list of "real cures."

Most of the "real problems" of their patients fell into these categories:

- ✓ *Fear and anxiety*
- ✓ *Depression and despair*
- ✓ *Lack of emotional stability*
- ✓ *Low self-esteem*
- ✓ *Feeling out of control*
- ✓ *Lack of self-care*
- ✓ *Loneliness*

✓ *Repressed anger*

✓ *Not knowing how to say no*

I was amazed that not one doctor in the audience wrote that drugs and surgery were the "real cure." Instead, they wrote that the most effective remedies included:

✓ *Education*

✓ *Positive attitude*

✓ *Healthy relationships*

✓ *Learning to get angry*

✓ *Having someone listen to their feelings*

✓ *Finding hope*

✓ *Assertiveness*

> *When a nurse in the cancer ward tells me we have a cantankerous patient in Room 214, I respond, 'Good, they'll live longer.' — Dr. Bernie Siegel*

Lamonte's Story

I met Lamonte when he was in college. He inspired me, and we became good friends. When I offered to host his graduation party at my home, he told me that he had never had a party with cake and decorations. I wanted to share part of his amazing story with you to open our eyes to the painful and powerful emotions that many carry silently inside.

I grew up in a rough part of Chicago in the '90's. *When I was in elementary school, there was never enough to eat. Because my mother did not have her high school diploma, there weren't many decent paying jobs for her. So instead of being gone all the time to make enough money for us, she went on welfare.*

We lived with my Grandma and my uncles in a small home. The problem was that there were seven of us in a house that was really meant for two. The noise level was something else. Outside there were people shouting and constant sirens, while inside there were TV's blaring in every room. Add to that the fact that my Grandma loved to have the police scanner on all the time so she could hear the police reports of where the criminal activity was, and you can imagine how loud it was.

In order to study, sometimes I'd take the bus to Barnes and Noble. I also really liked it when it rained, because then I could walk in the rain and it would be quiet because everyone else was inside.

We never had enough to eat. I'm sometimes asked why I didn't reach out for help during those grade school years. That's easy. The one time in second grade when one of my teachers asked if I had eaten supper the night before and I said I hadn't, we had child welfare services threatening to come and search our home and put my mom in jail.

Let's see, lie, or watch my family get split up? That was an easy decision. I got really good at making up stories about how much we had to eat.

Because we didn't have any food at home, I also got really good at figuring out ways to find it or make money to buy it. I joined choir because they gave out bagels and juice every morning. I joined violin because they had coffeecake. I'd shoot hoops with anybody dumb enough to compete with me and win a quarter. That would pay for my reduced lunch the next day.

But I also needed money for things like tennis shoes for me and my little brothers. In 4th grade I figured out a new plan. I'd get a ***Sports Illustrated*** *magazine — back in those days there were always stories about the Bulls or Notre Dame — and then I'd rent* *it to the kids in my homeroom. They could keep it all homeroom period for a quarter, and then they had to give it back. We had homeroom twice a day so that really added up.*

Pretty soon, with back issues of the magazine, I was renting out ten issues a day twice a day, so I was able to buy stuff like socks, underwear and toothpaste. I sold the old magazines for a dollar when they were done. It helped out a lot.

By seventh grade I was a mess of rage and depression. I'd do anything to make a dollar, shoveling snow for people who hadn't asked me to do it just so I could get a tip, raking leaves, walking dogs…but it still wasn't enough to really change anything.

I looked around and noticed that none of the kids in my neighborhood who were going to the local high school were making anything of themselves, so I decided to go for my dreams big time. I got out a phone book and started calling every private school I could find.

I'd talk to anyone: coaches, counselors, principals, or deans. My Ma said I was using too much phone time, but I knew this was my only way out. Then I'd write them letters, on cardboard or notepads, whatever I could find to tell people about my situation and ask for a scholarship.

I decided to tell my seventh grade teacher that I wanted to go to a university and needed to figure out a way to get into a good high school. I remember she laughed at me and said, "Oh, that's ridiculous. The local high school will do just fine." I'm glad I didn't let people like that get me down. My anger motivated me to just keep writing.

> *There is no instinct like that of the heart. — Lord Byron*

Unfortunately, even though I established lots of relationships with my letters, I still didn't have a scholarship. Finally, during my 8th grade summer, I did get an invitation to attend a summer basketball camp at Notre Dame High School, ninety minutes away by bus.

I knew I had to get their attention and help them know I could be "one of them," so every morning I dressed up in a suit jacket and tie I bought at Goodwill. Then I rode the bus the ninety minutes to practice, walked into the locker room, changed into my gym clothes, practiced, then changed back into my shirt and tie and rode the bus back home.

It got their attention. The last day of camp the coach asked me why I came in a suit and tie every day and I told him. He asked me to wait a minute and he walked down the hall to the principal's office to try and get me a scholarship.

When he came back he apologized and said they didn't have anything right now, but that he'd keep trying. I didn't hear anything for a week. Then at 6:15 the morning I was supposed to start at my neighborhood school, the phone rang. "We've got an anonymous donor that's going to fund you for four years," he said. I was ecstatic. Two days later, the first day of school at Notre Dame High School, I was enrolled as a student.

I graduated with lots of honors and two trips to the state basketball championship. I also got a scholarship to a great university. But I still had to be resourceful because the scholarship didn't cover food or books. The first semester I had to choose between food or sheets and blankets for my bed, but after that it got easier.

*Through all this, **Feeling All My Feelings** has been really important. For example, when the movie **Pursuit of Happyness** came out in 2007, I went to it with a couple of my buddies. The* *entire movie I could feel myself holding back, almost shutting down at the emotional parts of the film. It totally reminded me of my experiences, but I didn't feel comfortable crying around my guy friends.*

So right after it was over, I drove them home, turned around, and went back to watch it again — this time with lots of tears and cheers. There was no way I could tap into the passion and power of that film if I didn't allow my emotions to be felt.

Now I have my finance degree and a really good job. One of my dreams is that I will sell the old house my Ma and Grandma and uncles still live in and buy them a nicer one. Life is what you make it. I'm glad I took the high road.

Allowing the Feelings of Children

When my daughter was getting ready to move out, I had a discussion with my eleven-year-old son about the fact that when young adults prepare to leave home, they often get angry at their parents for every little thing.

"Why?" he asked.

"I imagine because they're afraid if they don't stay angry, they'll cry," I said.

That led to a good talk about sadness during which I reminded him of the importance of tears when we experience the loss of someone or something we love.

"If you died, Mom, I'd probably cry a whole week," he shared. "Or maybe even more. But I'd be crying happy tears, too, because I'd be so glad you're in heaven."

His comments helped me cry happy tears as we hugged. Allowing our kids' feelings, both mads and sads, can help us heal the future. Learning to **Feel All Our Feelings** in their presence can heal the present.

> *I am Me. In all the world, there is no one else exactly like me...However I look and sound, whatever I say and do, and whatever I think and feel at a given moment in time is authentically me... I own me, and therefore, I can engineer me. I am me, and I am okay. — Virginia Satir*

Putting Feel All Your Feelings into Practice

Journaling can write your childhood wrongs.

Catherine L. Taylor

Journaling

I have found that journaling feelings is the best entry into the world of accepting them. This kind of writing has no rules. The only guidelines are that you don't share it with anyone and you refrain from editing your writing. Whatever comes out, comes out, spelling errors and all.

A middle-aged woman credited my class with giving her "a ton of energy." A week later, I discovered the only thing she'd done differently was journal her feelings.

"Wow!" I said. "If you're having that much more energy, you must be journaling a lot."

"Not always," she replied. "On Wednesday I just wrote one word, 'Damn!'"

Feelings are often just underneath the surface, patiently awaiting our permission to come forth and free us.

One Rung at a Time

Below is a list of feelings from the phenomenal book ***Ask and It Is Given*** by Jerry and Esther Hicks. The feelings at the top of the list are how we feel when we remember our power. The further down the list, the more powerless the feelings. In other words, you could say this is where the emotions would be placed on the Power Pyramid.

Joy, Empowerment, Gratitude, Love
Passion, Enthusiasm
Optimism, Hope
Contentment
Boredom
Pessimism
Frustration, Impatience
Disappointment
Doubt
Worry
Blame, Anger
Hatred, Revenge, Jealousy
Guilt, Shame
Fear, Depression, Despair

A couple of notes about the above list:

1. Notice that anger is not at the bottom of the emotions/ power list; it is one-third of the way up. In other words, we might assume that an angry teenager has "fallen down" from joy and gratitude when he has actually "climbed up" from depression and despair. A despondent young person is much more of a concern than one expressing anger.

2. We cannot ascend this ladder of emotions in one large leap. What we can do, and encourage others to do, is move up one or two feelings (rungs) at a time.

For example, when I am feeling depressed, feeling revenge is actually two steps higher and therefore would actually be a positive and feasible step. Likewise, when I am able to choose thoughts that move me from guilt to anger, I am making important progress toward the empowered feelings of joy, gratitude, and love.

No one lives at the top of the Power Pyramid. We all experience a range of emotions in a day, a week, or a year. But as we've seen, embracing and honoring each of them for their unique gifts can weave a wonderful tapestry of a fully-lived life.

This being human is a guest house. Every morning a new arrival. A joy, a depression, a meanness, some momentary awareness comes as an unexpected visitor. Welcome and entertain them all!

Rumi

Q & A on Feel All Your Feelings

This topic can be heavy, so I thought we'd start with something light.

A friend of mine is a mortician, and he says one of the questions he's asked most frequently is, "Are you sad a lot?"

His answer is always, "Sure, I'm sad, but then someone dies and I perk right up!"

Okay, now let's get to some wonderful questions about feelings.

Q: How do I know if I'm feeling all my feelings or if I'm just poor-pity-me-ing?

A: This is a valid question to ask ourselves. Am I crying for attention or for release? My litmus test is whether or not I want people to *see me* cry. If I want them to see me, it's likely I'm tearing up for attention or pity. If I don't want them to see me or don't care, I am more comfortable that I am feeling in order to release, with no hidden agenda.

Q: Where do apathy and laziness fit into the feelings equation?

A: First let me respond to the question about apathy. Does anyone care about everything? Heck, no. That isn't healthy or realistic, but if someone contends that they don't care about *anything*, that's another issue. There's always a deeper truth underlying their seeming boredom.

When a family, company, or organization doesn't want to deal with anger in their midst, they'll soon be dealing with apathy. When teens or spouses get angry but are shut down by those who don't want to listen to their "emotional outbursts," they'll move forward in one of two ways: *exploding* into rage or *imploding* into depression or apathy.

As for laziness, I get agitated when I hear people talk about "lazy" teenagers. I've never met one. The only teens I've met who are referred to in that way are those who set such high goals for themselves that they've given up any hope of attaining them. They're not under-motivated as much as they're over-motivated. They need encouragement to follow their real dreams rather than their parents' "shoulds."

No one wants to be a couch potato. It results from having really big dreams with no one to coach them through the success process. ***8 to Great*** is the perfect solution for turning couch potatoes into powerhouses!

Q: I want to call this guy who just broke up with me. Is that stupid?

A: No. What I hear you saying is: "I'm not quite over him. I have lots of unresolved feelings." The only thing *not* to do in that situation is to stay stuck. Go ahead and call him. Get mad, feel jealous, or whatever you want to — just don't stay stuck in sad. Calling him may bring you two closer or it may help you realize the distance between you is too great. One angry woman, after an unpleasant call to her ex, joined two singles groups the same day. Action is often the result of feeling our angergy. You go, girl!

Q: I cry all the time. What's that about?

A: Crying is healthy, but if it's all the time, you're feeling helpless and powerless. Repeat over and over to yourself this week, "I'm in charge of my life." Journal about the things that make you angry. Unleash your angergy. Own your power. If you're suicidal or find yourself nearing a "9" out of "10" on the sadness scale, let someone know *immediately*.

Q: *Lately I've been kind of frozen, not wanting to work or talk or cry or be angry - just numb.*

A: When we feel frozen, it's because a big feeling is ready for healing. If you're frozen, you're in survival mode. With feelings, *the best way to a new one is through the one you're having*. Journal about it with phrases like "right now I'm feeling frozen" and let the pen take you from there to places like, "The good thing about being frozen is..."

> *If you're going through hell, keep going.*
> *— Winston Churchill*

Q: *How can I get my daughter angry enough to leave her abusive relationship?*

A: Take a deep breath. I'm going to coach you in a skill that will take you out of your comfort zone. You're feeling anger for your daughter, thereby robbing her of the angergy she needs in order to start over. **We're all half-jerk, half-jewel,** and I'm assuming that when you talk to her, you've been bringing up all of his "jerk" qualities, which has forced her to defend him.

The next time you talk, focus on his jewel points. Mention that he's in great shape, that he holds the door open for you, or that he's knowledgeable on a particular subject. This will almost always angergize her into action, and then she'll take care of the rest.

Q: What would an educational setting that encouraged healthy awareness and expression of emotions look like?

A: When my son was eight years old, he was extremely sad over a death in our extended family. As I drove him to school one morning, I noticed his grey mood and offered to let him stay home. He declined and after a half-hearted hug, walked slowly into his Montessori school. Later in the day, I was relieved to hear how his grief was honored.

According to his teacher, that morning during reading time he asked to sit in a quiet corner. With a book on his lap, he sobbed for nearly an hour amid occasional tissues and hugs from his instructor. When I picked him up at the end of the day, the little boy who got in my car laughing and asking questions was one who'd been shown that it was healthy and normal to **Feel All Your Feelings.**

> *If you suppress grief too much, it can well redouble.*
> *— Moliere*

Q: How do I tell people I'm getting a divorce? I hate how awkward it makes them feel and the downer discussion that follows. I even had a friend start to cry yesterday.

A: When I was in the process of getting divorced, I just said, "I've been meaning to tell you we're getting a divorce."

I'm not sure there's a softer way. Yes, people will cry, but their tears will be more about them than about you. It's like when you get to the sad part in a movie and you have tears come up about some completely different issue that you haven't cried about. I cried for two hours solid after watching the movie *E.T.*. Remember, tears are good. You're not making anyone cry. You're helping them cry.

Q: Why do you only mention mad and sad? What about all the other feelings?

A: These are the two feelings we "should on" and shut down from most in our society. They're neither more nor less important than the others. Joy, fear, confusion, elation - every one of them is part of a healthy life.

Q: When I started out working the High-Ways, it was the highest high I'd ever experienced, but now when I have a day that's not as "up," I get worried that I'm doing something wrong. Why do the grey days come?

A: Thank you for reminding us all that the road to success is bumpy for everyone. Oprah's been working these concepts for decades, yet she is open in her articles and interviews about how she gets discouraged and angry and sometimes uses food for comfort. Many TV talk show hosts and guests wept in public at the death of Robin Williams. There are many good models for healthy emotional expression.

Let's say you have a "blue" day - low energy, sad, and unenthusiastic about upcoming events. First, realize that you may have these feelings for many reasons. For example, there's a phenomenon known as "anniversary grief." It may be the day your dog died when you were five. Although you don't recall the date with your left brain, you remember the sadness with your right brain.

Maybe you're highly sensitive and pick up on the sadness

of others. One day I was immediately saddened as I entered a room where I was to speak. Halfway through the talk (when we got to the High-Way 4), I discovered that their leader, who had retired a year before, had abruptly died the previous day.

When we learn to allow feelings rather than judge or analyze them, it lessens their impact and helps move them through us with greater ease.

Q: You've told us that anger is healthy and that we should allow ourselves to feel it, but you're also telling us to be grateful every day. How can I do both?

A: Let me first express my gratitude for the great question. It shows that you're digesting and integrating the information.

There's always trouble in River City. No matter where you live or who you are, life has its challenges. You may choose to see them as a curse or realize that each difficulty offers opportunities for hidden blessings.

Recently I had a driver cut me off on the highway. I was angry at first, jolted into awareness. Then, for the first time in years, I became aware of the hundreds of cars around me driving safely and courteously, and immediately felt immense gratitude. My anger at the driver was followed by a pull into the present moment, and I felt gratitude for my wake-up call.

One way to look at a day in the life of our emotions is to compare it to riding bumper cars. When we hit a wall - feel anger at what we *do not* want - it helps us be clear and focused on what we *do* want. All our dreams come from our desires, which come from our adversities. And who isn't grateful for a ride on the bumper cars?

The best and most beautiful things in the world cannot be seen or even touched. They must be felt with the heart.

Helen Keller

5

High-Way 5: Honest Communication

Send and Receive the Highest Truth

Happiness is when what you think, what you say,
and what you do are in harmony.

Gandhi

Honesty is essential for a well-lived life. Without honesty there is no integrity. Without integrity there is no peace. Without peace there is no restful sleep, no relaxation, and no deep connection with others because we are so disconnected from ourselves.

Sadly, hiding the truth from ourselves and others often starts early, and if it remains unchecked, can spread across our lives. For some children it's hearing a parent say, "Don't tell your Dad/Mom. It will just upset them." As students the message from our peers is clear, that "everybody" cheats on tests. As young adults we hide behind electronic screens in an effort to avoid deeper open-hearted sharing.

As a result, hiding the truth can become the norm, and we discover that rather than providing protection from pain, hiding our true selves from others intensifies it, resulting in a self-imposed sentence to a prison of isolation.

Oh, what a tangled web we weave,
When first we practice to deceive!

Sir Walter Scott

The good news is that we hold the key to our prison cell. Freedom and peace are only one courageous decision away. When I ask my audience members to complete the phrase, "If I had no fear, I would..." the most common response *among all age groups* is, "I'd tell people what I really think/want/feel."

A woman who was in my **8 to Your IdealWeight** course recently shared that she had secretly admired a single coworker for years. When she encountered this High-Way, she courageously emailed him, asking him to coffee. He was thrilled, and they set a date to meet.

But what if her willingness to be more honest had *not* resulted in reciprocated interest? If he'd said "No thanks," after an initial pang of rejection, familiar to us all, she would have moved on, her risk muscles strengthened. Despite the risks, the rewards of honesty are among life's greatest gifts.

Despite the risks, the rewards of honesty are among life's greatest gifts. So how do we reclaim our integrity? The good news is that by the time you've embraced the High-Ways of **Risk, Full Responsibility**, and **Feel All Your Feelings**, you're well prepared for this next segment of your High-Ways journey.

> *I was angry with my friend: I told my wrath, my wrath did end. I was angry with my foe: I told it not, my wrath did grow. — William Blake*

The River of Life

Think of the abundance life offers as a river of love/grace/energy. When we have integrity with ourselves and others, we "grow with the flow" and the current is strong, carrying us swiftly to our next dream destination.

Each time we lie, it's as if we come to a fork in the river where a large portion of the water is siphoned off to a stream. One lie always requires another to cover it up and another stream veers off to feed that new untruth. With each falsehood, the river grows weaker and is slower in carrying us forward.

We have a choice. When we choose truth, the current in our lives remains strong and we are in the flow of all things good.

The End of the Cold War

Communication comes from two words: common and union. When we honestly communicate, we unite with our highest selves and feel closer to those around us — even when we don't agree with them. Two figures from a recent chapter in history who didn't agree, though they were phenomenal communicators, were Ronald Reagan and Mikhail Gorbachev.

Margaret Thatcher once referred to President Reagan as "the man who beat communism." Many historians contend that it was Ronald Reagan's honesty and openness in his personal conversations with Russia's top leader, Gorbachev, that brought an end to the Cold War.

It's worth noting that Reagan didn't soften his truth to find peace. On the contrary, he publicly confronted Gorbachev before the two met privately. In 1987, *against the counsel of his top advisors,* Reagan spoke the following words in front of the Berlin Wall:

"General Secretary Gorbachev, if you seek peace, if you seek prosperity for the Soviet Union and Eastern Europe, if you seek liberalization, come here to this gate! Mr. Gorbachev, open this gate! Mr. Gorbachev, tear down this wall!"

That same year, the two leaders were talking across a table and referring to each other as friends. Decades later, former first lady Nancy Reagan summed up their relationship this way: "From the moment they first sat down with each other there was a connection. You could feel it. When they left [the bargaining table] they would go down to the little place where the fire was going and stay there for about an hour. All the others were getting worried. What is he doing? What is he giving away? But taking that time turned out to be very, very successful."

> *We are each of us angels with only one wing, and we can only fly by embracing one another.*
> *— Luciano de Crescenzo*

That success not only earned Reagan ***Time*** Magazine's "Man of the Year" and Gorbachev the Nobel Peace Prize, but immense personal rewards as well. When Reagan died in 2004, Gorbachev attended his funeral, openly weeping as he embraced the first lady.

"In terms of human qualities," he later told reporters, "he and I had, you would say, communicativeness, and this helped us carry on. I take the death of Ronald Reagan very hard."

In this High-Way we'll define **Honest Communication** as speaking your truth in a fully responsible and respectful way, and listening with respect and compassion to the thoughts and feelings of others. It's a High-Way that can bring peace to your world.

Honesty with Self

I've known for years that I get major heartburn over the dishonesty of others. Unfortunately, because of High-Way 3, I have to assume **Full Responsibility** and constantly look to see where I can be more honest with myself. What I've discovered over the years is that the more honest we become with ourselves, the more we recognize when we're being less than completely honest with others.

I cited one example of my little white lies in my first book. I would sometimes hear myself say things like, "Oh, yes. The kids and I would love to come over for dinner on Friday." Meanwhile, thinking to myself, "And watch Barry Manilow specials on TV while we eat? No thanks!"

Honesty with others starts with honesty with ourselves, and that can start anywhere. In High-Way 4 we looked at the biggest hurdle — facing and allowing our feelings — but honesty can also begin with:

- ✓ *balancing our checkbook*
- ✓ *opening our mail*
- ✓ *cleaning our living or work areas to face what's in those piles*
- ✓ *acknowledging our age*
- ✓ *facing the fact that we over-schedule ourselves to avoid intimacy or commitments we don't want to keep*
- ✓ *stating our opinion in a calm way, even when it's unpopular*
- ✓ *admitting we need help*

Once we start to see ourselves more clearly, we're ready to be honest with others.

> *Be who you are and say what you feel, because those who mind don't matter and those who matter don't mind. — Dr. Seuss*

Honesty and Love

How does honesty interface with being loving? Prior to my experience in a domestic violence shelter, I might have said something like: "Love is feeling connection and affection, demonstrated through acts of kindness." However, spending time there, I redefined it as: *"Love is being authentically myself with you and encouraging you to be authentically yourself with me."*

One of my favorite authors once put it this way:

Love is the process of my leading you back to yourself.

Antoine de Saint-Exupery

When I moved away from defining love as doing things for others, I was free. I began to see that so much of what I was doing for others wasn't in their best interest and often was not even on their wish list. My efforts were really attempts to manipulate them into connecting with me. When I became more honest with others, I found greater peace.

One year on Valentine's Day as I was addressing a group of couples, I separated them by gender and asked, "How important is honest communication to a healthy marriage?"

The women took less than thirty seconds to respond: "100 percent."

The men took three minutes to come up with "94.5 percent." As we had a good laugh about the differences between men and women, one thing was clear — they all considered honest communication one of their highest values! So what keeps us from being more honest, and what would living with greater honesty look like?

The goal of this chapter isn't to give an overview of the rudiments of good communication. Instead, we'll focus on seven common areas that prevent loving connection and then offer processes for each:

Process 1: *The L.A.D.I.I. Formula for Deep Listening*
Process 2: *Sharing Fully Responsible Feelings*
Process 3: *Learning to Say No*
Process 4: *Asking for What You Want*
Process 5: *Constructive vs. Destructive Criticism*

Process 6: *Ending Third Party Communication*

Process 7: *Stopping Sarcasm*

Any one of these processes can quiet your mind and open your heart to the power and good feelings that honesty brings.

> *Honesty is the first chapter in the book of wisdom.*
> *— Thomas Jefferson*

The Honest Communication Process:

I know you think you understand what you thought I said,
but I'm not sure you realize

that what you heard is not what I meant.

Alan Greenspan

Learning to Listen

In today's world, there are a thousand experiences vying for our attention. Whether it's a text, a tweet, three people talking at once, or an urgent Facebook message, it takes effort to focus on one person or experience at a time. We listen three times as much as we talk, so it's clear that learning to truly *hear* the message the other is sending is vital for successful communication.

After working with men and women who were in various stages of anger over the years, it's become clear to me that the main cause of anger on the planet is feeling disrespected or "dissed." Understanding that, what is the *most respectful* thing we can do for another human being? The answer is to listen. No matter what triggered the anger in the first place, listening from the heart is the balm that can calm.

In order for listening to have a healing effect it must involve *open-hearted attention* — hearing and honoring the thoughts *and feelings* of the person who is speaking. Most of us are pretty good listeners when someone is telling us good news or talking about us, but once someone starts sharing a painful emotion, we're tempted to want to fix it, talk them out of it, or just ignore it. I often use a poem by Ralph Roughton to draw a picture of open-hearted attention:

Please Listen

When I ask you to listen to me and you start giving me advice,
you have not done what I've asked.
When I ask you to listen to me and you begin to tell me why I
shouldn't feel that way, you are trampling on my feelings.
When I ask you to listen to me and you feel you have to do
something to solve my problem, you have failed me, strange as
that may seem.

Listen! All I ask is that you listen. Don't talk or do - just hear me.
Advice is cheap; I can do for myself; I am not helpless.
Maybe discouraged and faltering, but not helpless.
When you do something for me that I can and need to do for
myself, you contribute to my fear and weakness.
But when you accept as a simple fact that I feel what I feel, no
matter how irrational, then I can stop trying to convince you and
start understanding what's behind my irrational feelings.
And when that's clear, the answers are obvious and
I don't need advice. Irrational feelings make sense when we
understand what's behind them.
So, please listen, and just hear me.
And if you want to talk, wait a minute for your turn — and I will
listen to you.

As we see in this poem, we can dismiss another's feelings as "irrational." That's because when one feels strong feelings, they sometimes exaggerate the facts to get our attention to their heightened emotions. Learning to listen to them from the heart can help that person feel whole, validated and accepted.

> *Listen long enough and the person will generally come up with an adequate solution. — Mary Kay Ash*

Defensiveness vs. Deep Listening

When I speak to struggling families, I ask both parents and teens, "What's wrong?" Parents answer, "They won't talk!"

Teens respond, "They won't listen!"

> *It takes courage to stand up and speak. It also takes courage to sit down and listen. — Winston Churchill*

The same scenario often happens when asking women and men what's wrong. People will only talk when there's someone who will truly listen.

One of the most common and damaging errors we make as listeners is becoming defensive during a disagreement. Think back to the last time you got defensive in a discussion. Did it help? Of course not. The reason is because you couldn't hear what the other person was trying to say. You may have been listening to their words, but you weren't hearing what they needed you to hear — their feelings.

Process 1: The L.A.D.I.I. Formula for Deep Listening

We call this initial process for Honest Communication **Deep Listening**. I learned a lot about listening rather than defending from relationship therapist Harville Hendrix, Ph.D., the author of many enlightening books on relationships, such as ***Getting the Love You Want, Keeping the Love You Have*** and his most recent book, ***Marriage Made Simple*** which he wrote with his wife of forty years.

When to Use the L.A.D.I.I. Formula

When there is anger that's dangerous or physically threatening, always remove yourself to a safe place until the other person calms down, and then get to a counselor, coach or hotline to know how to secure your safety.

The following skill is for those times when it is *only* verbal accusations, not physical threats, being shared. When the other person is using rage language (without violent threats), that is when the **L.A.D.I.I.** formula can help.

There are three signs that the individual speaking to you is in a rage. The three Rage Phrases are "you always," "you never," and "you are such a..."

As you hear them, it's important to remember that these words are not about you - you're just the "match" that ignited the kerosene inside of the other person. Since none of those phrases are ever true (You don't "always" do that thing, for example) we want to defend ourselves with our almighty facts. But when rage is present, **facts** will only pour more kerosene on their fire. The other individual is exaggerating with "always" and "never" in order to get your attention to their **feelings**.

Let's take an example from a couple I worked with and apply the **L.A.D.I.I.** formula.

Her statement was, "You never make time for me these days." His response using this formula was:

L. — "**L**et me see if I got that."

A. — (**A**cknowledge what they said). "It feels like I never make time for you these days."

D. — "**D**id I get that?"

Although this may feel awkward at first, it will calm the person who is using "You never" language when they see that they have your full attention. They will appreciate that rather than correcting their exaggerated "facts," you tuned into them on an emotional level.

Now, wait for them to reply. If their answer to "Did I get that?" is "No," then calmly asked them to repeat what they said, and be sure to use their exact words in your acknowledgment.

Note: One phrase to **avoid at all costs** is, "I'm sorry you feel that way." It infers that a "normal" person wouldn't feel that way, and that their emotional response is invalid. This leads to them feeling even more disrespected.

I. Is there more?

Once you've acknowledged that you hear their feelings/ accusations, asking if there's more will often catch them off guard. In the past, we've usually been quick to defend ourselves, and here we are asking to hear more! It is powerfully honoring to let them know that their feelings are worth listening to. Prepare to be surprised by their response. It will often tell a story that you have never taken the time to hear.

I. I can Imagine that feels... Putting words to what they *might* be feeling is a risk that is worth taking. Even though we will often guess wrong, they will appreciate our efforts. Another version of this statement is, "I hear that you felt/are feeling ________ and you have every right to feel that way."

We all have a right to our feelings. Remember that when you use this process, you are not agreeing with their facts, you are simply *acknowledging their feelings as valid.*

The Surprise behind his "You Never"

> *We are never angry for the reason we think.*
> *— A Course in Miracles*

When Kelsey, my coaching client, started dating Kyle, she noticed two idiosyncrasies about him. First, he hated it when she got up from the table while they were eating. Secondly, he ate slowly, at least compared to Kelsey.

One Tuesday afternoon, Kyle called to say he was getting off work early and asked if she was free for supper. Kelsey was delighted. "I have a meeting tonight, but 4:30 would be perfect!" she replied. They decided on a restaurant close to his work and not far from her meeting.

As soon as they sat down, they started chatting, never noticing that the waitress didn't ask for their order for twenty minutes. After ordering, they continued their lively discussion, unaware that the food took another thirty minutes to get to the table. At 6:10, Kelsey noticed that although she'd finished her meal, Kyle hadn't. At 6:15, she told him she had to go.

"I'm sorry to have to go, but I need to get to my meeting..."

"I thought your meeting was at 7:00! I'm not finished yet!"

"I forgot to tell you that it was at 6:30, and I've got to give a treasurer's report. I'm so sorry. Call me tonight so we can talk, will you?"

He didn't respond as she headed out the door.

The L.A.D.I.I. Phone Call

That evening, knowing he'd be upset, Kelsey was determined not to take his anger personally and to use the L.A.D.I.I. process to hear his feelings. She was grateful when the phone rang and it was Kyle.

"I just can't believe you did that today," he began.

She acknowledged him. "**L**et me see if I'm hearing you, Kyle. **(A)**You can't believe that I left before you were finished eating. **D**id I get that?"

"Yes."

"**I**s there more?

"Absolutely. Every time we're together, whether we're out to eat or you're jumping up to get something out of the refrigerator at your house, it's the same thing. It's ridiculous that you can't stay seated until I'm finished!"

"I hear you. It seems like every time we're sharing a meal I jump up before you're finished. Did I get that?"

"Yes!" For the next five minutes, she heard many "every," "always," and "never" statements from him, but she kept reminding herself that she was just the match to his kerosene.

Finally, when she asked, "Is there more?" his answer was, "No." Now it was time to move to the final step.

"I'm so sorry I upset you, Kyle. You have every right to every one of your feelings," she said. She truly meant it.

Immediately the conversation changed tone. In a softer voice, he thanked her for being such a great listener. Then he shared that he regularly had to sit alone at the table as punishment when he was a child. He often had to watch as his older brothers went outside to play baseball while he was confined to the table. "I should be over it, but I'm not. I still hate sitting by myself."

Kelsey thanked him for sharing and promised to be more aware. Over the next few dates, things changed and Kyle started noticing. She made a real effort to stay seated, until one day, a month later, she forgot. Kyle didn't even notice. Her deep listening had dried up the kerosene from his childhood that was in his mad bowl.

> *It is not our purpose to become each other; It is to recognize each other, to learn to see the other and honor him for what he is. — Hermann Hesse*

Hearing Unspoken Feelings

By the time Shelley and Don came to me for coaching, they'd been to many counselors, but nothing had helped. They were walking through their marriage in isolation, hardly speaking. That was because when they did speak, no one was listening. Here was a typical defensive exchange that they were able to turn around:

Shelley: "Honey, I have good news. While you were gone on your fishing trip, I had a garage sale and sold your old gear."

Don: "You what?"

Shelley: "I sold your rusty old fishing gear and I got $75 for it!"

Don: "You what?"

Shelley: "You told me you liked the new stuff I bought you for your birthday. Were you lying?"

Don: "I can't believe that you would do that. But then you're *always* doing things without asking me. Why should this be any different?"

As soon as Shelley heard Don use one of the Rage Phrases ("You're *always*..."), she was able to practice **L.A.D.I.I.**:

Shelley: "Let me see if I got that. You're saying I'm always doing things without asking you. Is that what I'm hearing?"

Don: "Yes, and get this, that was my Grandad's. He could have given it to any of his grandsons, but he gave it to me, and now thanks to you, it's gone!"

Shelley: "Oh Honey, I had no idea. I can only imagine how upset you must be that it's gone. That makes so much sense. I'm so sorry. Maybe there's an address on his check and we can get it back..."

At the following appointment they shared that with the new skills, their arguments were few and far between.

We Don't Understand

I steer individuals, couples and co-workers away from the overused phrase, "I understand." We don't understand. Each person's experience is unique, so therefore the phrase can sound disrespectful. Instead, when you hear someone's strong emotions, consider one of these optional phrases:

> *That had to hurt.*
>
> *I can tell you're really upset.*
>
> *You have every right to be angry.*
>
> *Go on, tell me more*
>
> *Ouch.*
>
> *I care about you and I care about your feelings. Thank you for sharing.*

Whenever someone starts using one of the Rage Phrases, think of it as an open door to their heart. In that sacred moment, you have the ability to help them heal a deep wound. That's what happens each week in 12-step groups around the country. Millions of people come together in small rooms to speak their unedited truth to open-hearted listeners. As a result, lifelong addictions are healed.

The word "heart" even has an "ear" in it! There's truly no substitute for hearing with our hearts.

> *The most called-upon prerequisite of a friend is an accessible ear. — Maya Angelou*

Process 2: Sharing Fully Responsible Feelings

B.C.ing when we feel angry or hurt is as common as it is destructive. Instead we can take **Full Responsibility** when we're communicating strong feelings. Which of the following are you more likely to say?

> *A. "You make me so mad."*
>
> *B. "I'm really mad."*

C. "I'm feeling mad and hurt right now."

D. "Something has triggered a lot of anger and sadness in me right now. I'd like to talk about it."

Notice the increased responsibility and objectivity in the above phrases.

Statement A isn't owning any responsibility and is trying to blame the other person for how we feel. This victim mentality is at "5" on the Power Pyramid and can lead to staying stuck in misery.

Statement B, while an improvement, tells our brains we *are* our feelings. That can prevent us from stepping back and looking at our emotions objectively, which means we can feel engulfed and overwhelmed by them.

Statement C moves us to a healthier place in two ways. First, moving to "I'm feeling" from "I am my feeling" gains a distance that helps us become more aware and accepting of our feelings. Also, we admit that we're feeling both mad and hurt, which can help calm us. (Remember, sadness releases excess angergy.)

Statement D is the most empowered way to communicate. It takes **Full Responsibility** while admitting that we're not even sure of all the triggers of the emotions we're feeling. It asks the listener to help us sort them out, rather than accusing that person of creating them, thus minimizing the chances of the listener getting defensive.

Honest Communication doesn't come naturally for most of us, but it's a skill we can learn and practice until it does - and the rewards of fewer and shorter arguments are well worth the effort.

Process 3: Learning to Say No

> *Let your "yes" mean "yes" and your "no" mean "no."*
> *— Matthew 5:37*

Have you ever noticed how the healthiest and happiest people are really good at saying "no?" They use phrases such as, "No, I won't be doing that, but thank you for asking." Try saying that right now, out loud. Don't you love it? You don't have to give a reason for saying "no." As soon as you do give a reason, an argument could break out about the reason.

Learning to say "no" is powerful, but it can be so foreign that sometimes we have to warm up to it. If you're not quite ready for the big N.O. here are some possible alternatives:

"I'll consider that in the future, but right now, no."

"Ask me later. I need to think about it."

"I won't be able to. I'm busy that evening." (Busy reading a book or relaxing in the tub!)

Another favorite for beginners: "Oops! Gotta go (because you're uncomfortable). We'll have to talk about this later." That phrase gives you time to work up the nerve to say you're not interested.

Face it. You're going to pay a bigger price for saying "yes" than the momentary discomfort of disappointing someone. Making "no" your friend is saying, "Yes, I respect myself."

Meanwhile, when someone offers you unsolicited advice, you can set clear boundaries with a phrase such as, "Thanks for sharing. When that decision comes up for review, I'll let you know."

> *It's hard for people to understand that you can disagree with them and not be against them. That you could be for something without being against something else.*
> *— Abraham-Hicks*

Process 4: Asking for What You Want

In the next few pages, I'm going to share a powerful skill for getting what you want. So why do only 10 percent of the adults and students I coach use this skill after they learn it? I'm told, "It's new," "It's a risk," or "I might do it wrong." The fact is that of the 10 percent who use it, 90 percent say it works wonders.

Pre-step: Have you got a minute?

This preparation step for asking is crucial in today's fast-paced society. I use it to begin almost every phone conversation because I never know what I've caught someone in the middle of. Inviting someone to sit down with you for a minute or to go for a short walk signals that you need their undivided attention.

Step 1: "When _______________ (describe one recent time and one place)..."

Oftentimes this will start out with something like, "When I didn't hear from you last night" or "When you interrupted me just now." Be sure to stay as calm as possible. Most importantly, steer clear of "you always" or "you never" phrases. Giving one example of the thing that upset you from the past forty-eight hours will get your point across the best.

Step 2: "I felt (a little)..." (mention one or two of your emotions)

The temptation when we're upset is to use phrases like, "I felt like" or "I felt that," but neither of those are feeling statements. They're judgments, exactly what you don't need if you want someone to keep listening. Using the phrase "a little" after you state your feeling will keep you from veering into opinion territory, such as, "I *felt* you were making a huge mistake." The truth is, you *thought* that they were making a mistake. Instead, say something like, "I'm feeling a little concerned about your decision." Their ears and heart are more likely to stay open.

Step 3: "Because..." (include your perception)

In this step, explain what your perception of the situation is, and remember, it's *only your perception*. It usually works best to use "it seems like" or "because it looks to me" to remind yourself (and them) that you're only checking out the facts.

Step 4: "Therefore..." (request a realistic desire)

This fourth step isn't always necessary, but sometimes we need to be clear as to what behavior would work better for us. A new spouse might say, "Therefore, if you can focus on a few things you like about the meals I fix, it'll help my confidence." A friend might say, "Therefore, if you can drive every other time, I'd feel more comfortable." A parent might say, "Therefore, if you'd like to go to the game tomorrow night, you'll need all your chores and homework caught up."

Always end with "Thanks for listening."

If you don't ask, you don't get. — Gandhi

Process 5: Constructive vs. Destructive Criticism

There are two kinds of criticism: one is respectful, the other isn't. One is constructive, the other is destructive.

C is about **B**: **C**onstructive criticism is about a **B**ehavior
D is about **C**: **D**estructive criticism is about **C**haracter

Destructive criticism is always disrespectful. When you make statements such as "You always," "You never," or "You are such a..." they're never true about the person you're berating, and when they hurl such phrases toward you, they're never true about you.

Constructive criticism, however, can be wonderful. After completing a 12-step program, one young mother would often ask her children, "Is there anything Mommy could be doing differently?" Their answer was usually, "No," but at her birthday dinner, as her children went around the table sharing one thing they appreciated about their mom, her six-year-old blurted out, "Mommy, one thing I don't like is that you lie down too much."

The woman's husband tried to shush the little one and encourage her to say something nice, but that amazing Mom immediately said, "She's right."

Tears ran down her cheeks as she relished her daughter's constructive and honest communication and admitted to herself that she often slept to avoid dealing with life. She remembers it as a turning point in her recovery. She had been told that a big part of her fatigue was due to her sugar consumption. She started a new food program and going to counseling the following week.

I'm grateful for those people in my life who have offered constructive criticism. Cindy Osterloh, a high school principal from a nearby community who helped make this book possible, was one. I'll never forget her email one morning as we were launching ***8 to Great*** at her school:

MK,

I wanted you to know that when you said on the phone yesterday, "You need to get the mayor or superintendent to introduce the assembly on Friday," it didn't work as well for me as "What do you think about this," or "Do you think this would work?" Yesterday, it felt like I was being told what to do. You're the expert on this program, but I know the people in this town. Thanks for listening.

Cindy

I replied:

Cindy,

Thank you. My sincere apologies. Please help me catch when I am coming across as demanding like that. I want to offer my ideas as simply that — ideas not demands. Your honesty with me is perhaps the greatest gift you have given me so far. I feel blessed by your courage to speak your truth.

MK

Her constructive criticism was clear, but not shaming. She shared something she perceived that I *did* wrong, rather than that I *was* wrong. She also gave me a picture of what would work better, and finally, she said it didn't work as well "for her," taking **Full Responsibility** for her feelings. She's a master communicator in that regard.

Process 6: Ending Third Party Communication

How destructive is Third Party (XYZ) Communication? You know the triangulation routine: X is mad at Z, but instead of telling Z, she tells Y. Then Y goes and tells Z.

I've seen it take down marriages, extended families, church choirs, businesses, and even small towns! If you've been bothered by XYZ games recently, that means you were a participant. The good news is that if you're a participant, you have the power to withdraw, and once you get out of the game, the game is over.

The big misunderstanding in Third Party Communication (also called gossip) is who the real culprit is. When X has a problem with Z and goes to Y with her complaint and then Y runs to Z to tell her what X thinks, the biggest troublemaker is *Y*, who will do her level best to convince Z that the problem is X. Don't believe it.

How to Avoid the XYZ Game

When you find yourself in an XYZ situation, there are easy ways out, depending on which part you're playing. Here are guidelines for never getting caught in XYZ again:

1. If you're X, just go talk to Z. You have the skills: "When you," "I felt a little," "Because," and "Therefore." Share your feelings rather than your judgments. Chances are Z will be more open than you think.

2. If you're Y and X comes to you B.C.ing about something Z did, simply tell X, "You need to go talk to Z about that." If they protest, say something like, "No, really. You're making good points and I'm sure Z will benefit from hearing your concerns." When you make it clear that the ball is in their

court, they'll never come back to you whining about that situation again.

3. If you are Z and Y comes to you saying, "Do you know what X said about you?" Simply smile and say something like, "So, do you agree?" **Y never carries a message she doesn't agree with.** In fact, whenever Y tells you about X's problem with you, it's almost always Y's agenda and Y is using X as an X-cuse! Don't give Y any encouragement for their behavior or you'll get a lot more of it.

To summarize: If you're X, go to Z with a "When you, I feel" statement. If you're Y, encourage X to go to Z. If you're Z, ask Y, "Do you agree?" and watch them do a dance while backing out the door.

And one final thing: don't feel bad if you are Z. I've found that in life, either you will talk about others because their lives are more interesting or they will talk about you because yours is. Be glad it's the latter.

> *A lie gets halfway around the world before the truth has a chance to put its pants on. — Winston Churchill*

Process 7: Stopping Sarcasm

Sarcasm: *A cutting remark intended to wound or demean. Often thought of as "witty" by the user, sarcasm can be poisonous and can cause permanent relationship damage.*

The first few times I encountered sarcasm I was tricked into thinking that the person using it was witty and intelligent because they could wordsmith their jabs to perfection, often adding sneers or a shake of the head at the "stupidity" of their prey. Over time I came to realize that sarcasm is nothing more than a desperate attempt by a frightened individual to gain attention at any cost.

Examples of sarcasm could be:

"Right. You didn't say that. I was hallucinating."

"Oh, did I step on your teensy-weensy feelings again?"

"No, it's not my real name. I'm just breaking it in for a friend."

According to Dr. Richard L. Williams, "A person who regularly uses sarcasm is nothing more than a verbal bully. The sarcastic bully uses words rather than physical threats to try to gain an advantage over the other person."

Those who use sarcasm fight a losing battle. Looking for more power through their cleverness, their sarcasm results in less. Looking to be "one up" in social stature by putting someone else down with verbal barbs, the perpetrator ultimately loses the admiration and trust of others along with lowering their own self-esteem.

The "butt" of the sarcasm also loses. The mockery can make us feel inferior if we *don't* respond and sorry if we *do*. We often feel helpless at first and infuriated later. We eventually withdraw from the perpetrator, leaving that person more alone, lonely, and frightened than ever.

Being around someone who uses sarcasm is like trying to walk through a war zone. You never know when the sniper is going to jump out of the bushes and fire an insult in your direction. It may be that their main goal is to get you to respond angrily to keep the game going. Remember that people would rather be unlovable than invisible.

How to Stop the Sarcasm

If you're ever the recipient of sarcasm, you have options. Start by observing how and when it's used and what feelings it brings up for you. Once you have at least two clear-cut examples of someone's sarcasm, sit down with that person when you're both fairly calm. Use the "When you, I feel" process noted earlier in this chapter.

For example:

"Have you got a minute?"

"When you interrupted what I was saying a few minutes ago with 'don't you have anyone else you'd like to bother right now?' I felt uncomfortable because it seemed a harsh way to say you wanted alone time. Therefore, I'd like to talk about taking sarcasm off the options list when you're communicating with me."

If you're the one who's been using sarcasm, start your healing by becoming aware of your tendency to judge. For example, how often do you find yourself talking about the incompetence or inabilities of others? Then once you see what you're doing, look at how you're feeling. Judging looks like arrogance but is always rooted in low self-esteem. With time and patience, we can all learn to love ourselves again.

It will take humility to admit that the "know-it-all" the world sees in you is just a cover for your insecurities. It will take patience to discover how loveable you are, and it will take courage to admit how hard you've been running from your pain. But no matter how challenging it is to release sarcasm and judgment, doing so will allow close, loving relationships back into your life.

Why We Don't Honestly Communicate

Honest communication means responding with what is true for you, regardless of how someone may react to your answer.

Byron Katie

Secret Keeping

Years ago, I spoke with a friend who was learning Russian. When she asked about the Russian word for "journal," she got into a deep discussion with her instructor. She discovered that the English word "journaling" didn't exist in their language. Her instructor made it clear that no one living in Russia would ever do such a dangerous thing as to write down their true thoughts and feelings on a sheet of paper.

We don't have to live in the Soviet Republic to keep secrets. I've seen similar patterns in the relationships of those around me.

- ✓ *A young woman who was deeply ashamed of her anger at her alcoholic parents went into denial by cleaning the entire house regularly, often into the wee hours of the morning.*
- ✓ *A wife who kept hundreds of secrets from her husband while she "did nice things" for him was eventually served with divorce papers.*
- ✓ *A man who worked extra hard while silently becoming more and more upset with his boss one day just up and quit, later regretting it.*

Over-Promising

One way we're dishonest with ourselves comes back again to High-Way 3. We make bigger promises than we can keep.

Living with integrity means doing what you say you'll do, when you say you'll do it, to the best of your ability. When you don't, you admit it, and make amends. (More on this in High-Way 6: **Forgiveness of the Past.**)

We are as sick as our secrets. — AA Member

It's like a child learning not to take more on his plate than he'll eat. If we find ourselves in an over-committing pattern, we need to stop and take **Full Responsibility** and make amends. When I over-commit, I do my best to make amends that are costly to me. For example, if I'm late, "The next meal is on me," or if I missed a deadline, "I'll drive the document over myself this afternoon." That pain wakes me up — and makes me promise myself to be more honest by not taking on so much the next time.

The Approval Addiction

Another reason we hide our truth is Fear of Rejection. We want people to like us, but we forget that we only like the people we respect, and everyone respects a person of integrity. No matter how much we want to impress others with the number of balls we can juggle, our reputation can come crashing down after a few broken promises.

Another piece of the Approval Addiction is a penchant for perfectionism. When this sort of striving takes over, a person is unable to feel satisfaction and joy because in their own eyes they never do things well enough to warrant feeling good. At their worst, perfectionists set impossible goals and measure their worth in terms of productivity and accomplishments.

Since perfectionists tend to be "all or nothing" thinkers, they often put too much effort and attention on small details and miss the larger picture.

> *I was always fearful of failing. It seemed no matter what I did right, I always saw something I was doing wrong. I never felt good enough, no matter what I did. I felt God was displeased with me. I was deceived! — Joyce Meyer*

A wonderful story about the challenges of all or nothing thinking is described in Robert Pirig's ***Zen and the Art of Motorcycle Maintenance.*** It's known as the "South Indian Monkey Trap."

The story tells of villagers who were desperately trying to curb a growing monkey population. One day someone came up with the idea of placing rice grains inside a long narrow hole that had been widened at the bottom. The thinking was that the monkeys would grab the grains of rice, and since the hole was just big enough for them to put their hands in, but too small for a fist full of rice to come out, the monkeys would be trapped. It worked. Like the perfectionist, the monkeys hung onto something insignificant while losing something precious — their freedom.

Nice vs. Kind

On the other side of the honesty fence are those who have trouble admitting when something doesn't feel good. Some of us were brought up hearing, "If you can't say something nice, don't say anything at all." In doing so, we lost our voice. We could no longer speak our truth because the truth might hurt. Little did we realize that lies hurt much more.

In our ***8 to Great*** seminars, we refer to the overly "nice" person as one who is "on-ice." My theory on Overly Nice (O.N.) people can be described as follows:

1. O.N. people have had all the passion squished out of them. Because I've been there myself, I can easily spot those who have to know how *you* feel before they can figure out how *they* feel. The danger for O.N. people is that they wear a mask so long they lose touch with who they really are.
2. O.N. people are scared. They will say they agree with you when they don't because they're frightened — of rejection, of hurting someone's feelings, or of being seen.
3. O.N. people will break promises. Sooner or later, it's not nice to be around O.N. people. Because they have no "no" in their vocabulary, their "yes" means nothing. Friends of O.N. people have to work hard to figure out what they really mean and they get tired of it, so they eventually leave, which is one reason that...
4. O.N. people are lonely. O.N.'s do too much for others while never asking for what they need. Therefore, other people assume they don't need anything, leaving O.N.'s high and dry. This can lead to a final characteristic...
5. O.N. people are angry. Because they smile when they're angry or hurting, O.N.'s have to push their pain down — but it eventually erupts. They're angry that they're alone, that they've had to swallow their truth, and that all they do is give. Because they've been quiet for so long, their anger often all comes out at once. When that happens, the O.N. feels ashamed, which leads to more dishonesty, which leads to more shame.

I find it interesting that some of my Christian friends who are the most active in church work tend toward O.N. behavior.

I'm not sure why. Jesus wasn't afraid of calling a Pharisee "a white-washed sepulcher" or telling Peter to "get thee behind me, Satan." He was passionate, fearless, and he got angry.

I thank God for the friends and counselors over the years who knocked the O.N. out of me. They may have saved my life. I know they gave me back my serenity.

> *Compulsively proper and generous people predominate among cancer patients because they put the needs of others in front of their own. — Dr. Bernie Siegel*

Honest Communication Success Stories

If I lose mine honor, I lose myself.

William Shakespeare

She Faced Her Fears

Laura's mom noticed that something was wrong. Lately Laura had been coming home from her part-time job calling people "stupid." Her mom had never heard that level of blaming and name-calling from her daughter, so she asked for a time to talk about it. When they sat down, she asked Laura if anything had changed with the job she had loved when she started the year before. Why the B.C.ing?

After Laura had finished telling her how frustrated she was at the paltry effort most of her co-workers put forth, her mom asked, "Is it possible you want to quit and just don't feel comfortable telling your boss?"

To Laura's credit, she thought for a minute and then admitted that she felt she'd be letting everyone down if she quit. Together, mother and daughter looked up statistics on how many jobs the average person holds in a lifetime and agreed that learning to bring honest closure to a job was a life skill worth learning. Laura gave her notice the next day and sat down to write a letter of thanks to her employer.

The first time I shared that story with young adults, I was amazed at the response. *One-fourth* of those in the session had experienced similar challenges, but rather than admitting their discomfort, had gotten themselves fired for absenteeism or tardiness! Leaving a job with ill feelings drags us down to a "5" on the Power Pyramid and makes attracting our next "95" job much harder. It pays, both emotionally and financially, to tell the truth.

> *When the whole world is silent, even one voice becomes powerful. — Malala Yousafzai*

No Longer Living a Lie

I'll always remember the high school senior who took the risk of writing on the anonymous feedback form after their first class: "I lie all the time. I lie so much that I can't even tell when I'm lying. Can you help me?"

The next time that class met, I unfolded the paper and read the comment aloud to the group. Holding it up I said, "Whoever wrote this, you just told the truth. You must feel a lot better. Congratulations! You're right on track." A few classes later the author introduced himself and thanked me for starting him on a new path to a more honest and happier life.

> *Honesty is the cornerstone of all success, without which confidence shall cease to exist. — Mary Kay Ash*

The Courage to Claim Our Truth

I recall training a group of high school seniors. As we ended the second day, I asked students if they'd be willing to share what they were going to take with them from the training.

A beautiful young woman looked at me with misty eyes and said, "I'm ready to tell my mom the truth. I have a scholarship to Julliard in clarinet, but I've known for a while it's not where my passion lies. I want to play the guitar professionally. I know it will be hard, but ***8 to Great*** has helped me see that taking the risk of being honest with myself and her will ultimately turn out for the best."

Julliard did not withdraw the scholarship when they heard of her decision. Can you imagine the kind of guitarist her truth unleashed?

The $20,000 Error

Another example of the rewards of honesty involved a friend who worked as an administrative assistant to a successful CEO. She had many responsibilities and some included working with large sums of money. One day she realized she'd made a $20,000 error. It took days to get up the courage to tell her boss, but she finally walked into his office and shared the painful truth. Crying, she said she understood that she'd have to be fired, but he stopped her mid-sentence.

"Fire you? Why would I do that? I just spent $20,000 training you!" **Honest Communication** is worth its weight in gold to bosses, co-workers, friends, and family members. It's a High-Way that can truly take you where you want to go.

If you tell the truth, you don't have to remember anything.

Mark Twain

Putting Honest Communication into Practice

If honest communication between two people isn't extended to the point of resolution and peace, the energy will appear again as wounding in another relationship.

Marianne Williamson

The Honesty Workout

"I hope this one works out," a new friend shared at the end of our conversation, referring to her latest romantic relationship.

The reality is that every relationship works out. They give our hearts and minds a workout like nothing else can. The goal is not to "win" him or keep from "losing" her, but rather to do the real work of intimacy and love — integrity.

Integrity is when we share who we truly are with another human being; when we're the same person in and out of that person's presence. It's a risk that requires a high level of courage, but when encountered, is deeply healing. Perhaps the most beautiful part about the love-work of integrity is that its success rate has nothing to do with the other person's response to us.

Holding another person while *withholding* from them isn't loving, but many people have never allowed themselves to be emotionally naked with another human being because they've never been fully honest with themselves. The great news is that we can learn to release attachment to another person's response. As we do, we can allow them the gift of "in-to-me-see."

We all fear abandonment on some level, but as Marianne Williamson reminds us, no one can "leave" anyone. We're all one on this playground called life, together for an eternity. You can't even be untrue to yourself for any length of time — your truth will come oozing out when you least expect it.

The Three Questions

Quantum Learning Network, an education and training corporation based out of Oceanside, California, helps people who are feeling distant from or angry with each other to communicate safely with three simple questions. See its power for yourself.

First, select a partner. Then ask your partner the following three questions. After each one, answer the same question yourself.

1. Tell me something I don't know about you.
2. Tell me something we agree on.
3. Tell me something you like about me.

I used this with my son while he was in college and our worlds seemed light years apart. It's amazing how this open-hearted attention heals. Have you told the truth in love today?

Because It Doesn't Feel Good

Perhaps the best reason to tell the truth is that it feels better than the alternative. If "when we feel good, good things happen," obviously when we *don't* feel good, we're attracting and manifesting things we don't want. Lying feels awful, and because lying always requires more lying, the cycle continues itself until a radical shift is made.

If you are in need of a cleansing, I suggest watching the film ***As Good As It Gets***. Jack Nicholson's character has been dishonest with himself and with women for decades. At first, he can't imagine ever coming clean, since it would require too great a change. Yet, after a massive heart attack and a glorious week with a woman who is completely honest, he decides to face the truth and finds peace and joy. You will find, as he did, that honesty is as good as it gets.

Teaching a class to recovering addicts for more than twelve years, it's been my blessing to watch men and women step out of the dungeon of despair into the light of day by simply telling the truth.

The first truth is usually that they're angry. Once they find out that they're not struck by lightning for sharing painful feelings, they move toward telling the ultimate truth, being honest about their gifts, their unlimited potential, and the profound goodness of life.

I was recently informed by a good friend that we cannot measure cold, only the absence of heat. Later I heard a speaker remind us that there is no "dark switch" when you enter a room, only a switch for light. As I wrote the words below, I was comforted that you and I do not need to battle the cold, dark elements of life. Instead we can choose to let our warmth and light shine through.

> *If there is no cold, only the absence of heat, and there is no dark, only the absence of light, and there is no despair, only the absence of hope, then there is no hate, only the absence of love.*

The Pen Is Mightier Than...

Finally, if you have not discovered the power of writing letters to your spouse, friend, teenager, or sibling, let me make one final appeal. Whenever you are having a hard time communicating with them, write them a letter. Tell them what's on your mind. Tell them what you are grateful for about them. Share your dreams for your relationship. They will often write you back, but even when they don't, the door is open for greater integrity and intimacy.

"I decided not to join the gang because of my teacher," said the young Latino student after he completed the ***8 to Great*** course at his high school. His teacher, Danelle, was indeed exceptional. When she first gave her freshmen time to write in their journals, most used it to share their innermost thoughts and feelings, but some, she could sense, were holding back.

"So one day I decided it wasn't fair that I was reading what they were opening up about, but they weren't getting to read *my* thoughts and feelings. I began doing my journaling on the board. It was very hard at first because it was around the anniversary of my father's death. But I knew openness and honesty were the best gifts I could give those kids."

I have had hundreds of teachers tell me of students who *wrote* what they could not *say*.

- ✓ *"My parents are both dying of AIDS. I'm an only child and have never told anyone..."*
- ✓ *"My mom and I are getting kicked out of our house on Friday and don't know where we'll live..."*
- ✓ *"My grandpa is dying and I'm the only one home at night to care for him."*

I beg of every teacher, parent, or youth minister reading this: give your students a half sheet of paper, some instrumental music, and five minutes to write once a week. We cannot meet the needs of our youth when we don't know what their needs are. Journaling helps us hear their needs and then find ways to help meet them.

Likewise, wonderful movements like World Wide Marriage Encounter (WWME) report divorce rates **under five percent** when couples use a ten-minute writing technique each week to communicate their love and/or concerns. Writing is a positively powerful way to break down barriers and strengthen connection.

Finally, let me add a lesson I have learned the hard way. Writing a letter is very different from writing an email. Whereas the old rule of thumb: ***criticize privately and compliment publicly*** is solid and true, I would add: compliment in an email but *never* criticize using that medium.

I once had one of my work team ask in an email how I thought he could improve. I mistakenly replied to him in an email. Although I did not write anything close to "You always," or "You never," even constructive criticism can sound like yelling through a text or an email. The next time I saw him, the pain in his eyes was my wake-up call. I have been vigilant never to do it again.

> *Be honest to those who are honest, and be also honest to those who are not honest. Thus honesty is attained.*
> *— Lao Tzu*

Q & A on Honest Communication

Q: I want to improve my relationship with my mom, but she doesn't trust me when I tell the truth because I used to lie a lot.

> *Being straight with people will get you in the best circles. — Anonymous*

A: You've dug a pit with your lying, Dear One, and now you'll have to re-earn her trust. It's good that she doesn't trust you right now, you haven't earned it. Have you made amends for your past mistakes? You can start by telling her the truth about being sorry for what you've done. You may want to write her a letter of apology, offer to make amends, and show your appreciation. You probably won't get all of your privileges back right away, but once you do, you'll be able to appreciate how good it feels to tell the truth!

Q: I want to join the military, but my parents would rather I go to college right away. The military will pay for my tuition, books and lab fees after I've served my time. I've used ***Honest Communication*** *to tell my parents what I want. Should I do what I want to do and ignore what they're saying?*

A: Let's look at "what you want." I always encourage young adults to follow their dreams, but I don't hear your dreams. I hear your *fears* about not having enough money for college. If someone else offered to pay for all your tuition, books, and lab fees, would you still be passionate about joining the military?

I recall a young man of twenty-two who couldn't decide between joining the priesthood and marrying his sweetheart. When I asked what appealed most about both options, he told me he wasn't sure where he'd ever get a teaching job if he got married. In other words, the life of a priest had more job security!

This is a case of discerning between running from and running to. The military and the priesthood are looking for men and women who are running *to* their calling. What will your decision-making process look like?

Q: Do politicians ever tell the truth?

A: I've met both ethical and unethical people in the world of politics. The more successful a leader is perceived to be, the higher their perceived "cost of failure." They often begin to fear being seen as human, so some stop taking risks, including the risk of telling the truth. For some, lying becomes a way of life.

If what we think about we bring about, we need to turn our focus to the brave truth-tellers at the top. If "we spot it, we got it," each time we point a finger at a liar, we need to see that we're pointing three fingers back at ourselves.

One story during the 2008 presidential campaign that didn't make front page headlines involved Mark McKinnon, chief strategist for Republican candidate John McCain. When it became clear that Barack Obama would be the Democatic nominee, Mark resigned from the campaign.

Honesty is an absolute prerequisite to service to the public. Unless a man is honest, we have no right to keep him in public life; it matters not how brilliant his capacity — Teddy Roosevelt

In an interview, McKinnon said that although he had policy differences with Obama and believed McCain was best suited for the presidency, "I just don't want to work against an Obama candidacy. I believe he is honest. Obama's election would send a great message to the country and the world."

Mark McKinnon turned down a five-million-dollar paycheck that campaign year, but it was a price he was willing to pay in order to be true to himself. There are thousands of people in politics we can all be extremely proud of.

Q: I often feel like I don't belong. Is that because I don't know how to communicate? Do other people feel this way sometimes?

A: Members of every group I've ever asked have told me that they often feel that way. We feel like we don't belong because we look at people's outsides rather than their insides. That was one of the messages of September 11, 2001. When everyone had grey dust from the towers on them, from executives to sewer workers, they were all the same.

> *The reason we struggle with insecurity is because we compare our behind-the-scenes with everyone else's highlight reel. — Steven Furtick*

It could be that you feel like you don't belong because you're not sharing who you really are with others, or not listening to who they are. Do more of the courageous risk-taking you did when asking this question and you'll find out just how alike we all are.

Q: How do you get a friend to open up when you know he has problems?

A: People aren't like cans. We can't just open them at will. First, we have to earn their trust. Keep reminding your friend that you care and that he can count on you to be there for him.

Consider sitting down with him and sharing that you've noticed some things and that you're concerned. Let him know you have time to listen if he wants to talk. If he doesn't respond, do the most loving thing we can ever do for a friend…honor his choices.

Q: I was recently asked to lunch by an old friend who said she wanted to get together to catch up. I was shocked when she then made a multi-level marketing sales pitch. I felt very disrespected. Should I call or write and tell her?

A: It sounds like this is the first time it's happened to you. The good news is that you learned your lesson quickly. Take responsibility for the fact that you didn't ask her clearly about the goal of the lunch. Let it go as a lesson learned, and the next time a friend asks you to coffee or lunch, get clear about their intentions before you make your decision.

Q: What if I'm being criticized so much by someone that it's affecting my life?

A: The first question I would ask is, is their criticism constructive or destructive? Remember that destructive criticism and sarcasm are not acceptable at any time from anyone. If those are occurring, consider seeing a counselor or finding a coach to help you protect yourself or leave the situation.

If their criticism is constructive, releasing the relationship is an option, but you have others. First, review the section in this chapter on asking for what you want. Have a courageous conversation with them about the pattern and ask clearly that changes be made.

Remember that everyone who has ever communicated anything to you has only been saying one of two things: "I love you," or "I'm scared and hurting, please help me." This will give you more compassion.

Second, remind yourself that they have no power over you. We are like Dorothy in ***The Wizard of Oz***, running from the wicked witches of our fears. If we just turn and face them, we see that the meaner people are, the more desperate and lonely they are.

I recall a time when my son was eleven and one of his friends came over to play while I was speaking across town. When I got home to relieve the sitter, my son was crying.

"He said awful things to me, Mom. He even said awful things about you, that you were a bad Mom."

"Look who he's talking about, honey," I said as we hugged. "He lives with his grandmother because he hasn't seen his own Mom for years." My young and very wise son was able to see the boy through new eyes.

Finally, realize that they're continuing to criticize you because it's achieving its desired effect of upsetting you. I challenge you to claim your power. We think that a word spoken (or not spoken) can deal us a fatal blow, but it can't. We're so much bigger than that.

This pity, insecurity, and self-indulgence is unbecoming of the Great Soul that you are.

Bhagavad Gita

6

FGH

The World's Simplest Positive Attitude Formula

High-Way 6: FGH: Forgiveness of the Past

The Power of Release

Defining Forgiveness of the Past

We may not know how to forgive, and we may not want to forgive, but the very fact we say we are willing to forgive begins the healing practice.

Louise Hay

Forgiveness is the ultimate remedy for what ails us. As Marianne Williamson writes: "The practice of forgiveness is our most important contribution to the healing of the world." In her powerful statement lies another truth: like all the High-Ways, **Forgiveness of the Past** is a skill that can be learned through practice. Our ***8 to Great*** definition is:

Forgiveness is releasing regret, resentment, and the desire for revenge.

Releasing Regret and Resentment

The Aramaic root word for forgive means: "let go." Forgiveness isn't an admission that what someone else did was acceptable. It's a decision to release the weight of regret or resentment and the desire for restitution.

What does the alternative look like? In 2008, a Cambodian couple who separated after forty years of marriage took things literally when it came to "splitting" their assets: the husband cut their house in two and moved his half to his parents' property! When we decide to hold onto bitterness, it can take on a life of its own and, like the monsters of horror films, one day will have us in its grip.

Every so often I'll hear one of my coaching clients look back on what they attracted, like a car accident or a broken relationship, with regret, guilt or even shame. This is completely counterproductive because it will pull you down to a "5" on the Power Pyramid. When we're "5-ing," we're asking for more of the same.

Why We Forgive

We have all been there. We became angry and hurt about being lied to or disrespected. At first we were confused. Then, once the initial shock registered, we had to make a decision whether to go inward and find our peace or move outward into bitterness because of a belief that forgiveness might "let them off the hook." Unfortunately, in the latter state we were the ones who got "hooked," as our vengeful thoughts consumed us.

The alternative is release. It is forgiving them for our sake, not theirs. The harm they did to us can't begin to compare with the harm we inflict on ourselves every day we hold onto judgment. Whether it's the physical and mental drain of living in the past or the inability to function in the present moment, the only person who pays a price for unforgiveness is you, and that price is your life energy.

> *Unforgiveness is like taking poison and hoping the other person dies. — Anonymous*

We only have so many thoughts and so much energy to invest in each day. If we choose to invest, say, 40 percent of that precious resource in thoughts of regret ("I should have") or bitterness ("they should have"), we'll find ourselves waking up tired, without sufficient energy to build our futures.

Just as the other person isn't harmed by our harboring resentments, we aren't doing them a favor by forgiving them either. Most, if not all, of those people have already moved on. Some may never admit that anything bad happened. Because their feelings are completely out of your control, all you can do (as High-Way 3: **Full Responsibility** reminds us) is stay in your business and forgive.

Your business is to feel good, and that requires making peace with the past so that we can come home to the power of the present.

How to Forgive

"All right," a female client asked me. "I want to forgive him for what he did to me years ago, but where do I begin?"

I recommended beginning with a simple formula:

The Forgiveness Formula
We were all doing the best we could at the time with the information we had.

How can we absolutely know that we were doing the best we could at the time? Think back to an incident you feel regret about. Then ask yourself: "If I would have known *then* what I know *now*, would I have acted the same way?" Of course not. It's not that you were a bad person then and you're a good person now. You were a good person then as now. You just needed more information.

You're reading this book because you are seeking more information. You're right on track.

Whom to Forgive

When I ask my audiences, "Who is the hardest person to forgive?" they all respond in one voice, "Yourself."

We can go one step further and remind ourselves we're the *only* person to forgive, because as we learned in High-Way 3, what we despise in others are those things we despise in ourselves. Whatever upsets us most in others is a reflection of those pockets of pain within ourselves that we haven't yet forgiven. Once we realize this and accept **Full Responsibility**, it's easier to move into forgiveness of our "in-a-me" — ourselves. The more we understand this universal truth, the more it shines light on our darkest memories. We were *all* doing the best we could.

I've been lied to and betrayed, just like you, but I was always able to go back and see that I had first lied to and betrayed myself through denial. We are not victims. In telling and owning the truth now, we move to a new place on the Power Pyramid and therefore attract different people and experiences into our lives.

> *We have met the enemy and he is us. — Pogo*

Who do you need to forgive? That person (living or deceased) or group of people you consider hardest to forgive is the best place to start. It has been very hard for me to forgive legislators who put test scores before the needs of children. On my best days, I see them as scared and hurting children themselves. However, on my worst days, I see them as rigid and blind. It's then that I realize it's time for me to use the Forgiveness process.

Why Forgive? The Mary Read Story

Mary Read was born in South Korea in 1988 to Air Force Lieutenant Colonel Peter Read and his wife, Yon Son Zhang. Mary was a "fun-loving nineteen-year-old" who had been voted "Best Smile" by her band at Fairfax's Annandale High School in Virginia. She was on the lacrosse team, had gotten good grades, and dreamed of becoming an elementary school teacher.

In 2007, her aunt shared the following story with **The Washington Post**:

"The last time I saw her, a year ago Thanksgiving here at my house, she kept disappearing. I finally said, 'Mary, what are you up to? Are you reading a good book or something?' She was knitting a beautiful scarf — a multicolored fluffy scarf like the girls wear — for her grandmother for Christmas. My mother still wears it. She often did thoughtful things like that."

On the evening of April 15, 2007, as Mary was sitting in her dorm room, she got out a red notebook and journaled some of her thoughts about life. In a section where she kept her favorite quotes, she wrote: *"When a deep injury is done to us, we can never recover until we forgive."* The next day, Mary was gunned down in her Virginia Tech classroom, along with thirty-one others.

The more we love, the greater the temptation to hate when what we love is taken from us — but as Mary reminded us, we must forgive, because hate kills love. Hate killed Mary Read. Forgiveness is the path to the peace we seek.

Research on Forgiveness

According to Dr. Fred Luskin of the Stanford University Forgiveness Project, there are dozens of reasons to forgive, including many for our own health and well-being: Forgiveness...

- ✓ *can help you enjoy the present by freeing you from the past;*
- ✓ *can help you concentrate on work or school;*
- ✓ *can help you distinguish between bitterness and resentment about old issues and anger and sadness about current events;*
- ✓ *can help you make better decisions (choosing to run to rather than from);*
- ✓ *can improve your relationships with others;*
- ✓ *can restore the energy drained by bitterness and resentment, thereby helping you accomplish your goals and dreams.*

Meanwhile, Dr. Luskin writes, those who make a practice of forgiving on a regular basis report improved health:

- ✓ *fewer incidences of heart disease*
- ✓ *better, deeper sleep*
- ✓ *fewer incidences of cancer*
- ✓ *lower blood pressure*
- ✓ *stronger immune systems*
- ✓ *less muscle tension and disorders such as TMJ*

What researchers all agree on is that whatever you're missing in your life can be attained or recovered more quickly when you forgive.

> *We are not held back by the love we didn't receive in the past, but by the love we're not extending in the present.*
> *— Marianne Williamson*

When to Forgive

The time to forgive and allow the flow of good feelings back into your life is always now. Signs that you still have Forgiveness work to do include:

- ✓ *angry outbursts over small incidents;*
- ✓ *avoiding family gatherings;*
- ✓ *warning people not to trust others;*
- ✓ *feeling depressed or anxious most of the time;*
- ✓ *using food, drugs and/or smoking to try and ease your emotional pain.*

The Power in Forgiveness

When Lucille came for coaching she told me things were "fine," but her body language told another story. I asked her what she was grateful for lately and the closest she could get to gratitude was, "Grateful I only have to work four days this week!"

As her feelings found words, I heard her passionate cry for a new job. I helped her see that from where she was on the Power Pyramid, she couldn't attract a new position that would fulfill her, just more of the same. I invited her to think of one thing she *could* be grateful for about her present situation. After a long silence, she said, "I really can't think of anything."

"Not even the regular paycheck?"

"No. I'm a really good saver. I don't really need the paycheck. No, not even that."

"Then why haven't you quit?"

"Oh, I'd never hear the end of it from my father."

I asked her if her use of the word "father" indicated a lack of warmth in their relationship. Theirs, according to this young woman, was frozen shut.

The more I listened to her story, the more curious I became. "Have you ever wondered why he gives you so much advice?" I asked. She shook her head. "Perhaps it's because he thinks you waffle and are unsure of yourself."

"That's true enough."

"So what might happen if you stand your ground, look him in the eye, and let him know you're quitting no matter what he thinks?"

She couldn't imagine doing any of those things, so we got out some paper and envelopes. First she sat and wrote an angry Feelings Letter to him using the strongest language she could muster. When she was finished, we placed it in an envelope and burned it.

Then I invited her to write a Forgiveness Letter. Her tears flowed as she wrote her long letter forgiving her father for not being the kind of father she'd dreamed of having. As she sealed that letter and walked with me once more to the fire pit, there was a new purpose in her posture. The following week she told her father of her plans and was able to find gratitude for lessons learned at the job she left. Feeling and forgiving is freeing.

> *If you had not suffered as you have, there would be no depth to you, no humility, and no compassion.*
> *— Eckhart Tolle*

What to Forgive

It's important to distinguish between forgiving something and dismissing it. In our humanity, we all forget things, break things, and step on an occasional toe, but not all of those things need forgiving. When a child spills milk at the dinner table while company is present, for example, it doesn't require forgiveness, just acceptance.

I am sometimes asked, "But on the other end of the spectrum, aren't there things I *shouldn't* forgive?" (I am most often asked this by women married to philanderers.) I refer them back through the first three High-Ways. I invite them to 1) **Get the Picture** of the life they want. 2) Ask themselves what they would do if they had no fear. 3) Answer Byron Katie's 4 Questions for **Full Responsibility**.

By the time they have completed those steps the original question has been answered.

The Forgiveness Challenge

I congratulate you on making it this far into the High-Ways. When it's time for forgiveness, don't give in to thoughts of "this is too hard" or "I can't do it." You're the most powerful being you know. It's okay to be angry at the process, but don't let that stop you! Claim that power within to get you through this transforming step and join the thousands of us on the other side in gratitude!

> *Everything can be taken from a person but one thing: It is the last of human freedoms — to choose one's attitude in any circumstances, to choose one's way. — Victor Frankl*

The Forgiveness of the Past Process:

Face it, Feel it, Forgive it

An eye for an eye leaves the whole world blind.

Gandhi

The Three Steps to Forgiveness

The process of Forgiveness has three distinct steps:

1. Face it
2. Feel it
3. Forgive it

It's often tempting to run from the first two steps. Forgiveness is a risk, and when we don't want to face it, we can make ourselves extremely busy or create new crises that keep us from dealing with our feelings and healing our pain.

Unfortunately, if we can't face it and don't feel it, we can't forgive it. Forgiveness is heart-work, as is the entire FGH formula. It can't be done in the head. That's why **Forgiveness of the Past** comes after High-Way 4: **Feel All Your Feelings**. We must be in touch with our feelings to truly forgive.

If you haven't yet faced your pain and given yourself time to feel your mads and sads about what has happened to you, go back and review High-Way 4. Soon you'll see that the more you practice the three steps of Forgiveness, the quicker you'll be able to work through *new* painful issues as they arise.

How Forgiveness of the Past Works

Forgiveness of the Past frees us not only from our past, but also from the unhealthy connection with those we have held in judgment. An anonymous poem entitled, "Reason, Season or Lifetime," starts with "Some people are in our lives for a reason, others for a season." Once you've forgiven someone, you're free to stay or go. Until you forgive them, however, that person has a hold on you. Do you want an energetic leash connecting you to someone who has hurt you?

Remember, the goal of forgiveness is to get to a place of detaching with love and releasing resentment. One way to describe it is that we're forgiving them for not being the way we wanted them to be. That brings us to the final "peace" of the **Forgiveness of the Past** process.

> *Enlightenment is putting down a burden and not picking it up again. — Peter McWilliams*

How to Know if You've Forgiven Someone

The test I've used over the years to see if I've fully forgiven someone is as follows:

If good things happen to them and you celebrate, or bad things happen to them and you commiserate, you've forgiven them.

If bad things happen to them and you celebrate, you have not.

I don't believe the axiom "time heals all wounds," because I've seen too many people who've wasted decades of bitterness and regret over a word spoken in haste or a solitary painful event. I do believe that forgiveness heals all wounds. I've experienced it hundreds of times in my own life and have seen it in the lives of my coaching clients. Take the test for yourself. If you still have Forgiveness work to do, this chapter will show you the way.

Appropriate vs. Inappropriate Guilt

I'm one of those who believe that discomfort or guilt over wrongdoings is okay. Do you have moral values? Of course you do. Imagine a circle around where you're sitting right now that's four feet in diameter. Think of that circle as your "moral boundary." If you step outside of that circle, it's natural to feel remorse.

My friend's son stole some things in his middle school years. Her greatest concern was that he didn't seem to feel guilt or remorse, and therefore his apologies sounded shallow.

One day he came to her and had a good cry. He could clearly see the person he wanted to be and the life he wanted to live, and he felt badly about his behavior. It was the first day of the "best" of his life and allowed him to stop stealing. That's healthy guilt.

I continue to discover layers of guilt I've heaped upon myself and must continue to release. When the big G of Guilt looms over me, I sometimes remind myself that anger feels better than guilt. (It's higher on the Power Pyramid), and I allow myself to feel angry it happened.

Why We Don't Practice Forgiveness of the Past

When one door closes, another one opens, but we often look so long and so regretfully upon the closed door that we do not see the ones which open for us.

Alexander Graham Bell

Over the years I've heard a litany of paltry reasons not to forgive someone. I call them:

Forgiveness Fallacies

People say they can't forgive someone because:

- ✓ *that person hasn't apologized or isn't remorseful*
- ✓ *then the other person will "win"*
- ✓ *the person has died*
- ✓ *justice must be served*
- ✓ *if they're forgiven they'll do it again*
- ✓ *forgiveness is a sign of weakness*
- ✓ *I have to understand why it happened first*
- ✓ *it needs to stop hurting first*
- ✓ *others don't hurt as much as I do*
- ✓ *there is too much to forgive to ever work through it all*

These are all excuses to stay stuck in our misery. When we're ready, we can replace these inaccurate assessments with:

Forgiveness Truths

- ✓ *Forgiveness is something you do for you, not for the other person.*
- ✓ *Forgiveness is a proactive decision to take your power back.*
- ✓ *Forgiveness is refusing to live in the past.*
- ✓ *Forgiveness is a skill you can learn.*
- ✓ *Forgiveness is freedom from the burdens of the past.*
- ✓ *Forgiveness is refusing to give the offender power over the present.*
- ✓ *Forgiveness is a choice.*

✓ *Forgiveness is running to rather than running from.*

✓ *Forgiveness is a process. Once you begin, it gets easier and easier.*

> *Bitterness is like cancer. It eats upon the host. But anger and forgiveness are like fire. They burn all clean.*
> *— Maya Angelou*

When You're Not Ready to Forgive

As I was speaking at a young women's rehab center, 16-year-old Shawna was sullen and resistant to my message. When we got to this **Forgiveness of the Past** High-Way, her emotions boiled to the surface.

"There's no way I'm forgiving him!" she said firmly. "He left us with no warning. We lost the house and we had to be split up! He used to beat my mom and was drunk all the time. There's no way I'm forgiving him!"

As tears spilled onto her desk, I knelt down and thanked her for being so honest. Then I reminded her that she didn't need to forgive him now and that her feelings were completely valid. Shawna was clearly working through High-Ways 4 and 5, **Feel All Your Feelings**, and **Honest Communication**, and was exactly where she needed to be. While the rest of the young women wrote Forgiveness Letters that afternoon, I invited Shawna to write a letter expressing her angry feelings to her father and then burn it.

That's what she did. After she burned it, she told me, "I feel like a kid again." She eventually went on to complete the ***8 to Great*** program and make peace with the choices her father and mother had made.

Your Pain Isn't Special

A middle-aged woman in a homeless shelter helped me understand that our pain is never unique. At the completion of her recovery program, she stood to give a testimonial.

"I walked into this shelter believing no one had ever been hurt as much as I had. Therefore, I gave myself permission to wallow in my misery and continue using. My greatest insight, for which I have all of you to thank, is that now I understand my pain is not special."

When we release our excuses, we're the ones who are released.

Forgiveness of the Past Success Stories

Forgiveness is not an occasional act; it is a permanent attitude.

Dr. Martin Luther King, Jr.

When we learn to forgive, life gets easier. Our dreams can manifest more quickly because much more of our energy is in the present moment. We are "95-ing" more often, and what goes around comes around effortlessly. Classroom teachers who come to my ***8 to Great*** Institute to learn our program are often surprised by the level of healing they personally receive along the way.

> *Happiness is nothing more than good health and a bad memory. — Albert Schweitzer*

Forgiving Her Ex-Husband

After one such weekend, I received this beautiful testimonial from a teacher:

MK,

I wanted to share that after I left, I had a very personal experience with forgiveness. I'd been struggling for years with forgiving an old debt (money owed me from years of past due child support). I felt like I should forgive and move on, since both of my children are grown and married with families of their own, but I didn't want to. After the training weekend, I knew that I'd be a happier person if I released that part of my past, so I wrote a Forgiveness Letter to him, burned it, and then did the legal paperwork required to release it for good.

The very next day, I felt so much happier and freed from a heavy burden from the past (more than just money). What was just as amazing was that less than twenty-four hours later my (second) husband and I received word of an inheritance totaling $1,500 more than the debt and the interest from the child support combined! It was just as you described. Forgiveness gets us back in the flow! I am so grateful for that weekend and these 8 High-Ways!

- Janice

Judge not, lest you be judged. — Matthew 7:1

The Sins of Others

A Catholic priest friend of mine usually chooses not to wear his clerical garb when traveling.

He once found himself on a plane sitting next to a well-known radio commentator who casually made comments about the Catholic author Andrew Greeley. He concluded with, "Father Greeley is a good man, not like those other priests who mess with kids."

My friend later remarked, "I felt like I had a target on me for the next two days. No matter what was going on, my thoughts seemed to return to that judgment, which had felt very personally about me. I realized that I needed to forgive that man in order to regain peace with myself."

On the flight back home, my friend had a very different experience. A woman walked down the aisle mid-flight and stopped at his seat.

"Excuse me, but did I overhear that you're a Catholic priest?"

When he replied that he was, she told him she'd made a promise to herself never to encounter a priest or nun without stopping to thank them for the wonderful education she'd received in Catholic schools while growing up.

> *If her past were your past, her pain your pain, her level of consciousness your level of consciousness, you would think and act exactly as she does. With this realization comes forgiveness, compassion, peace. — Eckhart Tolle*

What many people don't realize is that the Roman Catholic Church hasn't just been in great need of forgiveness, but it has also been a great model of forgiveness over the centuries. In 1984, Pope John Paul II walked into Rebibbia prison in Rome to meet prisoner Mehmet Ali Agca, the man who had tried to kill him just months before. During their time together, the Holy Father took the hand of the man who had fired a bullet at his heart and forgave him.

Years later, when news came that the pope had died, the press reported that his would-be assassin wept. "They had declared brotherhood when the pope visited him in prison," Adnan Agca said of his brother's meeting with the Holy Father. "The pope was Mehmet's brother. Wouldn't you be sad if you had lost your brother?"

> *There is no revenge so complete as forgiveness.*
> *— Josh Billings*

My Father

My father was a very good man. He worked hard, loved his family, was honest to a fault, and generous to all he met. However, forgiveness didn't come easily for him. There were times in his life when he held grudges against family members, not speaking to them for years at a time. It was just accepted in our home as "the way it was," and no one ever questioned it.

Just after Dad turned seventy, he was told he had lung cancer and had only a few months to live. We were all devastated. Because he lived in Florida and my four siblings and I were sprinkled around the United States, we alternated weeks to be with him, flying to Florida when it was our turn.

The second time I flew there, Dad was hospitalized. I remember one difficult day very clearly. He was coughing hard for long spells, so I kept calling the nurse. She finally pulled me aside and explained that his lungs were filling up with fluid. She said she was sorry, but there was nothing she could do. The next time Dad went into a coughing spell, I just held him in my arms.

When it was finally over, he looked up at me and asked, "Am I going to die today?"

"I don't know, Dad," I replied. "I don't understand this disease, but if this is the big day, you're ready, and I'll be right here with you."

Just then the phone rang. It was my sister in North Carolina calling to talk to him. As I held the phone to Dad's ear, all he could say was, "I love you, I love you, I love..."

As soon as I hung up the phone, it rang again. This time it was my brother in Seattle. Again their conversation was short and full of "I love you's" from Dad. Then it rang again. This time it was my brother in Iowa.

Tears ran down Dad's cheeks as he said again and again, "I love you, I love you, I love you."

When I hung up the phone after that conversation, I knew there was one more phone call to make — to a family member Dad hadn't spoken to for years — but I also knew I'd have to dial the number, and I did.

As soon as Dad heard who was on the line, he began to sob, "I'm so sorry. Please forgive me. I love you, I love you, I love you." When the phone call ended, Dad was quiet for a moment, and then asked, "Why did you do that?"

"Dad, do you remember Jacob Marley in ***A Christmas Carol***, carrying around all those chains? You don't want to carry those chains any longer."

He thanked me and cried some more, this time from relief. From that day on, there was a new peace about him. One month later he was gone, but I'll never forget the lessons he taught me in those final weeks. Forgiveness frees us to love and be loved. Although he wasn't cured, I believe Dad was healed. I know I was.

What could you want that forgiveness cannot give?

Do you want peace? Forgiveness offers it. Do you want happiness, a quiet mind, a certainty of purpose, and a sense of worth and beauty that transcends the world?

Do you want care and safety and warmth of sure protection always?

Do you want a quietness that cannot be disturbed, a gentleness that cannot be hurt?

A deep abiding comfort and a rest so perfect it can never be upset?

All this forgiveness offers you.

You who want peace can find it only by complete forgiveness.

A Course in Miracles

Putting Forgiveness of the Past into Practice

One secret of a long and fruitful life is to forgive everybody, everything, every night before you go to bed.

Ann Landers

At the beginning of this chapter, we defined Forgiveness as releasing regret, resentment, and the desire for revenge. Just as we asked in High-Way 2, **Risk**: "If you had no fear, what would you do?" we ask in this High-Way: "If you had no regret or bitterness, who would you be?"

The Forgiveness Letter

When you're ready to take the physical steps of forgiveness, get out a journal and write down the names of those you haven't forgiven, including yourself, God, or anyone else, living or deceased. Then decide who to write your initial Forgiveness Letter to.

You won't be sending it. This process is for you, not them. After you complete it, you'll burn it to signify that you've released the person. You may want to listen to some quiet music to get you started.

1. Take a few moments to think about the things you haven't yet forgiven.

2. When you're ready, begin your forgiveness or "release" letter with things like, "I don't know why you did it and may never know, but I don't care. I'm releasing the past and moving on."
3. When you're finished, sign it, fold it, put it in an envelope, and seal it.
4. Write a big "F" on the front of the sealed envelope, which stands for: "I Faced it, Felt it, Forgave it, it's going into the Fire, and now I am Free."
5. Burn it and feel the release as you do.

One of the most common questions I hear in my seminars is, "If I forgive them, will I forget?" The answer is yes and no. No, not right away, but as the **Forgiveness of the Past** process becomes more natural to you, painful thoughts will begin to fade, making room for more joy and appreciation of the present. Occasional memories may still arise from time to time, but they'll have less power to diminish your peace. If you're still having painful memories weeks and months after writing your Forgiveness Letter, you may want to consider writing another one.

"Thank You For-giving Me..."

A common benefit from doing your Forgiveness work is that many find themselves moving into Gratitude for the event that previously brought them pain. There are lessons to be learned from every adversity, and forgiveness frees us to find them.

Author Michael Beckwith describes the forgiveness blessing this way, "Thank you for-giving me this opportunity to grow."

We might also say it this way: "Thank you for being my mirror." It's so hard, yet healing, to remember that people treat us the way we believe we deserve to be treated. As we learn to take **Full Responsibility** for our lives, the tone of our

Forgiveness will move toward an increased self-awareness, self-forgiveness, and self-love.

> *Relationships do not cause pain and unhappiness. They bring out the pain and unhappiness that is already in us.*
> *— Eckhart Tolle*

It's possible to become grateful for every event. Each challenge has helped make you the **WISE** person you are today:

***W**onderful*
***I**nsightful*
***S**trong*
***E**mpowered*

One Woman's Light

Would you be reading this book right now if you'd never experienced adversity? I recall a wise woman at one of my seminars who lit up the room. I saw her coming toward me and before she could speak, I asked her, "What is your secret? You're absolutely glowing and radiant. What is it I'm sensing?"

"Many people make comments like that," she replied. "I guess it all started the year we lost the twins." She shared that her only two children were gone in the blink of an eye because the young man driving the other car was drunk.

> *All things work together for good... — Romans 8:28*

"Tell me more," I asked her in that crowded room.

"I cried and cried, of course, for weeks that turned into months. Then one day I looked outside and noticed that the sun had come up again. I walked out of the house looking for a new reason to live. Today my husband and I have a huge ministry to parents who have lost children. Our girls live on in our hearts and in our work. We're so grateful we had them for that time."

My personal reaction to hearing this story was dramatic. I have had many "disappointments" in life, when people promised things that they did not follow through on. I sometimes felt like I'd been "wronged." This story jolted me out of that life-limiting self-pity. How can I possibly be disappointed about anything *ever again* because *I have my two kids*.

Has *your* turn-around moment happened yet? If not, what is it going to look like?

Four Letters for Ending a Relationship

Romantic relationships don't end — but they are always transformed over time. Sometimes, during a growth phase, a couple stays together, and sometimes they do not. When the latter happens, there can be pain, either before the breakup or afterward. But just because our feelings are hurt, that doesn't mean we have to suffer or make the other person suffer. Although ending a relationship is one of the most joy-challenging experiences you can face, no matter who initiates the breakup, writing four letters can help you close the door and move on. After writing each one, burn it.

1. A letter of anger
2. A letter of sadness
3. A letter forgiving the other person and yourself (these are often separate letters)
4. A letter of gratitude for all the good times, which you may send or burn, depending upon the situation (this is often the longest letter)

When my coaching clients see this list, they sometimes ask, "Will letter number four make me want to get back together with the person?" There's a slight chance that it will, but for most people, it will not. It simply reminds them that there were good times and that we are all half-jerk and half-jewel.

"I Can Be So Controlling"

I still have trouble forgiving myself when I catch myself being bossy and controlling. One day my question to a good friend was, "How come I get so micro-manage-y at certain times and other times I'm fine?"

Her reply described exactly what was going on inside of me. "In your childhood you were unpleasantly surprised more than once. You then went on 'alert' and decided that if you were always on your toes you could prevent catastrophe. When you have the most to lose, you go into hyper-drive, just like the rest of us who have experienced such incidents."

"But I've heard all this before," I protested.

"You could only process so much of it at the time, but the seeds were planted then and now they're sprouting into a new level of awareness."

Her gentle words about a part of myself I have always had trouble loving helped me tremendously.

The Price of Judgment

I've worked with many women who were grieving an abortion years after the fact. In most instances, they had gotten pregnant while unmarried and had aborted the baby because they thought it would "kill" their parents to be so disgraced, "kill" their relationship, or that their parents would "kill" them if they found out. The result of those judgments was that those young women felt as if they had many lives to save and were pulled between them. It is one of the most powerful experiences I have had watching these women forgive themselves for doing the best they could at the time with the information they had.

Forgiving My Daughter's Stalker

Forgiveness is the key to freedom. — Hannah Arendt

One afternoon years ago, my twelve year-old was offered a ride by a stranger on her way home from school. She ran crying all the way home. We filed police reports and alerted the school. We hoped it was a one-time event, but he showed up again three mornings later.

It was traumatic — for her and for us all. That entire week I felt paralyzed. I had trouble working the High-Ways and became a raving robot to my fight-or-flight instincts.

"Should we move?" "Why aren't the police doing more?" "I should have..." "It's my fault...." "If only..." I felt caught on a merry-go-round of negative, fear-based thinking.

Then, on the fifth day, I saw what was happening and got off the carousel. I calmed down and breathed deeply again. I returned to my Gratitudes. That day I even laughed at a joke. Although we hadn't yet identified him, I realized I could choose to find peace inside me, if not around me.

I reminded myself that *the definition of peace is not the absence of war, but the absence of fear*. When I released my judgment of the situation, I was able to do my **Full Responsibility** work, accepting it as "how things are." I forgave the present circumstances for being painful. I went back to my FGH formula and became grateful for the excellent police team that was assigned to her case, for her safety, and for her courage. I regained my hope for our future.

The police contacted me the day before the last day of school to tell me, "We think he's going to show up tomorrow. We'll have six armed officers in hiding along the way — but we need you to let your daughter walk to school alone."

Watching her walk out the door that morning was one of the hardest things I've ever done as a Mom. I still remember it clearly. The night before she had told me she wanted that man found so the chaos could end. I was in awe of her bravery.

As predicted, two blocks into her five-block walk, he drove up and spoke to her. When apprehended, it was discovered that he was carrying a loaded gun.

Fast forward to his court date. I went with a friend to hear them set a date for the hearing and to look at his face for the first time. After the short proceedings, we began to file out of the room and I saw him glance at a couple as he was taken away by police.

Once in the hallway, I decided to approach them and introduced myself. "I'm Joanna's mother. I just want you to know that we mean him no harm. We only want everyone to be safe."

The woman almost collapsed in her husband's arms as she exploded in tears. "I'm so sorry. We're so, so sorry. Please forgive him. Please forgive us."

She continued sobbing loudly as her husband explained, "He's her brother. He lived with their parents all his life because he was so shy. It was a mistake and we can see that now. When they both died last year, he became totally isolated. We went over a couple of times and found him cleaning his guns. It just never occurred to us that something like this would happen. We're just so sorry for your family's pain."

Six months later I got a call from the judge. It was time to make a decision about charging him with a felony or a misdemeanor — and he was leaving the choice up to me.

"How has he been doing with his rehabilitation?" I asked.

The judge shared that he was responding exceptionally well, so I recommended a misdemeanor charge — and we never heard from him again. Forgiveness had freed us all.

Keeping a Clean Slate

Once you've written your Forgiveness Letters to wipe the slate clean, there are three ways to keep it clean.

> *When you make it a habit not to take anything personally, your anger, jealousy and envy, even your sadness will simply disappear. — Don Miguel Ruiz*

1. Don't take things personally

Although life experiences come to us as a result of the thoughts we think, the painful actions and demeaning words from others never come to us because they are true. What others say about us is more an indication of their current position on the Power Pyramid.

2. Fast from the past

The letters I get from truly unhappy people always include long lists of the calamities that have befallen them. Recently I received one that began with: "I've tried your program, but it isn't working. I've had a terrible life. I guess I should give you more details."

Here was my response:

"You're asking for my coaching. Well, here it is: Be done with it. Don't tell these stories ever again. Fast from the past. I know of no way out of your hell as long as you continue to recite these mishaps and misfortunes."

I suggested she read Byron Katie's book, ***Who Would You Be Without Your Story***? Then start sharing three Gratitudes with a partner each day. I never heard from her again.

When you're tired of your misery, you'll shed your past like an old coat and never put it on again. You're as free to do so as you believe you are.

3. Write Forgiveness Letters as needed

When you keep seeing a pattern of self-judgment, condescension, sarcasm, or judgment of others, write another Forgiveness Letter. It is a tool that I have used many times over the years, always with healing results.

Asking Forgiveness

Just as you can offer forgiveness to another in writing, asking forgiveness of yourself can be done in writing. Your letter or email can be as simple as: "I'm sorry. I didn't mean to hurt you. Please forgive me."

It's also possible to ask forgiveness of those who have died. Doing so with someone who is no longer in your life can help open your heart to loving those who are.

> *A stiff apology is a second insult.... The injured party does not want to be compensated because he has been wronged; he wants to be healed because he has been hurt.*
> *— Gilbert K. Chesterton*

The Only Thing We Need to Forgive

While writing this chapter, I came upon a quote by Abraham-Hicks that ended with:

"The only reason you don't love them is because you're using them as your excuse to not feel good." It struck me that you could rephrase that as: "The reason you need to forgive them is because you gave them power over how you felt about yourself and your circumstances."

Once we realize that we were the ones who gave away our power to the other person in the first place, we can move to a new place, remember our power, and forgive ourselves for ever forgetting.

Don't live life in the past lane.

Samantha Ettus

Q & A on Forgiveness of the Past

Finish each day and be done with it.
You've done what you could.

Some blunders and absurdities no doubt crept in;
forget them as soon as you can.

Tomorrow is a new day; begin it well and serenely.

Ralph Waldo Emerson

Q: Once I forgive myself, how do I get other people and their judgments off my back?

A: When you truly stop judging yourself, others will eventually stop judging you. It's how life works. In the meantime, listen to them with the same kind of listening you want them to offer you. Phrases such as "Have you got a minute to sit down and talk?" or "I know you want the best for me" may be helpful.

Q: I find myself apologizing all the time. Is that healthy?

A: I've always wondered why the most revered among us — Gandhi, Mother Teresa, the Dalai Lama, Thick Nhat Hanh — seemed to move slowly and talk slowly. I think I finally figured it out. That's the easiest way to stay conscious.

Years ago I started noticing how often I had been apologizing — sometimes half a dozen times a week. I wondered if I could go a whole week without doing anything I felt a need to apologize for. It slowed me down. Multiple apologies aren't bad, but they tell us we're not feeling comfortable with how we're living. Either change how you're living or learn to accept your best as good enough. Either way will help you feel better.

Q: I just did something that was mean-spirited and dumb. How do I forgive myself?

A: Let's call what you did "interesting." Like the child who's told not to touch the stove but touches it anyway, you didn't want to believe Mom when she said it would hurt you. Every adversity can make you bitter or better. What's going to be the outcome with this one?

As for mean-spirited, I'd change that word to fear-spirited. No one wakes up and says, "I can't wait to hurt such-and-such today." We may however, wake up and say, "I have to protect myself from that person." In the process of trying to protect ourselves from pain, we cause more. Deep down, we didn't mean to be mean. We just wanted to be safe. When we get that, we're already safe, and tendencies toward meanness melt away.

> *I have never met a greater monster or miracle than myself. — Montaigne*

Q: I want to forgive, but how do I get over a death?

A: Thank you for that courageous question. I suggest that: 1) You allow yourself to cry as much and as long as you want. 2) When you're ready, write them a goodbye letter. Then burn it and spread the ashes in a special place. 3) Find a grief support group to join so you don't feel alone.

I'm of the belief system that says *death isn't life-threatening.* That was helpful for me to get through my father's passing. I hope that you can find solace in your belief system also.

Q: Can you be too forgiving?

A: No, but you can be unloving to yourself.

When I'm not sure if I'm putting up with too much from someone, I ask, "What would I want my daughter to do in this situation?"

Allow your angergy to rise up. It may have powerful lessons to teach you. The lesson could be to set a boundary or confront your landlord. If something or someone is harming you, face it and feel it first, which often leads to healthy action. Then you'll be ready to fully forgive it.

Q: I'm sad a lot because of what has happened in my past and I don't know how to change that.

A: I was in a domestic violence shelter, one of my best friends got pregnant out of wedlock, and Oprah was sexually assaulted by a family member. Each of us had an "excuse" to stay stuck in shame and guilt for the rest of our lives, but imagine this with me:

Suppose your best friend wrote you a letter yesterday that told about all the rotten things that had happened in her life — and they were exactly the same as what had happened in yours! Now suppose that at the end of the letter she asked, "Can you still love me now that you know all of this?"

What would your answer be? Would you love her? Of course. Now allow yourself to love *you.*

Lord, today I am grateful that I have not been impatient, cranky, or irritable, that I haven't been jealous, rude, or judgmental, and that I haven't pouted, whined, or nagged. But soon, Lord, I'm gonna get out of bed, so I'm really gonna need your help. — Anonymous

Q: Why don't we send the Forgiveness Letters?

A: Your question indicates that you may still have a desire to change the other person. We do our best Forgiveness work when we detach with love from the other person. Sending the letter could stir up old issues they consider long gone or could get us caught up in wondering if they'll respond. Burning the letters is a powerful ritual of closure.

Q: How do you celebrate another person's successes and feel compassion for their challenges if they're deceased?

A: When you think about them, you'll feel the knot in your stomach begin to unravel and be replaced by peace.

Forgiveness is the answer to the child's dream of a miracle by which what is broken is made whole again.

Dag Hammarskjold

7

High-Way 7: FGH: Gratitude for the Present

The Power of Appreciation

Defining Gratitude for the Present

When a person doesn't have gratitude, something is missing in his or her humanity. A person can almost be defined by his or her attitude toward gratitude.

Elie Wiesel

Ever notice how people with lots of love, support, health, and wealth in their lives seem to be really grateful? Which do you think came first, the success or the gratitude?

One of the most exciting discoveries of the recent positive psychology research is that happiness isn't the cause of gratitude, it's the result. Gratitude comes *before* happiness and success in almost every case.

Growing up, most of us came to view gratitude as the "icing on the cake" of life. Back then, we thought of the "main course" as hard work, knowing the right people, or doing what others thought we "should" do every day. Now it's become clear that the main entrée of a happy, healthy and fulfilled life is *choosing thoughts that feel good*, and there's no easier way than being grateful.

A simple dictionary definition of gratitude is "a feeling of appreciation for something or someone." Like other emotions, it starts in our hearts and stirs up our senses. The phrase "overcome with gratitude" aptly describes our experience of welling up with tears of joy for blessings received.

My highest Gratitudes seem to be two-pronged. They acknowledge not only the gift, but also the giver, be it a person, nature or God. In that sense, it's very similar to the feeling of love – and love is as good as it gets.

Enjoy today: this is not a dress rehearsal.
— Refrigerator magnet

Why Be Grateful?

There are many good reasons to be grateful — with the primary one being because it feels good. Like drawing back the curtains to let the sun into a dark room, gratitude warms hearts and opens minds. Meanwhile, because it brings you happiness, others around you are blessed. I'll never forget my eight-year-old asking me what was different after I'd been doing my morning Gratitudes for just a few weeks. When I asked what he meant, he simply said, "You're so much happier!"

Researchers concur. According to a recent series of studies over a five-year span, gratitude positively affects practically every area of life. In *The Research Project on Gratitude and Thankfulness*, Dr. Michael McCullough and his colleagues at the University of Miami found the following attributes in adults young and old who kept gratitude journals or did regular gratitude interventions. They...

- ✓ *had more energy and vitality;*
- ✓ *were more optimistic;*
- ✓ *were more likely to make progress toward important personal goals;*
- ✓ *were more alert, enthusiastic, determined, and attentive;*
- ✓ *were more likely to help someone by offering emotional support;*
- ✓ *had higher life satisfaction;*

- ✓ *were more generous;*
- ✓ *were more responsible and committed;*
- ✓ *were less likely to judge others in terms of possessions;*
- ✓ *reported a heightened sense of mental well-being.*

According to their research, "Even the spouses of the subjects noticed the difference in the participants who did regular gratitude writings or verbal acknowledgments." McCullough also noted that grateful people don't deny the negative aspects of life; they simply don't choose to dwell on them. Many of my coaching clients notice that once they start making daily gratitude lists, they watch fewer newscasts. Focusing on the worst things that have happened in the past twenty-four hours is simply not a match for where they are on the Power Pyramid.

The Ultimate "All-Turn-ative"

Gratitude is extremely powerful because it has an immediate effect on our attitude. No matter what the situation, gratitude is the all-turn-ative that can turn all things around in just minutes. When we try *not* to think painful thoughts, we become a magnet for more of the same. Gratitude goes with the flow of life and gives us a new focal point. "What are you grateful for?" can yield an answer as simple as "I'm grateful I can choose to be grateful."

As a parent, my biggest disappointments haven't been in my children, but in myself. As a Type A personality, I've been impatient more times than I want to remember. (Thank heavens for High-Way 6: **Forgiveness of the Past**.)

Sometimes when I ask my children for forgiveness for my sharp tone or curt word, even their saying they forgive me doesn't return me to a "95." Yet as soon as I shift our topic to what I'm grateful for about them, the air clears. One afternoon I was on my son about leaving things lying around the house and we got into a shouting match. I later asked for his forgiveness and when he gave it, I was able to add, "I see you're reading that new book. I'm so glad you're giving it a try."

That evening at dinner, I added, "You know something I appreciate about you?" I had his attention. "When you called two friends today and neither of them wanted to go to the movie, you didn't give up. You called one more friend and now have fun plans for tonight."

A sincere "Thanks, Mom," and lively conversation was my resounding reward.

> *The question is not what you look at, but what you see.*
> *— Henry David Thoreau*

Gratitude and Work

The great little book ***How Full is Your Bucket***, by Tom Rath and Donald Clifton, is full of more proof of the power of being appreciated. One Gallup poll found that "65 percent of Americans reported receiving *no recognition for good work in the past year*." The poll also cited the following characteristics of co-workers who receive regular appreciation:

- ✓ *increased individual productivity*
- ✓ *increased social interaction*
- ✓ *greater longevity in their jobs*
- ✓ *fewer accidents on the job*

Perhaps their most astounding statistic was that the #1 reason people leave their jobs is because they don't feel appreciated. A pat on the back or recognition in a meeting can go a long way.

You'll never grow old until you've lost all your marvels.
— Merry Browne

Gratitude and Health

When you incorporate gratitude into your life, almost everything improves — even your health. In recent years, McCullough and Emmons have studied the effects of gratitude on psychological and physical well-being. They asked some groups of participants to list things they were grateful for once a day and other groups to make lists once a week.

As they were tracking the participants' self-reported emotional and physical states, the research partners were amazed to find that the participants who listed things they were grateful for even once a week not only improved in helpfulness and happiness, but spent more time exercising, slept better, and had fewer physical ailments. Those who shared daily Gratitudes enjoyed even greater health benefits. Evidence continues to indicate that when we focus on thoughts that feel good our level of wellness improves dramatically.

You've never met an ungrateful person who was happy, nor have you ever met a grateful person who was unhappy. — Zig Ziglar

The Top of the Power Pyramid

Gratitude is more than reciting thank yous. When we allow feelings of appreciation to flow through us, it changes us at our core.

The Chicago Cubs pre-game Gratitude ritual was shared with the press in October of 2017, while the Cubs were enjoying their reign as 2016 world MLB Champions. Each day before batting practice, their strength coach gathered the players on the field and let them know the honoree of the day. Then each individual expressed something specific they appreciated about them. Sometimes the sharing ended in laughter, and sometimes, in tears.

After first-base coach Barry Hyde was the focus of this deluge of affirmation, he shared, "At first I thought it would be a mess-around kind of thing, and then I realized it was sincere. It was emotional and overwhelming. It keeps going and going, and after a while, you're like, "Holy Cow."

Many wondered if their unique team-building practice could have been a secret to their success in the 2017 season as well.

Gratitude is at the very top of the Power Pyramid, along with joy, enthusiasm, and love. For those who want to rise to the top of their potential, gratitude is the ultimate "elevator." Once we're in the gratitude flow, things start changing for the better. In **Get the Picture**, we ask and believe. With **Gratitude for the Present**, we thank and receive!

Taking the Elevator to the 95th Floor

One of my favorite methods for explaining how gratitude works is to imagine being in a beautiful building with ninety-five floors. It's a building based on the Power Pyramid of life. Now imagine...

Yesterday you got your spirits and hopes "up" and your feeling good put you on an elevator to the top floor of your **Attitude Building**. Once there, you saw life more clearly and felt "on top of the world." You soon began to ask for the "highest" good in relationships, health, work, vacations, etc. As you did, you watched helicopters take off from the helipad going to get you exactly what you'd asked for (or better).

All was well until late last evening while you were waiting near the helipad for your deliveries to arrive. You became impatient and began to think about all the times you'd been disappointed. You wondered if your recent requests might not come to fruition. After all, asking and receiving seems so easy and you've always worked incredibly hard for what you wanted. You convinced yourself to be prepared for the worst and began to think of how you'd cope if you didn't receive your requests.

Before you knew it, you worked and worried your way down the stairwells. On the77th floor, you got distracted by an unpleasant headline in a newspaper lying on an end able. It upset you so much that you took the wrong escalator and were soon down on the 25th floor. Since the folks at the 25th floor had lots of crises to tell you about, you got caught up in listening to their unfortunate mishaps and forgot all about the delivery of your requests — which were, in the meantime, delivered to the 95th floor.

Unfortunately, since no one was there to sign for them, they were returned to sender.

Moral of the story: once you ask for a "95ing" partner, job, or experience, you'll want to be in a "95ing" mood to receive it!

At my home in Kyrgyzstan, I didn't have running water, a TV, a car, or most of the things I had when I lived in the United States, yet I was extremely happy. As a Peace Corps volunteer, you expect to go to another country where life is harder, poorer, and where people need your help. Sure, most people there are poor, but those I now call my friends are so rich in character that I never noticed how poor they really were. — Leslie Wakulich

Gratitude is Natural

It can be fascinating to discover the innate gratitude of the human spirit by studying indigenous cultures. If you've ever spoken with people who have worked in the Peace Corps, for example, their stories often carry an underlying theme about the immense gratitude of the native people in their assigned countries. In describing their experiences, volunteers love to remind us that those who have very little materially are some of the happiest people they've ever met.

Having doesn't bring happiness, but being *grateful for what we have* does. Hundreds of studies, such as those quoted in ***Thank You Power*** by Deborah Norville, reveal that once our basic needs are met, the average person's level of happiness does not increase with our income. We don't need more fortunes to be more grateful, but once we're more grateful more good fortune will be ours.

Many of us go through our days parched and empty, thirsting after happiness, when we're really standing knee-deep in the river of abundance.
— Sarah Ban Breathnach

What it Looks Like to Live in Gratitude

In her book, ***Mutant Message Down Under***, author, physician, and former Kansas beauty queen Marlo Morgan describes her months on a walkabout through the desert with Aborigines who refer to themselves as The Real People.

"I learned (on the walkabout) that the appearance of food was not taken for granted. It was first requested, always expected to appear, did appear, and genuine gratitude was always given.

"[One evening] The Real People explained how absurd it appeared to them when the missionaries insisted they teach their children to fold hands and give two minutes of grace before meals. They wake up being grateful! They spend the entire day never taking anything for granted. The tribe feels that if missionaries have to teach their own children to be grateful, something that comes innately to all humans, they should take a very serious look at their own society. Perhaps it is they who need help."

Oceans of Gratitude

Another way to understand our intrinsically grateful nature is by watching animals. Everyone has seen the gratitude of a dog when his owner takes him out to play. Is gratitude natural to all mammals?

According to a San Francisco Chronicle article from 2005, a female humpback whale was spotted by crab fishermen just off the Pacific coast wrapped in the nylon ropes that connect crab traps to each other. The traps were heavy and the whale was struggling to stay on the surface so it could breathe. Experts assessed the situation and concluded that the only chance the whale had was if rescuers could get into the water with her and cut her bonds, one by one. Any thrashing by the fifty-ton animal would have been deadly, but the crew decided it was a risk worth taking.

One of the divers, James Moskito, described the whale as remaining amazingly peaceful during the hour or so it took them to cut the ropes. When they finally finished, and the whale realized it was free, Moskito said it began swimming in circles around them.

"It felt to me like it was thanking us, knowing it was free and that we had helped," Moskito said. But that wasn't all. After the circles, "It stopped about a foot away from me, pushed me around a little bit and had some fun."

He said after the whale nuzzled him, it swam to each of the other rescuers as well. Talk about a whale of a hug!

Teach Your Children Well

> *When we develop a right attitude of compassion and gratitude, we take a giant step towards solving our personal and international problems. — The Dalai Lama*

Animals are great teachers of the pure essence of gratitude and the power of living in the moment. So how does this natural awe and wonder ever turn into boredom? When Zach was four, his dad gave me a beautiful rose. The day I put it in a vase, it was just beginning to open up. The following morning I awoke to a blaze of colorful glory on our kitchen table. I pointed it out to Zach when he awoke.

His response was, "Yeah, Mom, I saw it yesterday."

We had somehow given him the message that a tree was "just a tree" and a flower "just a flower." I'm grateful that we caught it early enough that, as a seventeen-year-old, that same young man often called me to the window to see a beautiful sunset.

The Gratitude Guarantee

Two minutes of sharing Gratitudes each day will not only bring you new blessings, it will help you solve whatever problems you face. Imagine that your present problem is a forest fire. Standing in the middle of the blaze, you can do nothing, but with the help of gratitude to "rise above" your feelings of hopelessness or panic, you can see your options more clearly.

Gratitude doesn't make what went wrong yesterday go away, but regretting or worrying about problems won't either. What it will do is make today better. Isn't that enough? Once you understand gratitude, you'll see that all your power and joy can only be accessed in the now.

The Gratitude Guarantee:

When you get grateful, you feel good. When you feel good, good things happen!

The Gratitude for the Present Process:

Daily Gratitudes

Gratitude unlocks the fullness of life. It turns what we have into enough and more. It can turn a meal into a feast, a house into a home, a stranger into a friend. Gratitude makes sense of our past, brings peace for today, and creates a vision for tomorrow.

Melody Beattie

I sometimes begin my talks with this question: "Is there anyone here who has something they could, if they wanted to, complain or worry about?"

Most hands go up.

Then I ask, "Is there anyone here who has something they could, if they wanted to, be grateful for?"

All hands go up.

I finish my point with, "Which of those categories occupy most of your thoughts? Your answer is an indicator of how your life is going these days. You have a choice about how it goes tomorrow."

The process of gratitude is simply choosing a focus of appreciation. Whether you do it at a prescribed time, such as when you first wake up, before each meal, or whether you allow your thoughts to gently flow back to gratitude throughout the day, feeling appreciation is as simple as it is powerful.

> *I check myself constantly for, you know, am I appreciating this? Why not, if I'm not. I pull myself back to what's happening right now. — Jim Carrey*

In High-Way 1 we said that a belief is "thinking it 'til you feel it." Similarly, thinking thoughts of appreciation without feeling the good feelings that go with them is like planting seeds without watering them. The fruits of gratitude are only harvested by getting to a place of humble acknowledgment of life's gifts, and that is one of the best feelings in the world.

Daily Devotion

Choose to devote yourself daily to gratitude. If you haven't started yet, begin with sharing three things you're grateful for from the past twenty-four hours with someone. Then continue every day, with no repeats. If you start to run dry, remember to include anything you'd miss if it wasn't there, such as the co-worker who always says good morning, the fact that you can Skype for free with a friend across the ocean, or that the person who cuts your hair is such a good listener. Your smallest movement in the direction of appreciation will reap huge rewards.

> *Enjoy the little things in life. One day you may look back and realize they were the big things. — Anonymous*

The Worry Eraser

When someone worries "all the time," it does not help to tell them to stop worrying. That only makes them worry about worrying! Instead, ask them to replace each worry thought they become aware of with appreciation for something or someone.

When worry threatens to overwhelm, you can also play something I call **The Alien Game**. Like Brad Pitt's character in the film ***Meet Joe Black***, players pretend they've just come to Earth and have been given someone else's body for the day. As an Alien, everything is foreign to them, not in a scary way, but in a delightful way.

Those who play this game best (by getting in touch with their inner Alien) marvel at how toothpaste tubes work, the sweet smell of fresh basil, how often children laugh, the way snow glistens in the moonlight, and how wonderful butter and cinnamon taste on a sweet potato.

When we pretend we have no past or future and are giving our body back to its owner in a week, we experience the ***now*** in a new way and meet life on her own terms. It's intoxicating!

Living in the Now

When we live in gratitude, our lives take on a gentler pace, and time often feels as if it's expanding. What good is all the manifesting in the world if we never stop and appreciate our gifts once we receive them? It's like downloading new music and never listening to it. Gratitude is a "stop and smell the roses" way to savor the fruits of our dreams.

How do you come back home to the present? Here's another simple method for achieving immediate results: Put down whatever is in your hands. Then, as you breathe, start to notice a tingling beneath your skin, perhaps in your hands or feet. Kind of tickles, doesn't it? (That's the way my friend used to describe it.) That's it. You're home. You're here...in the now. Just be.

Then throughout the day, come back to your awareness of being. It may happen when you hold a baby, pet a dog, meditate, make love, go fishing, plant a flower, sing a song or climb a mountain. All of these can pull you fully into the present.

Worry and time have an inverse relationship. The more you have of one, the less you have of the other. Yet curiously, both are suspended when you live in the now. — Mike Dooley

So next time someone asks, "What's new?" you can answer, "Now. Now is always new." In this moment, we can all say, "Never been here, never done this." It's in this moment that we can feel our feelings, taste our food, smell the coffee, and look our kids in the eye while they talk to us. In the now a whole new world opens up — opens us. There's really nothing like it. It's true freedom — and it's free.

Why We Don't Practice Gratitude for the Present

When you arise in the morning, give thanks for the morning light, for your life and strength.

Give thanks for your food and the joy of living.

If you see no reason for giving thanks, the fault lies with yourself.

Shawnee Chief Tecumseh

If gratitude is so glorious, why do some people read books like this one, yet never make even one daily Gratitude list? The excuses are many. Some people are full of resentment because they haven't practiced Forgiveness (High-Way 6); some are afraid of the tears of Gratitude that can well up (High-Way 4); some are addicted to busy-ness and are running from (High-Way 2); and others are frozen in jealousy, clueless to their own ability to manifest through asking and believing (High-Way 1). Fortunately, using the High-Ways can take us back home to gratitude's gifts.

Life's true goodness comes not from what you have, but from how much you value and appreciate it.
— Ralph Marston

We're Waiting for a Wake-Up Call

Those who remember the San Francisco earthquake of 1989 will recall a famous picture of a lone car straddling the edge of the Oakland Bay Bridge, barely hanging on. However, few people realize that the driver of that car was also in the Twin Towers on the fateful day of 9/11.

In interviews, that gentleman noted that he hadn't gotten the first wake-up call, but he had gotten the second one, saying, "Now I'm changing my life to one of daily gratitude, and am extremely grateful for a second chance."

What's it going to take for the rest of us to finally get grateful? You may have already had a wake-up call. After speaking with thousands of individuals on this subject, I've found that the three most grateful groups on the planet tend to be:

1. Those who've come close to a loss
2. Those who've had a loss
3. Those who know a loss is coming

The third category reminds me of my father's transformation after his diagnosis with cancer. Every sunset and bird song became precious to him in those final months. Having witnessed that transformation, I swore that I wasn't going to wait for a diagnosis to get grateful. I wanted to, as country singer Tim McGraw so beautifully puts it, "live like I was dying."

In his memoir, Senator John McCain wrote beautifully about his loss of freedom while spending five years in a POW camp that inspired his gratitude for America:

"In prison, I fell in love with my country. I had loved her before then, but like most young people, my affection was little more than a simple appreciation for the comforts and privileges most Americans took for granted. It wasn't until I had lost America for a time that I realized how much I loved her. I loved what I missed most: my family and friends, the sights and sounds, sports, music, information — all the attractive qualities of American life...They became all the more important to me."

As I was writing this chapter, hurricane Irma threatened my home state of Florida. I was staying with friends in Georgia just days before, hearing the forecast of ten to fifteen foot surges in my area. I had lots of time to feel my feelings and sometimes found myself in a state of grief as thoughts about the possibility of losing so much arose.

The storm took a surprise turn and missed my hometown. Returning home to a piano that was unharmed was one of many moments of intense personal gratitude. My neighbors and friends agreed, coming close to that loss had turned on the bright light of gratitude, and the issues that arose from the clean up could not dim it.

But what about those who were hardest hit?

Post-Traumatic Growth

Psychologist Jean Rhodes of the University of Massachusetts-Boston spent a decade looking at what happens to people after a natural disaster by studying the survivors of Hurricane Katrina. Her findings, compiled in a report called ***RISK: Resilience in Survivors of Katrina,*** show that the word "victim" is often a misnomer.

"Stress can precipitate our Post-Traumatic Growth. We begin to appreciate life more and feel a personal sense of strength from having endured the trauma. We see new possibilities. We begin to value relationships over things and have a spiritual awakening that psychologists believe often comes hand in hand with post-traumatic stress."

So hurricanes and earthquakes can result in the Gratitude Attitude, even for those who "lost" the most. What will be your catalyst? A stormy tale of woe or a simple turn to wisdom?

"I'll Be Grateful When..."

We often believe that we can't get grateful until our present challenge passes, but our greatest teachers have shown us otherwise. One of my favorite stories of gratitude amid adversity is that of Corrie ten Boom. In her book, ***The Hiding Place***, Corrie recounts that while in Ravensbruck, a Nazi concentration camp, she and her older sister, Betsy, read to the women from a tiny Bible each night.

> *In everything, give thanks. — 1 Thessalonians 5:18*

One night, Betsy read from First Thessalonians and insisted that they thank God for all things – even for the lice that infested their living quarters. Corrie resisted at first, but gave it her best. As the story unfolds, the women later discovered they had the freedom to pray each night because the Nazi guards hated the lice in their barracks so much that they wouldn't enter for the mandatory nightly beatings.

We Are Consumed with Work

When I ask employees and managers around the world what they'd like more of from their workplace, one answer tops the list. It's not more money or more time off. What they desire is more appreciation and recognition. I remind them that someone simply has to start the appreciation ball rolling. The result? Happier and more productive co-workers. Not a bad bottom line benefit!

> *The deepest principle in human nature is the craving to be appreciated. — William James*

We're Jealous

One of the weakest excuses for not giving thanks is that others have something we want. I recall sitting at the airport awaiting my plane when a gregarious family of four, two parents and two teens, sat across from me. They were noisy in the best sense — laughing, teasing, poking each other — and almost oblivious to those around them. I watched with fascination and eventually moved to another seat so I could "stare" a little less conspicuously.

I was most impressed with the parents. The man was physically affectionate toward his wife and there was a light in her eyes when she looked at him. As a single person at the time who was open to romance, I closed my eyes and put myself in her chair, sensing what it would feel like. Rather than being green-eyed, I was grateful-eyed. She helped me **Get the Picture** and get to an even better feel-good place.

We Fear We'll Lose Control

I recall working with a group of salespeople at a successful company. Throughout the day-long seminar, many of them shared powerful insights. As the experience neared its end, I sensed a blending of minds and hearts and took a risk. I asked if there was anyone who wanted to express gratitude aloud for their team, their employer, or an individual who had helped them. The room fell silent, but I saw many people look around as they considered speaking up.

Finally, I broke the silence with, "Are you not sharing aloud because you're afraid you'll get emotional?"

"BUSTED!" yelled the largest man in the front row.

The laughter that followed was an indicator that he wasn't the only one concerned about "losing" it in front of his peers. After we regained our composure, I encouraged them to take a few minutes to write a thank-you to someone in the room or on the team. They all did, and a few even took the risk of standing and reading theirs to the group.

If tears are a concern of yours as well, writing a thank-you note to those you love and admire is a gift you'll give them and yourself. Don't just email or text it. Write it. And no, Hallmark is not a sponsor of my programs...yet.

We Fear Surrendering to Gratitude

One day I stopped to ask myself why I was so fascinated by the study of gratitude. Knowing that we teach best what we most need to learn, I began to understand that it's because when I surrender to gratitude, it cures what ails me.

I've referred to my propensity for wanting to control things and people. Controllers love to give, but they're often uncomfortable receiving. We wear our "I don't need anyone" mindset like armor to keep ourselves from being hurt (again), yet that armor can keep us from letting love and life in.

We all need to receive. If we weren't receiving the gift of trees cleansing our air right now, we'd all die. Gratitude is our affirmation that an abundance of blessings are there for us, not because we've earned them, but as a free gift. One that we cannot, thank heavens, control.

> *Without receiving, we can't feel close to others.*
> *— Laura Doyle*

The idea of free gifts that we can't earn is more foreign to some individuals and cultures than others. In China, for example, there's a phrase: "You honor me a foot, I will honor you ten feet in return." It's a common practice for the Chinese to refuse a gift several times before finally accepting it. Many of us can relate.

Perhaps we feel that receiving puts us in a weaker position. Yet, in receiving gratefully, we become the giver, for receiving and being grateful is one of the greatest gifts we can give another person.

In the miraculous process of conception, a man gives and a woman receives. In her willingness to receive, new life is brought forth. Receiving in gratitude puts us in touch with our receiving feminine side. It reaffirms our interconnectedness. New life is born within us and greater love and peace surround us every time we allow, receive, and give thanks.

> *To these bounties, which are so constantly enjoyed that we are prone to forget the source from which they come, others have been added, which are of so extraordinary a nature that they cannot fail to penetrate and soften the heart. — Abraham Lincoln*

We're Afraid We'll Forget

Like putting on a seat belt, gratitude is a habit. At first, especially if your life has been on a downward spiral, it may seem challenging or awkward, but putting on deodorant or brushing our teeth felt foreign at first, yet they're habits we're glad we acquired.

If you're leery of starting daily Gratitudes for fear of forgetting to do them at some point, let me assure you, you *will* forget somewhere along the line. You may even forget for weeks or months at a time. But as mentioned in the first chapter, if you choose to, you can FGH: Forgive yourself for forgetting, be Grateful you remembered, and have Hope that you'll remember better next time. It will get easier and easier to remember. Trust me.

> *Thanksgiving pivots on our willingness to go beyond our independence and to accept the give-and-take between giver and thanks giver. The "yes" which acknowledges our interdependence is the very "yes" to belonging, the "yes" of love. — Brother David Steindl Rast*

We Fear We'll Run Out

The ***8 to Great*** daily ritual says "no repeats." It makes Gratitude-ing a lot more interesting and fun. We have to move from who we're grateful for, to what *about someone* we're grateful for. With a bit of brainstorming, we'll discover that we never run out.

Recently I created a list of "101 Ways to Open and Close a Meeting so People Will Stay Open and Close."* They're ways that any meeting facilitator can use gratitude as a focus to open or close meetings. Here are a few examples with Gratitude "themes":

What are you grateful for about...

- ✓ *The physical environment of our workplace*
- ✓ *The person to your left*
- ✓ *Our customers*
- ✓ *The gifts you bring to our workplace*

*Feel free to request the full list by emailing our office at info@8togreat.com.

Freedom from Behind Bars

I once spoke at the largest women's prison in our state. As I was waiting to go on stage, the warden came up behind me and startled me with her demands.

"Two things we need to go over, MK." She had my attention.

"First, no touching. I see that you touch people a lot. No reaching out with your hands and no hugging. You may not touch the inmates in any way."

"How do they get touched?"

"They don't."

"The second thing is, I don't want you talking about gratitude. These women have nothing to be grateful for, so I don't want..."

I turned away from her mid-sentence and walked on stage. "Good morning!" I shouted, and was greeted by an exuberant reply.

"My name is MK Mueller and they call me the Gratitude Guru. There are probably people in the world who think you have nothing to be grateful for, but of course we know better. Raise your hands right now and tell me some of the things you're grateful for."

Instantly, there were dozens of hands in the air, but a beautiful young woman in her mid-twenties had hers up the fastest, so I asked her to share first. She began to tear up. We waited.

"The dew on the grass...looks like diamonds in the sunlight," she finally managed to say.

After a moment of silent appreciation for her courage, I asked how she had noticed such a glorious gift.

"I just got out of solitary."

I received more thank-you notes from that presentation than from any before or since. Those notes meant even more to me knowing the sacrifice the prisoners had made to use money they could have spent on cigarettes or candy to purchase writing paper, an envelope and a stamp.

Not everything that counts can be counted.

Albert Einstein

Reflect on your present blessings, of which every man has many, not on your past misfortunes, of which all men have some. — Charles Dickens

Gratitude for the Present Success Stories

To speak gratitude is courteous and pleasant, to enact gratitude is generous and noble, but to live gratitude is to touch heaven.

Johannes A. Gaertner

As we travel the High-Ways of life, every so often we encounter individuals who live their values purely and simply. I'm privileged to call one such person my brother-in-law, Colonel Bruce Hurd. The following is a reply to a letter I wrote him shortly after he finished command of a unit at Robins Air Force Base in Georgia.

The Air Force Colonel's Story

Dear MK,

Thank you for your request to share what I've found to be helpful in setting the tone for good, positive, productive meetings. While many of the things I'll mention are not original ideas, I will take credit for having the good sense to "pick and choose" those ideas and techniques that appealed to me after twenty-three years as an Air Force officer.

1) I started off each meeting by asking the unit chaplain to conduct an opening prayer. I believe this set a good tone and helped us focus on appropriate priorities.

2) My first order of business was recognizing top performers throughout the unit by presenting them with the "Group Commander's Coin." The coin was something I had specially made for the unit. The only way anyone could get one was to do something, in or out of their job, very well. For example, if someone was recognized by an outside agency as being a top performer, I gave them a coin. If a crew flew a particularly impressive mission, I gave them a coin. I believe it helped set the stage for an enjoyable, upbeat meeting and served to remind everyone present what outstanding people we had.

3) The next thing I did weekly was recognize an enlisted person (usually a junior member) as "enlisted face of the week." He/she would come to our meeting and his/her commander would introduce them and tell the assembled staff about them. This not only gave the member a chance to be front and center in a positive light, but it also served to bring them to their squadron commander's attention.

4) After asking everyone present if they had anything to add/announce at the close of a meeting, I would announce any promotions and/or awards individuals or units had won since the previous week.

5) The last thing I would address was how much I appreciated the great work everyone was doing — particularly the leaders and supervisors who were present at the meeting. This would end the meeting on a positive note and send people off feeling good about themselves and seeking out award winners to congratulate them.

The things I mentioned above probably took five to ten minutes out of our formal weekly staff meeting, but I believe it was time well spent. While typically the "kick butt" method of leading will get results in the short term, I've seen how it is very detrimental to the long-term health and well-being of the unit and its members.

Appreciation Results in Appreciation

At Bruce's official going away party in Georgia, perhaps the greatest gift he received was seeing that the Gratitude Attitude he had lived had been picked up by his squadron.

That was made clear by the party game they created to surprise him — one they named BH (for Bruce Hurd) Bingo.

Here, again in Bruce's words, is a description of that tribute:

It revolved around a bingo sheet filled with common sayings I used every day. When I got up to talk that night, they all pulled out their bingo sheets from under their placemats. The idea was to "X out" a spot on the sheet when I would use the saying written in that block. Looking back at the sheet, I noticed that every one of the sayings was something positive, like "thank you," "thank you very much," "phenomenal," "outstanding," "great," "very great," etc. It was funny, because I really did use all of those phrases a lot.

At the end of the evening, one of my outstanding squadron commanders closed his remarks by saying, "Colonel Hurd is living proof that nice guys finish first!" I couldn't think of a better compliment from an officer that I respect very much. My heart was and is very full.

The Assignment

One day I was picking up papers off the dinner table when I found an open notebook of my daughter's. She was a junior in high school at the time and her English teacher had asked each student to write a short note to the other students in the class.

Most of the notes began, "Hey, Jo, Whaz Up?" and ended soon after that with, "Have a great year." However, there was one note from a classmate named Pearl that stood out from the rest. It began: *Joanna, You are a beautiful ray of sunshine that lights up the lives of everyone you meet.*

I started to tear up as I read the words that were so true of my daughter. Pearl went on to say: *The world is lucky to have you around. The universe is more balanced due to your greatness. Today is sunny and beautiful just for you. You should go outside and play in the world that has been created for you. Bask in the warmth of the sun. Lay in the grass and smile. Today is yours.*

Pearl had the incredible gift of seeing the magnificence, the heroism, and the perfection within each of us. I was unfathomably grateful for her loving note to my wonderful daughter, as well as for the exceptional teacher who was aware of the power of gratitude and willing to make time for it in her classes.

Surviving the Test of Teens

The following year was a challenging one. One day, that same sweet daughter stopped talking to me. It just happened. There were no arguments, but soon there were also no "thank you's" or "I love you's." I saw a lot of the back of her head and heard a lot of slammed doors. I didn't want to take it personally, so I turned to the High-Ways for answers. That led to the day I sat down and wrote her a letter.

> *If you ever want to mess your parents up, go up to them, put your arms around them, say "thank you" and walk away. — Chris Gardner*

Dear Joanna,

I wanted to write and tell you just how much I love you and how proud I am of the young woman you're becoming. Even your questioning me is a powerful part of your finding your own way.

It went on for about a page. Without mentioning the change in her behavior, I focused on all the things I loved about her. Then I folded it, put it in an envelope, and left it on her pillow.

I was truly surprised the next day when I got one back. I read (through my tears) not one, but three pages of how much she loved me and how glad she was that I was her mom. I made twenty copies and stuck them in every drawer in my bedroom so I couldn't ever forget the grateful spirit who lived inside her body!

What Goes Around...

Salina, Kansas pediatrician Ginger Senseman got a golden seat during a historical moment because she wrote a thank you note. When this wife and mother found out she had breast cancer in October 2008, she and her husband canceled a family trip to Hawaii so she could begin weekly chemotherapy treatments. Their sons William (ten) and Sam (seven) were especially disappointed.

Her cancer treatment was well underway in November when her boys' favorite presidential candidate got elected. To help salve the pain of the missed vacation, Ginger decided to risk contacting her senators about getting tickets to Washington for the inauguration of Barack Obama.

Both senators responded and she received five tickets in the blue section and five in the silver section. In addition to her immediate family, she was able to offer tickets to a sister and brother and to the physician who had been commuting to Salina to help keep her practice going during her chemotherapy.

She waited in line for more than an hour to pick up her inauguration tickets at Republican Senator Brownback's office. When it was finally her turn, she handed his staff a handwritten thank you note. As she was leaving, the senator's chief of staff chased her down the stairs.

"Ginger, Ginger, wait!" he yelled. Once he caught up with her, he said, "Mrs. Brownback can't make it. Do you want her ticket? It's in the gold section."

"Of course!" she said as she hugged him.

At five a.m. on inauguration day, her phone rang and she was told to go to Senator Brownback's office. While her family and friends faced the challenges of an overwhelmed public transportation system and hours in the cold, Ginger drank coffee for two hours and called everybody she could think of.

While there, she asked the staff how she'd had the good fortune to be selected to receive Mrs. Brownback's ticket. A secretary told her the staff had been handing out tickets for two days to people who were often ungrateful and demanding. When she came in with her note, the staff quickly voted that she should be the one to receive the ticket that would put her fifty feet away from the swearing in of the country's first African-American president.

> *Nothing new can come into your life unless you open yourself up to being grateful for what you already have.*
> *— Rev. Michael Beckwith*

Ginger was diagnosed with cancer, yet she lived in gratitude. Why is it that you rarely meet a motivational speaker who doesn't have a horrific story of overcoming a challenge?

While an event that lands you flat on your back isn't required for insight, it's definitely easier to see the stars from there.

I would maintain that thanks are the highest form of thought, and that gratitude is happiness doubled by wonder.

G. K. Chesterton

Putting Gratitude for the Present into Practice

When you feel grateful, you become great and eventually attract great things.

Plato

Her name was Dana. She walked up to me after a talk at a child care conference years ago and said, "I love your idea of a Gratitude Partner, but I live in a small town. I'm not sure where I'd find..."

"Email me," I offered. "Every day — three new Gratitudes. I'll write you back with mine when I can."

Her middle name must have been Faithful. For the next seven years, I was the grateful recipient of the most delightful Gratitude lists in my in-box, such as:

I am grateful...

> *for the ability to yawn.*
> *for being able to teach my girls how to follow a recipe.*
> *for buttons.*

Your friend,
Dana

Through the years, I got to know and love this incredible woman. Dana shared that her daily Gratitudes improved her health, her daycare business and her marriage. I know they also brightened my life immeasurably.

> *You can't feel blessed and stressed at the same time.*
> *— Anonymous*

The Gratitude Richual

So your daily homework is simply to **share three Gratitudes each day, no repeats**, for the rest of your life (but only on the days you want to feel good).

If after reading this chapter you're still not completely convinced, do the math:

> **Question**: *What have you got to lose?*
>
> **Answer**: *Two minutes per twenty-four-hour period.*
>
> **Question**: *What have you got to gain?*
>
> **Answer**: *Enjoyment of the present while manifesting every dream and desire for the rest of your time on the planet.*

It's a tough decision.

I recall a gentleman at one of my seminars remarking, "I can't wait to use Gratitude when I get home." We all had a good laugh as he realized what he'd just said. Gratitude can only help us be happy *now*. It makes every moment a very "right" now.

> *If you're feeling off balance or like your heart is broken, I guarantee you that keeping a gratitude journal will change your life. I absolutely guarantee it.*
> *— Oprah Winfrey*

When to Say Thank You

And you don't have to stop after your morning Gratitudes. The other most important times to say thank you are before, during, and after everything!

Before: As High-Way 1 attests, getting to a grateful place for something *before you receive it* is the fastest way to manifest that very thing.

During: Anyone who has ever cooked a meal knows the wonderful feeling a simple thank you from someone enjoying it can bring. One of my favorite vacation memories was when Zach turned to me and said, "Mom, if I forget later, thanks for this fun time!"

After: Whether you just completed a job interview, just went to a movie with a friend, just paid your bills with your spouse, just finished a big project at work, or just raked the leaves with your kids, a word, a text or a note of thanks is a golden investment in the hearts of those you live and work with.

30 Days to the Gratitude Habit

Like any other wellness activity, gratitude is a habit. Most of us are more in the habit of complaining and finding fault than we are of affirming, but that can change in a matter of weeks.

Give yourself this goal, 30 days to the Gratitude Habit.

> *Find a Gratitude Partner that you can phone, text or email your three Gratitudes to each morning. (Decide if you will do it five or seven days a week.)*
>
> ***Or** ask your spouse, child or roommate to share Gratitudes with you each morning or evening in person.*
>
> ***Or** use a Gratitude white board and write your 3 Gratitudes for your entire family to see each day.*

I heard from a Mom who wanted to impart the importance of gratitude to her ten-year-old daughter. They started by sharing their Gratitudes at dinner each evening. Two weeks into the process, she sent me this email:

"MK, I wanted to let you know that when we were stuck in traffic for a long time last night, Amanda turned to me and said, 'Mom, let's do Gratitudes,' and we did! I'm overjoyed knowing that she now knows she can take charge of her attitude, no matter what the situation."

> *Once we begin to look for what's right, our lives begin spinning in unimaginably exciting new directions.*
> *— Pam Grout*

Note: I know folks who share their Gratitudes on Facebook for all the world to see. While this is an option, I would also find a more personal sharing partner for those Grats you would like to keep more private.

Gratitude Comes Home

Every time I certify a new group of ***8 to Great*** trainers, they start their own Gratitude Group. Some have been going strong for close to a decade. A few of these groups share something they're grateful for about themselves on the **first** of each month. It could be something like "I stayed calm while the baby was crying today" or "I'm really good at recruiting new folks into my Rotary Club," or "I'm resilient!"

You could also share what you're grateful for about your partner on the **second** day of each month. If you're a parent, you could make the day of the month that's **closest to their birthday** the day your Gratitudes are about them.

> *You say grace before meals. But I say grace before the concert and the opera, and grace before the play and pantomime, and grace before I open a book, and grace before sketching, painting, swimming, fencing, boxing, walking, playing, dancing, and grace before I dip the pen in the ink. — G.K. Chesterton*

The Cyrano Solution

It can bring a blush to admit what we appreciate and cherish about ourselves, but loving ourselves is an essential element of feeling good. I wouldn't include the following letter *that I wrote to myself* — one of the hardest parts of this book for me to share — if I weren't absolutely convinced of its power to heal brokenness, prepare us to be loved by others, and align with our highest selves.

I got the idea from my favorite French play, ***Cyrano De Bergerac***, by Edmond Rostand.

Dear MK,

Please let me introduce myself. I've been a fan of yours for a long time. I'm not yet ready to tell you my name, but I can tell you that I'm very interested in getting to know you better.

You see, I've been watching you for years. I've seen how you came into our church community, manifested an incredible choir for more than a decade, and then gracefully turned it over when it was your time to go. I've also watched you raise two fantastic children under sometimes less than ideal circumstances, loving them no matter what they did or didn't do.

I've seen you fend off naysayers and accomplish dreams like the TV segment, the radio show, the KidSing Competition, and the Gratitude Gathering. Now look at this wonderful new book. Thank you for all you do for so many. But more than what you do, I love who you are.

MK, I know this is a bit odd, writing you like this, but I'm not quite ready to reveal my identity. Think of me as one of your favorite literary heroes (I know this about you, too), your Cyrano, who will admire you from afar for just a bit longer. Believe me, I don't intend to stay incognito as long as he did with the fair Roxane.

And speaking of fair, you looked so beautiful today. I love those patchwork overalls of yours. You have such a distinctive style! And mostly, I love your beautiful eyes that light up when you smile.

I hope you'll allow me to write you again. It would give me such pleasure.

Sleep well, dearest one.
Cyrano

Take a risk and find out how wonderful it feels to have your own "inner-Cyrano." Write yourself a love letter the next time you want to soar to "95." (I promise I won't tell!)

> *Appreciation of self and others are the closest match to Divine energy in the universe. — Abraham-Hicks*

Gratitude Games

Once you find out how good gratitude feels, you may decide to invent games to encourage it. One young family wrote down their Gratitudes and put them in an empty tissue box, taking them out each Sunday night at their family meetings to read them aloud.

In our middle and high school ***8 to Great*** curriculum, **The Gratitude Drill** is a student favorite. The facilitator invites five volunteers to come forward and stand in a loose circle. Then, beginning with the person with the longest hair, each individual must come up with something they're grateful for in less than two seconds or they'll be "gonged" (or buzzed) back to their seat.

Again, no repeats. If the person to your right says "family," you may say "sister" but you may not say the word "family" or you'll be ousted from the circle. You may choose to give a prize to those still standing at the end, but however you select your winners, be sure to have lots of prizes. I've found young people are especially hard to get out in this game once they get the hang of it.

Another favorite of mine is **Oh, Look**. Pretend something that you've taken for granted wasn't working yesterday but is working today. You can pick something that hasn't been broken, pretend it was, then get excited about it working again. For example, you could say, "Oh, look! The refrigerator is working again!" or "Oh, look! A postal worker is leaving mail in our mailbox now!" or one of my favorites, "Oh, look! The sun is shining again!" It may sound silly, but it's lots of fun!

Be grateful for what you have; you'll end up having more. If you concentrate on what you don't have, you will never, ever have enough. — Oprah Winfrey

One of the first times we played this, my son was twelve. "Oh, look!" I shouted. "You can hear again, Zach!"

To which the smart aleck replied, "What'd you say?"

Q & A on Gratitude for the Present

Gratitude is not only the greatest of virtues, but the parent of all the others.

Cicero

Q: I've gone back to work and am very grateful for my kids and husband making the necessary sacrifices to make it all work. How can I let them know how grateful I am and be there for them during the time we have together?

A: In his wonderful book ***The Five Languages of Love,*** Gary Smalley points out that everyone speaks their own language when it comes to love and appreciation. Ask your family members if they feel appreciated most by your words, your quality time, your acts of service, your touch, or your gifts. They'll appreciate being asked. Then you can "speak" your appreciation to them in a way they'll clearly hear!

Q: How do I get my children to write thank you emails or notes?

A: I have two children who are very different in this regard. Although both were raised hearing regularly about the importance of gratitude, they each have their own way of expressing it. My daughter is excellent at writing a thoughtful card or email, or posting her gratitude to her husband or family members on Facebook, but you don't hear as many thanks from her verbally.

We can complain that roses have thorns or be grateful that thorns have roses. — Anonymous

On the other hand, while growing up, my son said, "Thanks Mom" an average of ten times a day, yet he's less likely to send a thank you email or card. I'm so proud of and grateful for both of them.

The best teaching in this regard is modeling. No matter their ages, write them (and your spouse) little thank you notes and leave them in surprise places. Their appreciation of your taking time to do that will remind them that they can help others feel that good as well.

Meanwhile, if you perceive that your children have become ungrateful, consider going camping, volunteering as a family at a local shelter or food kitchen, or traveling to a third world country. It will give them a new perspective on the abundance they are surrounded by each day. Having some, but not all of what we want is the human condition, and it's a condition worth giving thanks for.

Q: Where I work, our clients regularly call to complain. How are we supposed to deal with such unappreciative clients?

A: Right now, they're ungrateful for you and you're ungrateful for them. When you're ready to see real change, get into FGH. First, clean the slate from the past. Start expressing appreciation for the things your customers do right. For example, you could express gratitude for their asking for what they want from you, and that they've stuck with you all these years.

Are you starting every day with your three Gratitudes? Put your customers on your list. For example:

I'm grateful:

1. That my phone/internet works.
2. That I've trained my clients to expect only the best from me.
3. That I'm learning not to let other people own my attitude.

Q: It seems that very young children don't need to be taught gratitude. At what age do you suggest starting gratitude activities?

A: It can be seamless. As your children hear you and your spouse share Gratitudes aloud (every time you get in a car, for example), it will be a game they'll want to play and will rarely tire of!

If you count all your assets you'll always show a profit.
— Robert Quillen

One Mom of two young boys was exasperated by their constant fighting. When it just got too loud, she'd walk into the room and yell "Gimme three!" She required them to say three things they were grateful for, and the final one needed to be *about their brother*!

She shared with me that after weeks of this, the boys never hesitated, and almost seemed relieved to do it. What absolutely melted her heart was the day she heard a ruckus and was heading toward the living room when she heard the older son say to the younger one, "Gimme three!" That is, to this day, one of my all-time favorite **Gratitude for the Present** stories.

Another is this story of a four-year-old sent by his young mother:

Noah is just getting to the point where I'll let him play outside alone. The other day — one of those beautiful blue-sky Indian summer days we've had — I peeked out the window to check on him. He was under the biggest tree in our yard. He had his arms stretched out, head thrown back, and he was singing and dancing. I could just barely make out the words. He was making up a song to the sky. I watched, wishing I had my phone to record it, but knowing that if I interrupted him, the moment would be gone. When he finished, I opened the door and asked what he was doing.

> *"I'm singing to the sky."*
>
> *"How does that song go, Sweetheart?"*
>
> *"It's over."*

Let us be like little children and embrace this moment with gratitude, before it's gone.

Life is not measured by the number of breaths we take, but by the moments that take our breath away.

Vicki Corona

8

High-Way 8: FGH: Hope for the Future

The Power of Surrender

Defining Hope for the Future

Don't worry about the world coming to an end today...

It's already tomorrow in Australia.

Charles Schultz

When I first started teaching the High-Ways, I defined **Hope for the Future** as "Having Only Positive Expectation." However, it soon became clear that there was even more, because that definition was so close to High-Way 1, and **Get the Picture** is not the antidote to despair that Hope is. I continued to be open to discovering the distinction between High-Ways 1 and 8, but after months and months of sitting at my computer waiting for inspiration, the answer wasn't coming.

I needed to finish this book, and move onto other projects, so I became frantic. Why wasn't this chapter coming to me as clearly as the others? Occasionally I would feel myself freezing up with fear. I could still do 100 Gratitudes at a sitting because I had my children, friends, family, freedom, health, and the 8 High-Ways process. I was still taking risks, staying out of Blaming and Complaining, and feeling all my feelings, yet I could sense myself losing hope. I had dreamt big, but it wasn't helping me feel better. I was spent.

Meanwhile, I had many well-meaning friends and advisors telling me what to do. Their "shoulds" only added to the din of my own. What I needed wasn't advice — I needed Hope. One day, it came to me, sweetly, during a morning phone conversation.

"You'll be successful, sweetie. Look, you've done everything right so far. Your project will be a huge success." Even as I write this, tears come to my eyes as I remember the relief I felt from my sister's reassuring words. She knew everything about me — my past victories and my recent challenges. Her words helped lift the cloud of self-judgment I'd been living under. Every time I repeated them to myself, I could breathe deeper.

Clarity rose in me like the sun that day. I began to understand that **Get the Picture** and **Hope for the Future** both require Positive Expectation, but that Hope included an aspect that only B.I.G. (Bold, Innovative, and Grand) dreamers need. The closest word I've found to describe the distinction is that Hope requires ***surrender*** — releasing attachment to the outcome.

To-do list for today: Inhale. Exhale.
— As seen on a college dorm bulletin board

B.I.G. Dreamers

Every hero, ancient or modern, could tell you of their journey through their dark nights.

We must accept finite disappointment, but we must never lose infinite hope.

Dr. Martin Luther King, Jr.

In the midst of winter,

I finally learned that there was in me an invincible summer.

Albert Camus

Optimism is the faith that leads to achievement.
Nothing can be done without hope and confidence.

Helen Keller

Hope is being able to see that there is light despite all of the darkness.

Desmond Tutu

I've learned from studying great men and women that *goal setters* don't need Hope because they have a roadmap of when, where, and how. Only B.I.G. dreamers who find themselves wandering in the desert looking for the Promised Land need it to fend off despair.

In this High-Way, we won't discuss ways to handle depression or the blues; we did that in High-Way 4: **Feel All Your Feelings**. Depression is of the mind and heart. Despair is of the spirit and soul.

Despair only happens on the way to our biggest dreams when our Positive Expectation starts to wane. When we ask, "Will it ever come?" or cry out in self-judgment, "What am I doing wrong?" we need to remember that we haven't done anything wrong. In fact, we are right where we need to be.

Hope for the Future and Get the Picture

To understand these two High-Ways better:

High-Way 1: Get the Picture - Asking and Believing

To review, **Get the Picture** is about learning to believe — thinking a thought until we can feel what its reality will be like. It's an *active* step that asks that we take time to visualize and have fun imagining our dream's manifestation.

I recall the day I announced to my office team at our annual meeting that I'd love to host a weekly call-in radio show. We talked about it for five minutes and I was even more excited when we finished. Once we broke for lunch, I checked my voice messages. The largest radio station in the state had left me a message, asking if I wanted to host a weekly call-in show. I asked, I believed, and I quickly received. That's the power of **Get the Picture.**

High-Way 1: Get the Picture is closer to...

Positive Expectation — **feeling the excitement of the final outcome**

Confidence — **the assurance that the Laws of the Universe work every time**

Visualization — **seeing the end result play out in your mind**

Imagining — **pretending that what you ask for has already arrived**

High-Way 8: Hope for the Future is closer to...

Trust — **the faith that there *is* an answer, even if it's not obvious at the moment**

Surrender — **yielding to the guidance of a person, Higher Power or process**

Openness — **relaxing into the now and allowing whatever shows up**

Time-Out — **taking a break from doing or "trying" in order to regroup and refresh**

> *If you want to have radical results, you must begin by displaying one the greatest human attributes — the ability to be humble enough to let go of the reins and hand them over. — Debbie Ford*

Letting Your Dream Find You

When all my visualizing wasn't feeling good, it was because my Positive Expectations were trying to survive amid my "struggle" mentality. I needed to relax and open up to allowing. When the process of following a dream feels painful, and we're looking too hard for answers, we simply need to stop and let our answers find us.

The Hope for the Future Process:

When hope is all you have, it's all you need.

Anonymous

In order to move into **Hope for the Future** we have to open ourselves to possibilities. To illustrate this process, connect your middle fingers and thumbs to make an "O" with your hands. Now imagine asking to receive a watermelon. The catch is that, whatever you request, in this case, a watermelon, has to pass through that "O" to get to you. Obviously, it's not going to happen, because you're not open enough for it.

Now make a new "O," this time by stretching both arms in front of you and interlacing your fingers. (This opening should be about the size of a basketball hoop.) What would happen if you asked for that watermelon now? It would slip into your life with ease. This is the gift that **Hope for the Future** offers. To be a successful B.I.G. dreamer, we have to be open enough and patient enough to let our magnificent dreams come through when they're ready.

Surrender isn't passive. It is the most active, assertive, creative, intelligent response we can make to any moment. — Dan Millman

Asking and Letting Go

When our biggest dreams don't manifest when we expect them to, we can get frustrated. Before we get too deep in despair, we must move into **Hope for the Future**, letting go of our need to control and our attachment to the outcome. When we free our dreams to come to us however and whenever it's time, like the release of a balloon, we find ourselves freed, as well.

The glorious "aha" of this process is that we are not surrendering *what* we want or *why* we want it. We are, however, letting go of the how, when, where, and who. The day we release and let go is the day we sleep better, laugh harder, and live more fully in the moment.

Going Along for the Ride

Once you move into **Hope for the Future**, it means you're letting something bigger than you, such as God, your counselor, or the Law of Attraction, do the driving. Once you've set your intention (decided on a "what"), you can let go of the steering wheel, move into a passenger seat, and get grateful for the scenery out your window.

Everyone has heard of the couple who "tried everything" to get pregnant, then finally decided to adopt, only to be surprised with a pregnancy shortly thereafter. The same universal law applies here. When you can't focus on a dream without stressing, *stop focusing on it altogether*, go enjoy the rest of your life, and stay in feelings of appreciation.

Pathways to Surrender

Surrender can take many forms. Four paths I've used and seen others use successfully are:

1. Stop and refocus
2. Trust a person or a process
3. Get playful
4. Get quiet

1. Stop and Refocus

I've learned the hard way that when I've done "all I can," and the end is still not in sight, I need to stop doing. Trying "one more thing" may result in my burning out or getting sick. Once we come to the point of surrendering our dreams, it's time to refocus our efforts in another direction, or, as the TV character Tony Soprano was known to say, "Forget about it."

There's a perfect example of this surprising road to success in a recent chapter in American history.

"At the age of forty," a politician reflected, "I began feeling the way I imagine an actor or athlete must feel when, after years of commitment to a particular dream, he realizes that he's gone just about as far as talent or fortune would take him. The dream will not happen, and he now faces the choice of accepting this fact, or refusing the truth and ending up bitter.

"I refocused on my work. I spent more time at home and properly cherished my wife, exercised, and read novels. It was this acceptance, I think, that allowed me to come up with the thoroughly cockeyed idea of running for the United States Senate. One last shot to test out my ideas before I settled into a calmer, more stable existence."

After releasing attachment to the "where" "when" and "how" of this young man's dream, it was revived. He held press conferences that no one attended and drove for hours to small towns to find two or three people waiting for him around a kitchen table. But he was not deterred. He had asked, believed, and let go. What followed, was that, through a series of surprising events, he won his senate seat that year. The dream of political success came back to find Barack Obama.

> *We've been warned against offering the people of this nation false hope. But in the unlikely story that is America, there has never been anything false about hope. — Barack Obama*

2. Trust a Person or a Process

Another way to surrender the outcome is to trust a coach. Over the years I've seen half a dozen friends surrender to their AA sponsors. Sometimes their sponsors said, "Don't date him, you're not ready," or "Take that job for now." My friends' willingness to turn over the reins to another person during the first years of their recovery has been a source of inspiration to me.

My very first life coach began our initial session with, "Are you willing to be coached?" I knew my answer would commit me to her guidance. I also knew that resistance would come up at some pivotal point and I'd have to decide to surrender to her wisdom or withdraw. Knowing all that, as soon as I said "Yes," I relaxed. I felt safe and at peace. That is the gift of trust.

Just as we can let a person lead us to a new place, faith in a *process* can also take us to our dreams. I have seen that coachability is the most important factor when taking women through my ***8 to Your IdealWeight*** program. I remind them that more than "willpower," it is "willingpower" that will make the difference in their success. Even while we're thinking to ourselves "this will never work," following a proven process is, in itself, surrender.

> *Sometimes it's holding on that makes one strong; sometimes it's letting go. — Sylvia Robinson*

Trust is Not Blind

The most effective Coaches offer us processes. While trust in that person or process is key, when hearing their coaching, be sure that it does not compromise your values.

Speaking of values, I always have a coach in my life in one area or another. I recently had an excellent business coach who began our process taking me through a clarification of my company's Core Values. It was a powerful process I highly recommend. Ours spell COACH and they stand to this day:

Courage ***(High-Way #2)***

Ownership ***(High-Ways #1 and #3)***

Attitude ***(High-Ways #6, #7 and #8)***

Coachability ***(Everyone at every level must be coachable.)***

Honest and Open Communication ***(High-Ways #4 and #5)***

Coachability is another way to say, "The ability to hear opinions of others and be open to change." Surrendering to any process or Coach, whether to grow a business, find your soul mate, or break your sugar addiction, opens us to allowing. We stop second-guessing ourselves. Faith in your sponsor/coach/trainer/counselor/program becomes a kind of compass to your ultimate success. *Giving up* is synonymous with losing Hope and does not feel good. *Giving over* is finding Hope, and once we surrender to it, it feels wonderful.

> *The creative process is a process of surrender, not control. — Julia Cameron*

My Cowboy Coach

Although depression has never visited me for long, I've had to face despair more than once. I vividly recall being so frustrated one afternoon that I threw down an issue of Oprah's magazine, thinking the last thing I needed was advice! It fell open to an article about Miraval Resort in Tucson and a man named Wyatt Webb. The article explained how he helped people discern their next steps in life by teaching them to work with horses. The idea fascinated me, and the next day I signed up to go.

That first morning at Miraval, Wyatt allowed each of us to choose a horse to work with. "Just remember," he drawled in a throaty voice that revealed decades of ranch life, "whatever challenges come up, and there's always challenges, it's not about the horse."

During my stay, I worked with Wyatt three times. I cleaned hooves next to Hollywood film producers, dancers from the New York City Ballet, butchers, bankers and veterinarians. The faces changed, but each morning I saw how we all had to learn to trust our coach and be in the moment. If we didn't, we couldn't get our 1,200-pound animals to acknowledge us, let alone give up their hooves for cleaning.

The lessons that came up were unique to each individual. For one man who couldn't seem to get the horse to lift its hoof, it meant admitting he was afraid of those "bigger" than he was. As soon as he faced his fear, the horse cooperated.

For the ballerina, it meant acknowledging her fear that she'd "get the steps (of cleaning the hooves) wrong" and look like fool. Again, the horse applauded her courage of coming clean by allowing her to clean his hooves.

For me, it was admitting that a part of me wanted the horse to like me, and that I didn't want to upset him or make him uncomfortable. As soon as I figured that out, I liked *myself* better and was able to get the job done.

Our biggest challenge wasn't our animals — it was surrendering to Wyatt's coaching. Once we trusted him with our safety and psyches, insight and renewed hope were our rewards.

> *Anyone who really wants to know who they are has to travel to uncharted territories all the time. So that kind of person has to live in a world of "I don't know," which is scary, but that's the only place you learn anything.*
> *— Wyatt Webb*

One of my favorite stories from Wyatt's first book, ***It's Not About the Horse***, was of an angry young man who hated his horse — just like he hated his life. He tried for half an hour to get the horse to budge and finally gave up, walked away, and began to weep. At that point, the horse walked up behind him and nuzzled his neck. That's what surrender looks like.

3. Get Playful

Hope relaxes us into an "I've got nothing to lose by asking" mentality. Here again, even when we don't believe, as long as we don't *not* believe, we are still open to receiving.

> *The difference between an optimist and a pessimist is that an optimist laughs to forget, but a pessimist forgets to laugh. — Tom Bodett*

Sometimes when my friends and I get playful, we put our dreams in an imaginary pink bubble, blow them out the window, and then forget about them. Every January 1st we write one intention on a white rock and set it on a bookshelf. Sometimes we throw "Come as You Will Be" parties, where we write our dreams-come-true on paper, attach them to our backs to be read by the other guests, and treat everyone at the party as their future version of themselves. When dreaming is fun, it's amazing how quickly dreams manifest.

Just as thoughts become things, stress becomes strings. Thinking about your dreams with no strings attached (expectations) is a glorious way to watch your fun become your future.

4. Get Quiet

Another powerful form of surrender is getting quiet. Go on a retreat if you need to, but stop giving, talking and doing — just be still and receive. We think of "being still" as stopping movement of our physical body, but that's just the beginning. A more challenging and rewarding stillness is when we stop our mental runnings-around. We do this, not by trying *not to think*, but by focusing on something so relaxing or boring to the brain that it just rests. That focus could be our breath, a candle flame, a mantra, or for my Dear Mom, the decades of a rosary.

More and more studies are showing that when we're in a meditative state, we stop aging, our immune functions increase, our pulse slows down, and our mind get a much-needed rest. That's on the physical plane. On an internal plane, we're like cork on a beautiful ocean of love and bliss, and we naturally float to the top of the Power Pyramid. Check out the look in a newborn baby's eyes. We were born blissing.

> *Ten minutes of meditation won't make you a better multi-tasker, there's no such thing, but it will make you more adept at switching tasks and returning to a deep level of concentration more quickly. — Daniel Goleman*

Giving Up vs. Giving Over

Remember the story of Abraham and Sarah in the Old Testament? They were in their 90's and yet held out Hope of having children. Miraculously, Sarah conceived and bore a son named Isaac.

Now let's fast forward to when Isaac was a young boy. One day in a dream, Abraham was told to sacrifice his only son to God. With the heaviest of hearts, father and son headed up the mountain. Once they reached the top, Abraham prepared an altar where the sacrifice would take place. Then, just at the moment when he lifted his knife in anguish, an angel reached out and stopped his hand, honoring his obedience to God, telling him he would be greatly rewarded. Father and son rejoiced and headed back down the mountain, and Abraham became the father of nations.

Whether you believe this story to be true physically or metaphysically, this story is our story. Like Abraham and Sarah, you have a dream — a big one. So big, in fact, that perhaps you haven't told anyone about it because you don't want to take any teasing.

Then one day you get a piece of your dream and start thinking, "This is great. Now I can do this and that and... " when suddenly, your dream seems to be taken away from you, and it looks as if it's the end of the road. At that moment, you have two options — give up (quit) or give over (surrender). When you do the latter, as Abraham did, you release your need to have something go your way in order to stay hopeful of the eventual outcome.

> *I know the plans I have for you. Plans of fullness, not of harm, to give you a future and a hope. — Jeremiah 29:11*

Once you release any bitterness about not receiving the original dream on your schedule, that is often when it comes back to you tenfold, or in Abraham's case, through generations of ancestors "as numerous as the stars."

Surrender vs. Submission — The Story of Ryan Vogelsong

Submission is the act of giving *up* and often results in tears of sorrow. Surrender is the act of giving *over* and often results in tears of relief.

As you can tell, I am an absolute nut for the sweet sport of baseball, and one of my favorite stories is about a gentleman who kept my Kansas City Royals team from a World Series win.

In October 2010, Ryan Vogelsong was 32 years old. He and his wife, Nicole, had a one-year-old son. He had had a very undistinguished major league career to that point, playing for short stints in San Francisco, Pittsburgh, Philadelphia, and Los Angeles, as well as *ten* different minor league teams in as many cities. He had even played in Japan for three full seasons when no contracts playing for U.S. teams were offered.

When the Los Angeles Angels released him that October, his father-in-law was very ill and Ryan had a decision to make. He asked his wife how she would feel if he "gave it one more try" in the Venezuelan Winter League playing for the *Tiburones de La Guaira*. He had **surrendered** his dream of making it big and just wanted to go out on a good note. "I think I have one more season in me," he told his wife.

She told him to go. He pitched well while there and the San Francisco Giants noticed his improved performance. They signed him onto one of their minor league teams, and after just two months, called him up to the Giants due to one of their pitcher's injuries. The following year he did so well he was selected for the 2011 All Star Team. When he described playing on a team with many of his childhood heroes, he said "It was like a dream."

In 2012, the Giants won the World Series in large part due to the four games he pitched.

He was also instrumental in helping the Giants win another World Series against the Royals in 2014. Meanwhile, he was awarded the coveted Willie Mac Award, given annually to the Giant who best exemplifies team spirit and leadership.

Over the years, Ryan Vogelsong became one of the Giants' all-time fan favorites. He retired at the age of thirty-nine, one week before this book went to press, having been released by the Minnesota Twins. But before he retired, the Giants signed Ryan to a ***one-day contract*** so he could take the mound one last time to a sustained standing ovation and officially retire from baseball as a San Francisco Giant. Only one other Giants player had ever received such an honor.

Ryan Vogelsong's "song" was a melody of hope, and his rewards are a testament to its power.

> *I was set free because my greatest fear had been realized, and I still had an old typewriter and a big idea. Rock bottom became a solid foundation on which I built my life. — J.K. Rowling*

Hope and the Darkest Night

Hope knows there is a light, even in the darkest night. The five-year-old son of a friend of mine once asked his mom, "Mom, what is night for?"

His wise mother replied, "So we can begin new all over again the next day."

I loved her answer, and I would add this: It's also so that we can rest in "not doing," trusting that the sun will rise again and, in the meantime, see the beauty of the stars.

> *Develop the spirit of surrender. You will then experience bliss. — Sri Sathya Sai Baba*

Why We Don't Practice Hope for the Future

Hope is both the earliest and the most indispensable virtue inherent in the state of being alive.

Erik H. Erikson

It's rare to meet any person who hasn't lost hope at some point on their journey. The reasons are many.

We Worry

I once met a school administrator who, when I asked him what his dream was, answered, "A day with no worries!" Worry felt bigger than he was, and, from his well-intentioned viewpoint, he felt he was responsible for fixing all the problems of his staff and students. Unfortunately, his health was beginning to suffer. The good news is, the only thing we are responsible for fixing is our focus.

Worry is a form of fear, and fear is near the bottom of the Power Pyramid. Yet according to **Emotional Intelligence** author Daniel Goleman, some of us have come to believe that worry wards off danger "like a magical amulet." We have convinced ourselves that worrying about something will stop it from happening — but nothing could be further from the truth. Worry actually makes our problems grow.

So what are you growing in *your* worry garden? Is it...

- ✓ *bills*
- ✓ *the fluctuating job market*
- ✓ *fear about your childrens' safety*
- ✓ *your health problems*
- ✓ *natural disasters*
- ✓ *making the wrong decision*
- ✓ *running out of time*

If what we think about we bring about, worry is using our imagination to **Get the Picture** of something we do not want! And not only does worry not feel good, being *worried about* feels almost as bad.

What are our options? The FGH formula reminds us to simply get grateful. Unplug from thoughts of what awful things could happen and plug into something you are thankful for. What else could you focus on rather than worry?

The list is endless: pet your dog, pet your cat, put on your favorite song, put on your favorite outfit, call a friend, call a radio show, take a nap, take a hike, change the channel, change your hairstyle, volunteer at a shelter, volunteer at a hospital, run a race, run for office, play eighteen holes, play the drums, write a song, write a blog, hug your kids, hug a tree…

In other words, focus on anything that feels good.

The late Zig Ziglar often asked his audiences, "What percentage of what we worry about do we have any control over?" His answer was .06 percent! We could not make a poorer investment.

A Worry-Free Parent

Many of us have bought into the belief that the more we worry, the more we care. It is a belief that does not serve us and can eventually seriously harm us. On the other hand, take a moment to think of someone you know who *doesn't* worry much. How do you perceive them? Do you label them as irresponsible and selfish or as relaxed and happy?

A counselor friend of mine learned an antidote to worry from his dad when he was eight. He overheard his father talking to their neighbor at the feed store in their farming community.

"Well, aren't you worried about it?" he heard the neighbor ask.

"Heck, no. Not my problem," said his father.

"Then whose is it?"

"I got a man who does that. I hired him awhile back to do all my worrying for me. I just don't have time for such nonsense."

My friend remembered that conversation as he got older, and he still uses his father's clever wisdom in his counseling career today.

We Doubt Ourselves

> *There's nothing more dreadful than the habit of doubt. It is a thorn that irritates; it is a sword that kills. — Buddha*

Another sign that we could use a heap of Hope is when we're doubting ourselves. Here's how it often happens:

We start to manifest wonderful things. One day we notice that something we've asked for hasn't arrived yet.

Which leads to our starting to doubt ourselves

Which pulls us further down the Power Pyramid

Which slows down what we've asked for

Which gives us more reason to doubt

Which pulls us further down the Power Pyramid, etc.

Ask yourself: "Where has doubt ever gotten me?"

The answer is, to the same place as worry — nowhere. I once heard: "If you're going to doubt it, don't do it. If you're going to do it, don't doubt it." I say, if you must doubt, *doubt your doubts*.

We Don't Understand Failure/Feedback

Sometimes we use failure in a business or a relationship as our excuse for doubting ourselves. What's needed in that case is a reframing of failure. Successful and happy people often refer to it as "feedback." There are four options every time we experience failure/feedback:

- ✓ *We can choose B.C. and blame our failure/feedback on others.*
- ✓ *We can busy ourselves enough to run from (ignore) the failure/feedback.*
- ✓ *We can let shame prevent forward movement, feeling as if we're "wrong."*
- ✓ *We can take Full Responsibility for the failure/feedback, learn from it, and use it as a springboard to move forward.*

Only with the last option can the feedback free us.

Sara the CEO

Sara Blakeley wasn't exceptional by many standards. As a young woman, at first she wanted to become a lawyer, but when she failed the LSAT, she realized she wanted to try her hand at business. Five years later, though she was making an adequate living selling copiers door-to-door, Sara got an idea for a new company. Even though she'd never taken a single business course, she knew all about failure/feedback.

While growing up, her father encouraged his children to risk by asking at dinner each night, "What did you fail at today?" If they hadn't failed at anything, he was disappointed. "I'd sometimes come home and tell Dad that I had tried out for something and had failed miserably, and he'd actually high-five me," Sara said in an interview.

Sara followed her dream. Today she's the CEO of Spanx, a multi-million-dollar undergarment business.

"If I hadn't failed the LSAT, I'd have been a lawyer and there'd be no Spanx," Sara said with a smile. "I now believe that failure is nothing more than life's way of nudging you. My attitude toward failure isn't attached to outcome, but to not trying. It's been liberating for me. Most people attach the idea of failure to something that doesn't work out or to how people perceive them, but seeing failure in this way is about answering to myself."

When asked if she ever wanted to give up, Sara replied, "I don't think one person told me that Spanx was a workable idea until two years after I began pursuing it. At times I stopped for a while out of discouragement, but I never lost confidence in the fact that it was a good idea."

Like almost all BIG dreamers, she lost her way but never lost her hope.

> *My life has been a series of endless crises... most of which never happened. — Mark Twain*

We Deny That We're Discouraged

Today Sara shares candidly on talk shows about the days when she was discouraged. BIG dreamers know that discouragement is just part of the menu you're going to sample along the way. Imagine trying to talk a woman giving birth out of feeling her labor pains. Her screaming would only intensify. Discouragement is a stepping stone toward surrender. Rather than deny it, we can accept that we feel what we feel.

Impatience and Hope

Have you been reading along and wondering when I'm ever going to deal with impatience? The most impatient readers have. We all get impatient from time to time, and from that lower place on the Power Pyramid, we often manifest "right now" rather than "right."

I recall reading an article about how many delays the original ***Star Wars*** film had, how over budget it was, how many people (including members of the crew) thought it was a kids' movie and had no faith in it, and how it almost got canceled at the last minute because it was so overdue. When it was finally released, only thirty-seven theaters in the entire U.S. agreed to show it.

Director George Lucas had stuck to his guns. He had a choice between getting it right or turning it in right now. George released ***Star Wars*** five months later than promised because he chose *right.* The result was the first film in history to gross one billion dollars in just twelve days.

> *Most damn fools quit on the one-yard line, one foot before the winning touchdown, one minute before the end of the game. — Ross Perot*

We Get Tired

When people ask if it's truly "darkest before the dawn," I say no, but it is coldest before the dawn. We give up so close to the finish line because we don't know how close we really are. The final mountain we climb on the way to our dream seems steeper because we're just plain tired.

There was a college science professor who, when explaining stress management to his students, raised a glass of water and asked his students, "How heavy is this glass of water?" Answers ranged from 20g to 500g.

The professor replied, "The absolute weight doesn't matter. It depends on how long you try to hold it. If I hold it for a minute, that's not a problem. If I hold it for an hour, I'll have an ache in my right arm. If I try and hold it for a day, you'll have to call an ambulance. In each case, the water weighs the same, but the longer I hold it, the heavier it becomes."

He continued, "That's the way it is with stress. If we try to carry our burdens day after day, sooner or later, they will become too heavy. It's crucial to our success to put down our burdens and rest awhile before picking them up again. When we're refreshed, we can carry on."

To surrender is to release working on our dreams, resting in the knowledge that there is a reason, a purpose, and a Divine Order to life.

Our Hopeless Habits

Years ago I realized that optimists believe that *ill* fortune is temporary, a fluke, and that it will pass, while pessimists believe that *good* fortune is temporary, a fluke, and that it will pass. As the marvelous work of author Martin Seligman attests, both are right some of the time, but optimists are happier, healthier, and statistically much more successful in the long run.

> *While writing **Eat Pray Love**, I fell into one of those pits of despair that we all fall into, and I started thinking "I should just dump this project." — Elizabeth Gilbert*

So what do you do if you've played the cynic over the years, debating everyone you can find to "prove" that hope is hopeless? It can feel like an overwhelming challenge to break your mold. Begin right now to forgive yourself for your pessimistic pontifications. Then you can be grateful that you now get to choose what to believe. Just as you un-learned that black cats are bad luck, you can unlearn a pessimistic attitude. One way of thinking may be how you were raised as a child, the other will be how you will raise your children.

The House of Surrender

There came a day when I realized that surrender and Hope are good friends who live together in a serene and quiet place on a mountain. It's a place any of us can go when we've exhausted our reserves and resources. We simply leave the busy doer that we usually are behind and climb to this place to listen and wait.

How long do most people stay there? It depends. The hardest part is simply admitting you're there, but then one day your resistance and denial disappear and you accept that you're right where you need to be. Time begins to pass easily and effortlessly. One day may be spent just breathing, another watching the clouds change shapes, and still another studying the beauty of your hands.

Then one day, when you least expect it and don't even have a pen handy, inspiration will hit you like a lightning bolt. "Oh, my gosh! It's so clear," you'll say to yourself. "How could I have missed it?"

You thank your hosts and head back down the mountain — into a time of focused and intensely creative activity. This chapter is for anyone who has been afraid to scale the mountain of surrender fearing that it was a valley in disguise. Those of us who have been there before you honor your process.

> *So what I have to keep telling myself when I get really psyched out is, "Don't be afraid. Just continue to show up." — Elizabeth Gilbert*

Hope for the Future Success Stories

Hope begins in the dark, the stubborn hope that if you just show up and try to do the right thing, the dawn will come.

Anne Lamott

The Rudy Reality

If you haven't seen the true story movie ***Rudy***, I encourage you to do so. If you have, answer this question: "Did Rudy ever quit?"

Very few of my seminar participants answer that question correctly. Re-watch the film and you'll see that on the biggest day of his life, Rudy didn't show up for football practice. When confronted by his custodian friend, he said, "I quit." When asked why, he said, "I wanted to prove that I was somebody."

His friend let him have it, saying, *"You're so full of crap. You're five feet nothin' and you hung in with the best college team in the land for two years. And you're also gonna walk out of here with a degree from the University of Notre Dame. In this lifetime you don't have to prove nothin' to nobody except yourself, and after what you've gone through, if you haven't done that by now, it ain't gonna never happen."*

Rudy did dress for the final game of his senior year at Notre Dame. What happened as a result of his not giving up, is that he received an honor that has not been given before or since to another Norte Dame player.

> *I overcame my nightmares because of my dreams.*
> *— Jonas Salk*

Meanwhile, there was a behind-the-scenes story on the set of that film. The man who played that custodian — actor Charles Dutton — was an ex-con who had spent seven years in prison. While behind bars, he started to **Get the Picture** of being in movies, and to date he has acted in more than thirty feature films and has won an Emmy.

The Rudy Reality is that most of the greats had a time when it would have "made sense" to give up. When Rudy trusted his friend, his surrendering took him into the end zone.

Kurtis, the Checkout Boy

I love sharing the story of a young man from my own high school who had high expectations for himself as a football player. After college, he tried out for the Green Bay Packers and to his delight, Kurtis was signed as a free agent — only to be cut five weeks later.

> *Disappointment is nothing but taking score too soon.*
> *— Abraham-Hicks*

Kurtis still had the love of his life (his girlfriend, Brenda) and the love of her two kids. One of them had been dropped by his birth father when he was four months old and had suffered severe brain damage, but Kurtis loved the child as his own.

He stayed open to life and hope, and three years after being released from the Packers, he prepared for his marriage to Brenda and another NFL tryout — this time with the Chicago Bears. The wedding was wonderful, but while on their honeymoon, Kurtis was bitten on his throwing arm by a venomous spider and wasn't able to perform at the tryout.

Fighting off despair, he went to the European league for a few months until he was picked up by the Rams as their third string quarterback. Two years later, when quarterback Trent Green was injured, Kurtis Warner stepped onto the field — and into the history books. He threw for a record 414 yards in Super Bowl XXXIV and was voted Most Valuable Player. In 2017, he was voted into the NFL Hall of Fame. For those who want to know where BIG dreams and Hope can take you, the first words of Kurt Warner's acceptance speech tell the story:

"I remember the moment I visualized this event for the first time (being inducted into the NFL Hall of Fame). Growing up, my Sundays were spent watching every game I could find on TV. Then I'd grab my "jersey," a t-shirt, and pull out the masking tape, write the last name of the star of that day's game, and put it on my back. Then I'd head outside to re-enact my version of the games. One afternoon, that all changed. I went through all the regular player suspects until I finally settled on one. It would be the first time I wore a jersey with this name on it, and the last name I ever wore on my jersey."

W-A-R-N-E-R. I'll never forget writing it the first time. A few little letters changed everything.

Kurt Warner

Expecting vs. Wanting

Kurt Warner didn't just want to play pro football – he expected to. Wanting is very different from expectation. When a woman wants to have a child, there's a longing which can, over time, get mixed with sadness if not realized. Once she's "expecting," even though her manifestation isn't fully realized, she has the excitement from knowing what's coming. With practice, we can get to expectation about anything our hearts desire.

Waiting Bells

Everyone who knew Katie knew that she'd been expecting "him" to show up all her life. She had just turned 48, and had never married when she found herself on her knees one Sunday after Mass, talking to God, again, about finding a husband.

"Okay, God," said Katie, "I know I'm supposed to be patient. I know he's out there looking for me, too, and I know that he'll come and find me when he's ready...but dear God, isn't he about ready?"

Two weeks later Randy Lee moved to town, and two years later I sang at Katie's wedding. Randy was her perfect match. While she'd been running major department stores, he'd been managing an island for a cruise line. While she'd been living her faith in a world that often nodded condescendingly, he'd been working for an orphanage in Mexico. They both loved God, family, and the outdoors in that order, and neither had ever married. Perhaps the biggest thing they had in common was they'd both surrendered their dreams, believing that faith was enough to find true love in a very small town in northern Minnesota.

These "Losers" Won Big

When teachers share ***8 to Great*** in schools, they give students a quiz. It's one they know the students will have trouble with because they never guess that:

- ✓ *J.K. Rowling was on government assistance (the British version of welfare) when she sold her first Harry Potter book. At this printing, she's the second wealthiest woman in the world.*
- ✓ *Einstein was expelled from high school at the age of fifteen for poor academic performance.*
- ✓ *The Beatles were told by Decca Records that they should get a "real" job because guitar groups were on the way out.*
- ✓ *Franklin D. Roosevelt flunked out of law school.*
- ✓ *Mother Teresa had dozens of articles written about her accusing her of crimes.*
- ✓ *Oprah had run away from home a number of times when her mother tried to put her in a detention home, but all the beds were filled and she was sent home.*

Hope on the High-Ways

Sometimes our intuition can be our coach. I'll never forget the time my mom and I took a special road trip, just the two of us. I was a first-year high school teacher and wanted to scope out the Minneapolis Children's Theater for a possible field trip with my students. She said she'd love to join me, so off we went to the Twin Cities, except that both of us thought the other one was bringing a map! (In the days before GPS...)

The interstate got us to the edge of the metropolis but we faced dozens of choices as we approached the downtown area.

For whatever reason, I turned to Mom as we were barreling down the freeway and said, "We're gonna follow that white car. She looks like she knows where she's going." Mom wasn't convinced of my plan, but having none of her own, she just laughed and agreed. Our spirits were high as we continued on our adventure.

As the little car took one exit after another, it started to get dark, so we decided that if we passed a motel, we'd stop. Fifteen minutes later, we saw a cute little motel. The next morning, ready to continue our quest, we headed to the check-in desk.

"Excuse me," I began. "We've come to Minneapolis to visit the children's theater. Would you know where it's located?" The woman behind the counter looked at me like I was from Mars as I continued, "I'm not sure of the name of it, but it's world-renowned. Have you ever heard of it?"

With a sly smile, the woman walked over to the front window and pulled back the curtain.

"You mean this one?"

There, across the street, was the Minneapolis Children's Theatre.

Most people never run far enough on their first wind to find out they've got a second. Give your dreams all you've got and you'll be amazed at the energy that comes out.
— William James

Finding My Writing Assistant

I could have given up hope in finding the perfect person to help me write this book, but because I didn't, I was blessed with one of my life's greatest gifts.

That first year, I placed ads in the newspaper three times for a part-time writing assistant. However, I go at quite a pace and the first two assistants I hired told me they couldn't keep up. I was grateful for their input, but knew I couldn't change who I was, so I simply ran the ad again, believing "the one" was out there.

Worrying does not take away tomorrow's troubles. It takes away today's peace. — Anonymous

The third time, the first resume I read was Tessa's. With her journalism background and the fact that she'd worked on film crews (think: handling high-maintenance individuals) she was a shoo-in.

The part I remember most about her interview was when she pulled out a little slip of paper and showed me the first ad I had run for the position ten months earlier.

"I knew this was the perfect job for me," she shared, "but I was in the middle of a project and didn't want to let the person I was working with down. I've had this in my billfold ever since."

What we're looking for is looking for us in every instance!

I will never be able to express my gratitude for Tessa's years of dedication and her incredible gifts. When she came on board, she'd never read a self-help book or considered picking up one. Her openness to these concepts has been exciting to watch. Let me end this section with her own eloquent words:

In film and writing work, it is often feast or famine. At one point while working part-time for MK and freelancing, there was an abrupt and unexpected end to another editing project I was working on. After devoting months to this project only to watch it disappear, I was feeling anxious and a bit daunted. When I came into work the next day, MK and I discussed the fact that my last opportunity showed up out of thin air and the next one would appear the same way. With renewed hope I sent off a couple of resumes that evening.

Two days later I got a call about working on a film, and I was over the moon. Since then I have had the honor of working on many indelible films and even exploring my own passion in documentary film.

As this book has evolved, so have I. The insights I've cultivated through editing these chapters have impacted my personal and professional life. I feel privileged to have been a part of this process and am forever grateful to MK for trusting me with her words. She continues to show me that everything I could ever want or need is already within. I am proud to call her a teacher and a friend.

Genius is only the power of making continuous efforts.
— Elbert Hubbard

Putting Hope for the Future into Practice

There is nothing of which every man is so afraid as getting to know how enormously much he is capable of doing and becoming.

Soren Kierkegaard

Recess-ion

In 2002, entrepreneur Maria Pinto had an employee embezzle tens of thousands of dollars from her designer clothing business. That blow, coupled with a slowing economy, led to her filing for bankruptcy. A year later she suffered major health challenges, yet she found new hope, and with new investors she restarted her business. In 2007, she became one of the First Lady's favorite designers.

There are thousands of stories like Maria's, where what seems to be the end of the day was just a recess break. While we entrepreneurs have to deal with uncertainty regularly, tens of thousands in the corporate world learned to face it due to the economic shift across the U.S. in 2008. While many were losing their homes and their hopes, others were using the adversity, or their furlough days, to enjoy and improve their lives. They put the "recess" back in recession.

"It Fed My Soul"

Duane was a successful motivational speaker by the time I met him. His first twenty years in the work world had been spent selling vacuum cleaners door-to-door.

A day came when my family and I ran out of food. I'll never forget the day we had enough in the refrigerator for breakfast and lunch for my wife and kids, but no idea how we were going to buy food for supper. I said a prayer, putting it all in God's hands, but I was still nervous.

That day, I must have knocked on fifty doors. Not one of them even let me in for a demonstration. Finally, at 4:00, a woman was gracious enough to let me come into her home and explain what the machine could do, but forty-five minutes later, her answer was, "No, thank you."

I thanked her, packed up my stuff, and was halfway to my car when I heard someone yelling. I turned to see her on her front porch, shouting, "Young man, come back here."

Confused, I walked back toward the house. She then asked me the most amazing thing. "I was wondering. My husband and I just bought a side of beef and it wouldn't all fit into the freezer. Could you use two pounds of hamburger?"

Since I had told her nothing about my situation, this miracle not only fed my family, it fed my soul.

> *You know what happens right before the heavens open up and all your dreams come true? Nothing.*
> *— Mike Dooley*

Giving Hope a Hand

Author Mike Dooley is adamant about the power of giving Hope a hand. He goes so far as to suggest that if you're looking for a job, get up early, put on the coffee, then shower and dress for work. Then get into your car and drive to the area where such jobs exist. Mike's popularity and the half a million people who receive his daily encouragements are testaments to the fact that his principles work.

Mike's enlightened books and his "Notes from the Universe" have helped me laugh when I wanted to cry more than once. If you'd like a love note from "The Universe" five days a week that will make you smile, soar, and show up, sign on for his free daily Notes at www.tut.com.

Hope is a muscle, not a magic incantation. I have found that those who are truly committed to taking their lives to the next level not only sign up for daily reminders like Mike's, but they also find or start groups who help them focus more on what *can be* than what *is*.

How to Host a Magnificent Manifastations Group

Do you recall my reference in High-Way 1 to the ABCD of the **Congratulations Game**? The steps were:

Ask your partner what is one of their dreams

Buddy answers.

"**C**ongratulations!"

Dream interview your buddy about their dream.

Since this is one of the most magical and enjoyable activities in this book, here's how to make sure it's part of your weekly routine. Use these ideas to create your own ***Magnificent Manifasters*** dreams support group.

I suggest each group has three to five members who agree to meet or talk by phone at the same time each week or every other week. A suggested agenda is as follows:

Before each meeting/call, take a few minutes to write a list of ten things you would like to ask for/intend.

- Some Wee (find something I've lost, hear from an old friend, receive flowers)

- Some Wild (find a heart shaped rock, see a shooting star, catch a big fish)

- Some Wonderful (meet a new friend, find new opportunity, receive surprise income, experience a healing)

Be sure to always add "receive a delightful surprise" to your list.

Then, once you are together:

1. Start the meeting by each sharing three new things you're grateful for.
2. Next, read aloud the ten things on your written list that you would like to receive.
3. Pick one of them and play "*The Congratulations Game.*" After you share that "it" has happened (in the past tense), the members of the group exclaim, "Congratulations!" and then interview you with questions such as, "So what was it like?" "How did it feel?" "What was your favorite part?"

Week 2: Meet (Call) once a week

1. Share 3 new things you are grateful for, *at least one of which was manifasted from last week's intentions list.*
2. Next, read aloud the ten things on your written list that you would like to receive.
3. Pick one of them and play "*The Congratulations Game.*" After you share that "it" has happened (in the past tense), the members of the group exclaim, "Congratulations!" and then interview you with questions such as, "So what was it like?" "How did it feel?" "What was your favorite part?"

Remember Magnificent Manifastations can be from any of the following areas: family time, free things, support, fun and laughter, health, new friends, new customers, new invitations, order and organization, energy, confidence, romance, creativity, stillness, nature connection, prayer or meditation time, delightful synchronicities, etc.

The future belongs to those who give the next generations reason for hope. — Pierre Teilhard de Chardin

I will never stop participating in gatherings like the one described above, because new dreams and manifastations are what keep me young and "95-ing." It is a regular reminder that when you have a process, you have hope, and when you have hope, you have power. Added to that, the fun of gathering with friends and the thrill of watching dreams come true are a deep well of bliss that never fails to fill me up.

When new members ask for ideas of what to intend, we encourage them to start with things they believe could happen. One young woman wrote down that she would receive flowers, and a surprise bouquet was delivered the following week. As you ask and receive, your Hope muscle gets stronger and you begin to allow larger manifastations (watermelons) to come into your experience. After doing this for six months, one night at the meeting I wrote an intention as $25,000 of surprise money. I didn't expect it anytime soon, but wrote it down for the fun of it.

The following week, my son got a letter from his university of choice that he had received a $40,000 Presidential Scholarship that he hadn't applied for. While I know the scholarship was a result of his intending, believing, and his powerfully positive focus in high school, I was determined to pay for whatever he needed to graduate debt free, so it was a glorious win-win for both of us.

Rediscover Your Sense of Humor

Throughout these 8 High-Ways, and especially with **Hope for the Future**, it's important to retain a spirit of playful possibility. Humorist Jean Kerr hits the nail on the head when she says, "Hope is the feeling that the feeling you have isn't permanent."

> *Life is too important to be taken seriously. — Oscar Wilde*

T. Marni Vos is a humorist I'm grateful to know personally. My favorite line from her presentations is: "Time heals all wounds, but I say, why wait?"

"Humor and hope are inseparable," says Michael Pritchard, parole officer and professional comedian. He goes around the country delighting young adult audiences with questions like the following:

Q: What is the best thing about turning 100?

A: Total lack of peer pressure!

When You Have a Process...

If you found yourself stranded one night on a country road in a car with a spare tire, but with no knowledge of how to change it, you'd be stuck. If, however, someone had offered to teach you the **process** and you had taken time to learn it, you would be powerful. You would be free. You would be on your way.

You now know:

- ✓ *how to dream*
  *(**Get the Picture**: High-Way 1)*
- ✓ *how to risk*
  *(**Risk:** High-Way 2)*
- ✓ *how to take full responsibility*
  *(**Full Responsibility**: High-Way 3)*
- ✓ *how to feel all your feelings*
  *(**Feel All Your Feelings**: High-Way 4)*
- ✓ *how to communicate honestly*
  *(**Honest Communication**: High-Way 5)*
- ✓ *how to forgive the past*
  *(**Forgiveness of the Past**: High-Way 6)*
- ✓ *how to get and stay grateful*
  *(**Gratitude for the Present**: High-Way 7)*
- ✓ *how to have hope*
  *(**Hope for the Future**: High-Way 8)*

At the same time, if someone taught you eight steps to changing a tire, and you only used seven of them, would you want to drive away in that car? No. In the same way, if you want results, you need to work every step of this High-Ways process.

Over these years of living, speaking about and coaching this material, I have noticed that this process is *alive.* **Once you start working it, it will start working in you**. Has that started to happen?

Think back to what prompted you to select this book among the hundreds of thousands you could have chosen. Is it possible that this process chose you? Here is another glorious gift — now that you have this process, you can apply it to *every area of your life*. Like the 8 turned on its side, the 8 High-Ways are a journey that is *infinite,* always there to guide us, heal us, and remind us of the power and abundance within ourselves and others.

Q & A on Hope for the Future

I choose to make the rest of my life the best of my life.

Louise Hay

Q: How can I stay motivated after I'm finished with this book?

A: I use daily Gratitudes and weekly Manifasting with the Congratulations Game. I fill my mind and expand my heart with books, articles, TED talks, true-life movies and uplifting speakers. I only Facebook-friend those who stay positive and focus on what they want rather than what they do not want. I attend retreats and get-aways that refresh and reconnect me with myself and what I know to be true. Most importantly, I surround myself with like-minded persons at my church, in my social circle, and even on the pickle ball court.

Author Jim Rohn famously stated that we will become like the five people we are closest to. Whether you meet them through meet-ups, work or dating sites, we all get to choose who we hang out with.

As for staying in touch, you can join our ***8 to Great*** Facebook page and sign up for my free "Key-Mails" at www.8togreat.com. You can sign on for my Youtube channel, mk8togreat or for 8toGreat on Twitter. You can also e-mail us at info@8togreat.com with questions and comments.

Finally, we have a certification training in this material. If you'd like more information, contact us at the above email or by calling 828-242-9033.

Q: I need help. I'm not making a living for my family. I've spent lots of money on self-help materials, but still my excuses are many: not smart enough, no experience, not taking action on my goals, not worthy, and I could go on, but I think you get the message. Hope you can help.

A: Dear One, you're experiencing "Analysis Paralysis." You're so afraid of making the wrong decision that you're not making any decision. Here's the great news:

There are no wrong decisions.

So, if you're coachable today, I'd start with joining Dave Ramsey's Financial University to face and turn around your money situation. Then you have my 8 Steps in your hands/on your screen. Follow them. Get up every day and spend five minutes looking at your dream board and sharing your Gratitudes with someone. Your life can't help but change. Allow yourself to be coached and expect miracles!

Q: How can I teach my friend or my spouse FGH?

A: I have two gentle ways to share this message. The first is to wait until there is a "teachable/reachable moment" when they come to you with a challenge and ask for help. Then you can share the message or recommend this book. Just be sure *not* to check back to see if they used your suggestion. Offer it and let it go.

The second is to live it. When you do, if it's meant to be, your joy and freedom will have that person begging for your secret!

Q: If someone around you has lost hope, how do you help them hang on?

A: There are two levels of "losing hope." The first is rage and/or depression. If you have someone in your life who has been frustrated and complaining for a long time, chances are you have offered every possible "turn-around" tool, a dozen self-help books and numerous courses they can take. It's time to face the fact that you do not have *their* answer.

I recently spoke with a mother who said she was tired of feeling like a punching bag for her forty-year-old son's bad days. "He only calls to complain about his job!" she told me, "yet he won't take any of my advice on how to change things!"

In our coaching session, I first helped her get clear on how she wanted to feel. Her next step was to gently release her need to "fix" her son. She realized she was trying to be her son's "Higher Power" and that he could never connect with his real Source until she stepped out of the way. She decided to stop enabling him with expensive gifts and international vacations.

Then, when he would call to complain, she would listen in silence or simply restate what he was telling her. "It sounds like you're terribly unhappy with that job." Eventually he talked about other subjects.

Finally, she decided to limit her reaching out to him to encouraging texts ("thinking of you") and birthday cards rather than self-help suggestions and advice. It took quite a while to reset their relationship, but he is now healthier and happier, realizing he can stand on his own two feet. Meanwhile, their mutual respect for themselves and each other has helped her sleep better, lower her blood pressure, and live the life of her dreams.

The second level of hopelessness is much more serious. If they start talking about life "not being worth living," or start giving away their prized possessions, contact a suicide hotline immediately. If you are not a family member, alert their loved ones. If it's a student, tell the school counselor. If they're an adult, call a hotline for help. There are many suicide hotlines ready to assist you.

In either circumstance, worrying about them twenty-four hours a day is not an option or you could find yourself drowning in your own stress. Once you've done your best, surrender to what is, and live fully in your own here and now.

Q: I live in a small rural community and know how depressed the town sometimes feels. I don't know what I can do to rekindle hope for our little town.

A: One North Dakota community had a similar situation. The weeds growing around the stop signs were indicative of the mentality of apathy and discouragement.

One day, a resident who had just heard me speak got the picture that things could be different. She took a risk and invited some friends over for coffee. She suggested that they work together to trim the weeds back. Another woman suggested putting flower pots at each stop sign. A third woman said if someone could find the pots, she'd have her art students at the high school paint them.

A fourth person added, "I don't have any pots, but my brother has a Quonset full of tubs." As of this printing, the painted flower tubs are still there, years later, blossoming and blessing the town.

Q: Which of the High-Ways do you think is the most important?

A: There are many answers to your wonderful question. The High-Way I've seen have the most dramatic and immediate effect on the most lives has been Gratitude. It's the quickest and simplest way back to "95." Once it's in place, everything changes.

My other answer is that the most important High-Way for you could be the one you don't want to travel, because that's the one acting as an obstacle between you and the manifestation of your dreams. It could also be the one you can't wait to travel. Pick one. Any one. Follow your instincts and have fun. Remember, there are no wrong decisions, and every moment is the "right" now.

Curly: Do you know what the secret of life is?

Mitch: No, what?

Curly: This. (Curly holds up one finger.)

Mitch: Your finger?

Curly: One thing. Just one thing.

You stick to that and everything else don't mean shit.

From the film *City Slickers*

Our greatest happiness comes from following our greatest dreams.

In Conclusion...

MK, I want to apologize for doubting this program. Now I know it is possible to be that happy because I am that happy!

AA Member and *8 to Great* Coaching Client

If you have begun to use these High-Ways, you have discovered that the keys to greater happiness, health, love, wealth, peace and success lie not in self-deprivation and sacrifice, not in good fortune or good genes, not in hard work or heavenly intervention, but in the simple act of choosing a thought in this moment that feels good.

I grew up hearing a lot about eternal life, thinking that I had to be patient in hopes that it would be my reward when I died. It was only as I grew into my knowing that I realized that eternity "began" a long time ago. We're all smack dab in the middle of the eternal life we've been promised. Heaven on Earth is possible for those ready to claim it.

And so many of us are. This book has been a work of heart by myself and so many others. And it is time. We are at the heart of a deep change in the world, watching a new generation embrace the unlimited possibilities foretold ages ago. We need only open our eyes to see young and old rediscovering their passion and finding their compass in their compass-ion. It is such an exciting time to be alive.

The Final Fairy Tale

There will be those who rail against these truths with "if it were that easy..." and that is all perfect. Their rants remind me of a scene in ***The Wizard of Oz***. Near the end of the film, Dorothy's friend, the Scarecrow, listens to Glinda the Good Witch's shoe-tapping instructions and challenges her with, "If it was that easy, why didn't you tell her a long time ago?"

Her simple reply reveals a great truth: "Because she wouldn't have believed me."

The Wizard Within

As you become a believer that dreams really do come true, your path from victim to victor or average to awesome will look like Thomas Edison's, Mother Teresa's, Winston Churchill's, Rosa Park's, Harry Potter's and Dorothy's.

High-Way 1: *Get the Picture* — You will ask for something that feels like it exists "over the rainbow."

High-Way 2: *Risk* — You will dare to say (or sing!) your dream out loud.

High-Way 3: *Full Responsibility* — You will want to blame and complain about all the people in your life, like Auntie Em, who don't understand you and your dreams, or who, like the Wicked Witch, seem to be "monkeying around" and trying to hurt you.

High-Way 4: *Feel All Your Feelings* — You will feel elated and delighted, lost and scared, mad and sad as the new realities you've manifested on your yellow brick road take shape.

High-Way 5: *Honest Communication* — You will learn to be honest about what you need from those you meet along the way who you consider "wizards" (who are all half-jerk and half-jewel).

High-Way 6: *Forgiveness of the Past* — You'll start to forgive those from your past and see that the Lions are just "scaredy cats" underneath all that fur.

High-Way 7: *Gratitude for the Present* — You'll move into greater and greater appreciation for those around you as well as your own magnificent heart.

High-Way 8: *Hope for the Future* — You'll understand that the thing you have always desired in life, whether it's wisdom, courage, brains or love, has always been within you.

Finally, you'll understand that you've never been in danger, you've never left the heart-land of Kansas, and all roads lead to Oz.

By now you know this process can be your map to wherever you want to go. And although you'll be taking the same High-Ways that so many greats have taken before you, the winding roads and wonderful rewards will be uniquely your own.

None of us knows what we are capable of, but we do know that what we'll get from following our dreams will be nothing compared to what we will become.

Your dreams await.

Blissings and Blessings!

MK

Whatever you can do, or dream you can, begin it.
Boldness has genius, power and magic in it.

Goethe

The *8 to Great* High-Lights

The Power Pyramid

What goes around comes around. Misery loves company, but so does joy!

We're always somewhere between "5" and "95."

"5" is only using 5 percent of your power because only 5 percent of your thoughts feel good.

"95" is using 95 percent of your power because 95 percent of your thoughts feel good.

We are more energy efficient (have more energy) when we choose thoughts that feel good!

When we are at "95," what goes around comes around faster! When you feel good, good things happen.

High-Way 1: Get the Picture

A belief is a thought you keep thinking until you feel it.

The difference between a dream and a goal is that when you dream, you don't concern yourself with Who, When, Where, or How, only What you want and Why you want it.

High-Way 2: Risk

The four-letter word that the happiest people have been found to have in common is Risk.

The decision-making formula for every decision to be sure it's the right one for you: "If I had no fear, what would I do?"

What is a Risk? Running to, not from. (Running from is not a risk, but an escape.)

High-Way 3: Full Responsibility

What does Full Responsibility living look like? No B.C. (Blaming and Complaining) only A.D. (Acting and Dreaming).

You spot it, you got it, so exchange "You should" with "I could."

High-Way 4: Feel All Your Feelings

Mad (Angergy) and Sad (Release) are two sides of the same coin. You always feel them together to the same extent.

To stay out of depression, feel your anger (fire). To stay out of rage, feel your sadness (water).

When someone says, "You never," "You always," or "You are such a..." use L.A.D.I.I. (See High-Way 5 below.)

High-Way 5: Honest Communication

4 Steps for asking for what you want:

Pre-step: (Have you got a minute?)

1. When you... (1 time and 1 place)

2. I felt a little...

3. Because...

4. Therefore...

How to prevent defensiveness with L.A.D.I.I.:

1. "Let me see if I got that..."

2. Acknowledge what they said.

3. "Did I get that?"

4. "Is there more?"

5. "I can Imagine that feels..."

How to stop 3rd party communication:

If you're X, go to Z.

If you're Y, tell X to go to Z.

If you're Z, ask X if they agree with Y.

High-Ways 6, 7, 8

Positive Attitude is FGH:

Forgiveness of the Past

Gratitude for the Present

Hope for the Future

High-Way 6: Forgiveness of the Past

The Forgiveness Formula: We were all doing the best we could at the time with the information we had.

How to balance pride and humility: We're all half-jerk, half-jewel, no better, no worse than anyone else.

The Three Steps of Forgiveness:

Face it

Feel it

Forgive it

How to tell if you've forgiven someone: if when something bad happens to them, you commiserate rather than celebrate.

High-Way 7: Gratitude for the Present

The Gratitude "Richual:" Share 3 Gratitudes each day from the past 24 hours, with no repeats.

The Three Most Grateful Groups:

Those who just had a loss

Those who have come close to a loss

Those who know a loss is coming

High-Way 8: Hope for the Future

Hope is Having Only Positive Expectation and Surrender.

The Road to Success is **never** a straight line.

Author

Enlightened by experiences that led to her spending a month in a domestic violence shelter at the age of thirty-four, **MK Mueller** began a support group in her home called, "Taking Care of Me." Almost overnight, word of her empowering and uplifting message for men and women in all walks of life grew, and she became a highly sought-after speaker and trainer for businesses, community groups, and national conferences.

Her first book, ***Taking Care of Me: The Habits of Happiness***, was soon followed by her award-winning book, ***8 to Great: How to Take Charge of Your Life and Make Positive Changes Using an 8-Step Breakthrough Process***. Today she travels the world giving keynotes and seminars, and has over 2,500 Certified Trainers taking the 8 High-Ways into workplaces, health care organizations, schools, and community groups.

Meanwhile, Mueller has written ***8 to Your IdealWeight: How to Release Your Weight and Restore Your Power in 8 Weeks***. Today she trains and certifies life coaches in her 8-week ***IdealWeight*** and ***8 to Great*** process.

www.8togreat.com

www.coach.8toyouridealweight.com

www.8toyouridealweight.com

MK is the proud Mom of Joanna and Zach, and enjoys life to the fullest in Southwest Florida.